Author's P1___

These are my memoirs. One of the definitions given of a memoir in the *Concise Oxford Dictionary* is 'history written from personal knowledge or special sources of information.'

There is a problem in deciding the extent to which memory constitutes personal knowledge as anyone foolish enough to test his or her memory against an impartial record of a particular event soon discovers. The discrepancy can be alarming, especially if the story has been told and retold over a period of many years. When people start trying to remember what they think they thought, as opposed to what they think happened, their chance of getting it right is further reduced, to put it mildly.

So much for 'personal knowledge'. We now come to 'special sources of information', such as collections of letters to and from the author, papers and assessments, and the drafts of speeches and lesser talks. These should be more reliable than the author's memory, but it is possible that on occasions the writer of the documents has slanted the truth to suit the situation.

Such considerations might well deter someone from trying to write his, or her, memoirs. Luckily it does not always do so. If it did, there would be many fewer books available and a shortage of original sources for other writers to sift through, criticise and distort.

Before writing this book, I naturally gave thought to these matters. Although my memory may sometimes fail, I have access to an extensive store of special sources of information, which should help in establishing the truth.

Unfortunately truth alone can no more turn writing into literature, than painting into a work of art. For this to happen, the writer's words or the painter's brush, have to stir a deeper response. So far as this author is concerned, that may prove to be 'a bridge too far'.

Foreword
by General Sir Robert Pascoe KCB MBE

Frank Kitson's maxim in life was 'eyes and ears open, mouth shut'. This served him well throughout his long career although he was reputed to scare some people by his pointed questions or terse remarks.

That was not my experience when I served under his direct command on three separate occasions and I came to know him as a firm friend and generous host.

He was certainly a 'one-off' who really cared about people. As a senior officer and commander he was a tough, no-nonsense soldier who worked hard to deliver the best he could.

Promising junior ranks were picked out and encouraged to press onwards and upwards. He sought opinions and ideas from his riflemen whose soldierly outbursts would often leave him shaking with mirth.

Sycophants were not tolerated and he made it clear to preaching padres that ten minutes in the pulpit was long enough.

He was devoted to his family and a tolerant father, always full of fun. Under the uniform was a far from uniform fellow.

In professional matters however he was dedicated to the task in hand and ruthless in its pursuit. Although he was knowledgeable on many subjects and had a firm opinion on just about everything he was always a modest man, a characteristic which comes across clearly in this book.

Key to his success in a long and influential career was the priority he gave to acquiring information and intelligence in every situation he faced.

His ability to analyse problems and his attention to detail lead to innovative ideas and clear instructions which, over the years, had an immense and lasting effect on the army.

All this and more about the long and eventful life of Frank Kitson is revealed in this, his personal memoir. It is the last of many books written by a remarkable man who was an inspirational military leader.

Intelligent Warfare

Intelligent Warfare

The Memoirs of General Sir Frank Kitson
GBE KCB MC and Bạr DL

General Sir Frank Kitson

Pen & Sword
MILITARY

First published in Great Britain in 2024 by
Pen & Sword Military
An imprint of Pen & Sword Books Limited
Yorkshire – Philadelphia

ISBN 978 1 03612 291 1

Typeset by Mac Style
Printed in the UK by CPI Group (UK) Ltd, Croydon, CR0 4YY.

Pen & Sword Books Limited incorporates the imprints of After
the Battle, Atlas, Archaeology, Aviation, Discovery, Family History,
Fiction, History, Maritime, Military, Military Classics, Politics,
Select, Transport, True Crime, Air World, Frontline Publishing, Leo
Cooper, Remember When, Seaforth Publishing, The Praetorian Press,
Wharncliffe Local History, Wharncliffe Transport, Wharncliffe True
Crime and White Owl.

For a complete list of Pen & Sword titles please contact

PEN & SWORD BOOKS LIMITED
47 Church Street, Barnsley, South Yorkshire, S70 2AS, England
E-mail: enquiries@pen-and-sword.co.uk
Website: www.pen-and-sword.co.uk
or
PEN AND SWORD BOOKS
1950 Lawrence Road, Havertown, PA 19083, USA
E-mail: uspen-and-sword@casematepublishers.com
Website: www.penandswordbooks.com

Contents

Introduction

An original edition of this work was first published in 2011 and intended largely for the enjoyment of family and friends. In it General Kitson provided recollections of his childhood and, later, affectionate stories of his marriage to Elizabeth Spencer (later Lady Kitson OBE DL) and the arrival of their three daughters, best known in family circles as Kitty, Chiggy and Mo.

While this original edition of *A Different Sort of War* revealed a fascinating counterpoint to the general's army career, for the reader with a particular interest in an intimate military study of the second half of the twentieth century, such personal details pose something of a distraction. It was with this in mind that this revised work is published.

Any editing of the original has been done with a careful eye to retain the general's exceptional skill as an author. All those who have read his seminal work *Gangs and Counter Gangs*, or his biographical studies of Prince Rupert and Oliver Cromwell, will recognise his artistry in engaging the reader whatever the subject.

All lives have more than one narrative and it is worth recording that those who knew General Kitson particularly well, recognised that his attachment to his family formed the bedrock of life beyond the battlefield, while his love of field sports, riding in particular, and his enjoyment of a wide social life revealed a side of the man, disinclined to suffer fools gladly it is true, but above all sensitive, humorous and human.

Chapter 1

Early Days 1944–1953

That I should become a serving army officer at all is worthy of note as, on the day of my birth in December 1927, my father was promoted as a Royal Navy captain to command the newly built HMS *Rodney*, then one of Britain's most powerful warships. A year later, now a Rear Admiral, Henry Kitson (known throughout the navy as Jan) moved his family to Devon where my brother was born.

In 1929, now aged 50, Rear Admiral Kitson took command of the 3rd Battle Squadron in the Home Fleet and two years later he became admiral superintendent of Portsmouth Dockyard where my family lived for the next four years. In 1933 came further promotion as vice admiral and in 1935 he became a knight.

Despite my immediate naval credentials it was an army tradition that prevailed with my paternal grandfather holding a major's rank and his father serving in the Indian Army and on his death in 1939 at the age of 98 being the last surviving officer of the Indian Mutiny. Surpassing even this distinction my mother's brother Frank, a professional soldier in the Poona Horse, won the Victoria Cross at the First Battle of Ypres.

On the outbreak of the Second World War my father, now aged 63 and retired, was called back to service, taking charge of all naval forces operating round Cornwall in his old rank of vice admiral.

I was now at Stowe School and, along with my fellow schoolmates was keeping a close eye on the war's progress and each doing our bit as members of the Officers' Training Corps. By the end of 1942, now aged 16, the family agreed that I should give up all idea of joining the Royal Navy and settle for the army instead. A year later I became a member of the Home Guard in a unit close to our home in Devon. Such were the relative humble beginnings of my military career.

* * *

In February 1944, two months after my seventeenth birthday I had been to Oxford to enlist. As I had volunteered instead of waiting to be conscripted,

I could choose what branch of the service I wished to join and better still I could avoid being conscripted into going down the mines. For a moment I wondered whether anyone would be concerned about my asthma, but the medical examination was by no means exacting. A bored looking officer in the Royal Army Medical Corps (RAMC) looked up from his newspaper and seeing that I had two arms and two legs pronounced me fit. I was then marched into another room where I took the oath of allegiance to the King and was given a shilling by a sergeant. I was now in the army but I was instantly placed on the reserve and told to wait until I was sent for to do my training. This did not happen until the end of the year when I was just 18. Shortly after Christmas I arrived by train in York and that evening I reported to the guardroom of the Rifle Depot. In Europe the major German counter-attack, known as the Rundstedt Offensive, was petering out. As I entered the barracks I felt myself to be a grown up man of some significance. It soon became apparent that the army took a different view of my position.

On arriving at the depot I was put into a platoon with about thirty other recruits a third of whom were aiming for commissions. The rest would serve out their time as riflemen except for a few who might eventually become non-commissioned officers (NCOs). But for the first six weeks of our service we were private soldiers. Only when we passed our 'primary training' would we be entitled to call ourselves riflemen. Our surroundings were in every way suited to our humble status. We were all together in a barrack room down the sides of which were a number of double bunks. In the middle of the room was an iron stove with a long funnel, which served as a chimney. The stove when adequately stoked provided our only heating.

My companions were a diverse bunch. Although those seeking commissions were all from public schools, the rest were from the East End of London. They were young, cheerful, shrewd but uneducated having left school at 14. Indeed about a third of them were totally illiterate. One or two were in very bad shape physically with rotting teeth and venereal disease. They were of course more streetwise than the public school contingent and to start with I could hardly understand their fast cockney repartee replete with its rhyming slang. But we were now all in the same boat and the misery of the next few weeks soon broke down the barriers.

The first day was taken up with drawing kit and undergoing medical and dental inspections, which included being inoculated against a variety of diseases. For this purpose we were lined up in single file and called one at a time to a trestle table where a Royal Army Medical Corps doctor plunged a large and blunt needle into us one after another. After each person was injected the needle, which looked and felt like a bayonet, was held in a naked flame for a few moments and then wiped on a rag before being plunged into the next man. Most of us suffered reactions from the injections although we were expected to have got over them by the next morning. One poor man had all his teeth extracted, which entitled him to an aspirin and a whole day off.

My immediate superior was Acting Corporal Hole who was my section commander. Above him was Sergeant Capper who had joined the army in time to fight in the First World War but who was relegated to the depot owing to his advancing years for the second. The job of these two men over the next six weeks was to break us in to army ways and then to teach us a few basic skills to a very high standard such as the use and care of the rifle and light machine gun. The idea was to build up the confidence and self-respect that we might well have lost during the breaking-in period. NCOs in the Rifle Brigade were not supposed to swear at riflemen or to shout louder than necessary. At the same time it was no part of their job to sympathise unduly with the inevitable distress that we would be experiencing as a result of being chased around from 'rouse' to 'lights out' which was all part of the breaking-in process.

That is the background to the six weeks that I spent at the Depot in York. My main memory is one of discomfort brought about by the intense cold. We were only really warm in bed on the straw palliasses that served as mattresses. The worst moment was getting out in the morning into the freezing barrack-room, which had rapidly lost heat during the night once the stove went out. Every morning one of the two people in each double bunk had to get up five minutes early in order to erect the black-out screens before the lights went on. I slept on the lower bunk, which was unfortunate as the man above me was an habitual bed wetter. All the same I volunteered to do the black-out every day in return for his bacon ration at breakfast which he could not eat because he was an orthodox Jew. To my mind I deserved more than a bit of bacon for sleeping in what smelt like a stable, but he drove a hard bargain.

At the end of 'primary training' those of us who had not been back-squadded were deemed to have passed and were entitled to call ourselves riflemen. The band was on parade when we marched past the commanding officer, Lieutenant Colonel Poole, to the tune of the regimental march. We then said goodbye to Sergeant Capper and Acting Corporal Hole both of whom had, up to the previous evening, been assuring us that we were the biggest 'shower' they had ever had the misfortune to instruct. Now they actually said 'well done' and wished us 'all the best'. We were promptly despatched to the 9th Battalion of the Rifle Brigade (9 RB) which was stationed at Ranby Camp near Retford where we would undergo 'continuation training' for a further sixteen weeks after which we would be ready to join a battalion in the field.

Our platoon from York, less my bed wetting friend, moved en bloc to B Company, 9 RB. Now in addition to a platoon sergeant and section commander there was a platoon officer and a company commander to watch out for, to say nothing of a company sergeant major and a colour sergeant. The commanding officer was Colonel Vic Turner, nephew of my father's old friend Admiral Buller, whose losses at El Alamein had caused me to be propelled into the army in the first place. At Alamein Vic Turner had not only won the Victoria Cross, but he had also received a wound that left him with a large dent in the side of his head. He was greatly liked and respected by one and all.

At Ranby we lived in a Nissen Hut which was a tidy distance from another hut and which contained the ablutions (wash basins) and lavatories. As there was snow on the ground when we arrived, trotting across to the latrine in the night was unpopular. On the other hand easing springs outside the door left a nasty lemon coloured stain in the snow which laid one open to the charge of indiscriminate urination if one owned up, or an extra drill parade for the whole platoon if one kept quiet. It was a great relief when the snow melted. Another lingering memory is of the pungent smell in the ablutions caused by the mixture of steam and cigarette smoke. For some reason many felt obliged to light a cigarette on waking up and then leave it hanging from the corner of the mouth when washing and shaving, hence the repulsive stink. It is strange that this lingers in the mind when so much else lies forgotten. We all received fifty free cigarettes each week because they were supposed to be helpful in staving off hunger when the rations failed to arrive and steadying the nerves at times of stress.

The army takes no risks with the important aspects of training, which meant that we had to do all the lessons on the rifle and Bren gun that we had done at York, again. We were also subjected to numerous drill parades and much physical training including death defying scrambles and leaps across the assault course. To start with I was scared stiff by these antics but they soon became as much part of the routine as getting fed in the cookhouse. We were also obliged to undertake a series of route marches of ever increasing length culminating in one of 20 miles. These were regarded as being team events, which meant that everyone in the platoon had to complete the march. If anyone started to wilt, someone else had to help him by carrying his rifle and if necessary he had to be supported on either side and dragged along to the finish. For anyone to fall out was considered a great disgrace for the whole platoon. Depending on the circumstances the platoon might have to do the whole march over again.

For the first time minor tactics were introduced into the syllabus, which included judging distance, camouflage and stalking an enemy. I well remember one day sitting in the sun on the side of a hill and thinking that spring was in the air and I was not freezing cold. It seemed so strange. I even wondered whether certain aspects of soldiering might be enjoyable.

After we had been at Ranby for a month we were sent on ten days leave. Dressed in my uniform and carrying my kit bag I travelled in the train overnight arriving at Bovey Tracey station early next morning. Bursting with fitness derived from many miles of marching I practically ran up the hill to Higher Bowden where I arrived in time for breakfast. I had only been away from home for three months but it seemed as if I had travelled from another world. A few days later I was taken, protesting, to Newton Abbot to have my picture taken dressed as a soldier.

As time went on we were taught a wider range of subjects including the use of grenades, the 2-inch mortar, booby traps and mines and finally how to drive wheeled vehicles and motor bicycles. Once or twice we were given the task of escorting German prisoners of war from the railway station at Worksop to a nearby prison camp. At this stage of the war we rather expected that the Germans would be starved, exhausted and thoroughly dispirited but this was not the case. Although some were bandaged or had an arm in a sling, they swung along at a good pace singing their marching songs which sounded very different from the songs that we sung when we were on the road. Ours were ordinary songs such as 'Onward Christian Soldiers' or 'O Come All Ye Faithful' with the words changed and sung in marching time, or we sang what can best be described as pub songs that had been put together in the days before women patronised pubs. The Germans sang songs that had obviously been written as marches and they sounded impressive. Luckily we could not understand the words: they were probably '*Wir fahren gegen Engeland* [We're racing against England].' All I knew was that I had live ammunition in my rifle and I was quite ready to take a shot at anyone trying to break away.

We were still learning to drive when the war in Europe came to an end. On the day in question we were in the Derbyshire hills between Chesterfield and Matlock being waived at by bystanders who charitably credited us with having played an important part in winning the war. We even got bits of fruit given to us when we slowed down in one of the villages. Appreciation of this kind was not something to which we were accustomed. Normally it was only NCOs that spoke to us and usually to tell us to do whatever we were doing better or faster. Soon afterwards we lost some local good will when my great friend Livingstone-Learmonth who was in the driver's seat, got in a muddle with the pedals and went through the window of a shop. One good result of our driving instruction was that those who passed, received army driving licences, which automatically entitled us to hold full civilian licenses without taking a test.

At the end of our continuation training the platoon that had been together since our arrival in York, split up. Those of us who had been accepted for training to become officers were moved to a another company in which we would be prepared for examination by a War Office Selection Board (WOSB). The remainder were sent to battalions overseas. Our new platoon hut was at the other end of the camp and our training went on more or less as before with even more time devoted to physical fitness and marching. We were also taught to drive the Bren-gun carrier, a small tracked armoured vehicle, in which we constituted an even greater hazard to the civilian population than had been the case when we were driving wheeled vehicles.

We mostly passed the WOSB after which we were qualified to attend an Officer Cadet Training Unit known as an OCTU. Hitherto the Green Jackets had run their own OCTU in the Depot at York. Because the Rifle Brigade and the King's Royal Rifle Corps (KRRC) provided motor battalions for armoured brigades, their officers were trained differently to officers required for duty in ordinary infantry regiments. But with the end of the war in Europe it was considered unnecessary to run such an exclusive organisation and it was decided that we should be sent to an infantry OCTU. But as none of these had enough vacancies to take us immediately we were sent to another company of 9 RB at Stokesly which was doing combined training with tanks along the borders of Yorkshire and Westmoreland.

This company was organised as if it was part of a motor battalion so that each platoon had four white armoured personnel carriers; one for each section and one for platoon headquarters. At this time I was in platoon headquarters as the 2-inch mortar man. Each week we went off with a squadron of tanks to carry out an exercise, which lasted for three or four days during which we got the chance to fire live rounds from all the platoon weapons. In practice we spent most of the time digging in, that is to say preparing short term defensive positions, a task that is the bread and butter of soldiering.

It was in September 1945 that I finally reached the OCTU, which was housed in a disused Billy Butlin holiday camp outside Morecambe in north Lancashire. Now an officer cadet rather than a rifleman I was able to drive myself into Morecambe for a good meal occasionally after work.

After a few weeks the whole OCTU moved to an abandoned stately home called Alton Towers in Staffordshire where we lived in large Nissen huts instead of small wooden chalets. In the OCTU the Rifle Brigade cadets joined by cadets from the KRRC were spread around the platoons of a company so that in each platoon about half were Green Jackets, the other half being men destined for red-coat regiments. Some of these people were little different from us, but others having risen from the ranks, had battle experience and were also older than we were. One had been a sniper and he regaled us with horrible stories of his killings complete with the bubbling of his victims' blood as he went through their pockets.

The training was now more varied than it had been in 9 RB and included a certain amount of written and administrative work. We also went away to a training area in Wales for exercises. Early in 1946 the course finished but when our red-coat friends passed out as second lieutenants we were left behind for a further month to do special to arm training for motor battalions. This consisted mainly of learning how to use the wireless sets installed in armoured personnel carriers and high-speed map reading. In February it was our turn to pass out and we became officers. Even so we were still not considered ready to command riflemen and were sent to the new Rifles Training Battalion recently established at Ogbourne St George in Wiltshire, to do a six weeks young officers course. Only when this was concluded did I find myself heading off to the Depot to take command of a platoon of recruits.

*   *   *

With the end of the Second World War and the disappearance of the Americans, the Rifle Depot had moved from York to its traditional barracks in Winchester, the training company being in Bushfield Camp a mile or two to the south. It was there that I took over my first platoon. A few weeks later we moved to Barton Stacey by the River Test. The idea was that I would command this platoon for its sixteen weeks continuation training at the end of which I would go to 1 RB. Barton Stacey was a splendid place especially as I managed to get some fishing from a very hospitable lady who lived nearby.

By this time my parents had abandoned Higher Bowden in favour of Monk's Hill which I could easily reach on my motorcycle when it was in a good mood. This was by no means always the case but in those days we had to wear uniform all the time and any serviceman who broke down was sure to be helped by the next car or lorry that came along. On several occasions I was delivered to my destination in the back of a truck and once I was towed there on the end of a rope, a particularly hazardous business. Nowadays the idea of officers travelling round the country in uniform seems strange but then everyone took it for granted. Social events were starting up again and I remember going to Andover station on my motorbike in my green patrols and crossbelt, getting a train to Waterloo and on to a dance in one of the big hotels. Our table was next to the one where Princess Elizabeth was sitting with some Guards officers. In the course of the evening I retired to relieve myself in the men's lavatory. On emerging into the passage leading to the ballroom I found myself next to a slim naval officer.

Looking more carefully I realised that it was the King who had dropped in to see how his daughter was getting on.

At the end of the war most of the Rifle Brigade and KRRC battalions that had existed when we joined the army were being disbanded, leaving each regiment with only two. This meant that our regiments did not need as many officers as had been trained, so that the surplus had to be weeded out along the way. Some found homes in other regiments and others were sent off to do jobs such as re-burying soldiers in the new War Graves Commission cemeteries. I was therefore lucky to have been selected to go to one of our two battalions and in August I set off to join 1 RB stationed at Osnabrück in Germany. We travelled by troop-ship from Hull to Cuxhaven and then by a very slow train via Hamburg and Hanover to our destination. Scenes of devastation were everywhere with colossal damage evident in all of the built up areas through which we passed. The town of Osnabrück was no exception. Luckily 1 RB was in a barracks on the outskirts of the town in a relatively unscathed area. It was called Winkelhausen Barracks after some long dead German general but was soon re-christened Roberts Barracks, presumably after Major General Pip Roberts who commanded 7th Armoured Division. We were in 22nd Armoured Brigade which was one of the brigades of this division.

On arrival I was given 3 Platoon of A Company which by chance was the platoon that Alfred de Pass was commanding when he was killed in 1944. Johnny Walker was the company commander and Colin James who would later become one of my greatest friends was the second-in-command. There was no battalion officers' mess so the officers of each company lived in various nearby houses. A Company shared the upstairs floor of the local Post Office a few minutes walk from the barrack gate, with the officers of I Company. The commanding officer, Colonel Poole who had formerly been at York, shared a house with the battalion second-in-command, Peter Peel, and the adjutant. Of the thirty odd officers in the battalion only Peter Peel was married and his wife Pickles understandably decided to stay in England.

I had hardly settled in before I was told that I would have to go to Wilhelmshaven as a member under instruction of a war crimes court, which would probably last for a week. I would be housed by 22nd Light Anti-Aircraft Regiment which was stationed outside the port. It would be a full month before I returned to the battalion. During the intervening period I learnt a lot about the administration of justice in an international setting. The court consisted of five British officers and me, the president being a lieutenant colonel. The defendants were the three guards of a small concentration camp, which mostly housed European slave labourers who had misbehaved according to the Germans. The commandant was an SS warrant officer and of the others one was a corporal and one a private. As the evidence unfolded it became apparent that the private who was stupid if not sub-normal, had grossly mistreated some of the prisoners and that the corporal had exercised no restraint on him; if anything he egged him on. The warrant officer had been extremely lax in his supervision and had more or less left the other two to do what they liked. As a result a number of the prisoners had died. To cut a long story short the warrant officer was sentenced to one year, the corporal to fourteen and the private to death. I greatly disapproved of this as the deaths had been as much the result of the lack of restraint by the warrant officer and corporal as by the cruelty of the private. Luckily for me as I was under instruction, my vote given first, did not count so I did not feel in any way responsible for the outcome.

But I did develop a great dislike of the whole system of war crimes trials as the law seemed to be made up by the courts as they went along in order to convict people of crimes that did not exist when the people concerned committed them. This was particularly evident in the case of the major trials where crimes were invented in order to convict generals of doing things, which had never before been regarded as crimes. Thus General Jodl of the German High Command was convicted and hanged for helping to plan attacks on foreign sovereign states such as Poland and Russia although later, when it was too late, his conviction was overturned. Many officers in the British Army of the Rhine (BAOR), including myself, contributed money to pay for really good lawyers to defend General Manstein who was accused of some invented crime that he had allegedly committed in Russia. The fact is that war crimes were thought up for political reasons to appease the thirst for revenge of many people in Britain, America and Russia. All that can be said is that they prevented a lot of genuine Nazi thugs from being shot out of hand which would possibly have been less damaging in the long term than inventing offences for which they could be punished. It is interesting to note that attacking sovereign states seems to be legal again now since that is precisely what we have more recently done in Serbia and Iraq.

*   *   *

When I got back to 1 RB in mid-October I was able to get a feel for life in a regular battalion in the aftermath of the war. 1 RB was made up of two main groups. First there were those men who had served for some years in the war and who were gradually being released from the army. They were naturally disinclined to take much interest in peacetime soldiering and wanted to be left alone as far as possible although they mostly had enough regard for the regiment to put on a decent show on special occasions. The second group consisted of men who had been conscripted after the end of the war and who were also waiting to be released as they had no intention of staying in the army for longer than necessary. They lacked the military skills of the first group and also the motivation for developing them. A third, smaller group consisted of the long-term regular soldiers many of whom were senior NCOs and they were the people who kept the show on the road on a day-to-day basis. Because of the disinclination of the two larger groups to take much interest in soldiering the battalion was far less efficient than the training organisations in which I formerly served.

Some of the officers felt much the same as the men, although others were so committed to the well being of the soldiers that they laboured to make the battalion work on the grounds that an inefficient organisation is seldom a happy one. Dick Poole, who had joined the army at the end of the First World War and who had been a company commander in the early days of the desert war, was a strong personality. He was also so much older than the company commanders that they were a bit careful of him as indeed were most of the officers. On the other hand he intended to retire at the end of his period in command and was not out to make his name. He was also a very charming person whose main concern was that the battalion should not be bothered by outsiders, be they generals or administrative bureaucrats, during the transitional period between wartime and peacetime soldiering. Johnny Walker had not intended to become a regular soldier having joined from Cambridge when the war started. He had fought throughout and had been wounded at El Alamein. He was an excellent regimental soldier but he had no long-term military ambitions. He owned a large estate in Wiltshire, which he would have to look after in due course. Meanwhile he intended that the soldiers should be properly looked after and woe betide any subaltern who failed in this direction. From these two I would not learn anything much about the broader aspects of my profession but at least I would start out with a thorough knowledge of how to handle men.

One other aspect of soldiering in Germany in the aftermath of the war is worth mentioning. Although life for civilians in England was bleaker than it had been in the war itself in terms of shortages of food, petrol and building materials, the army in Germany wanted for nothing. An officer could live well and cheaply with gin at two shillings and sixpence a bottle and white wine was virtually free. Meals in the officers' club in Osnabrück were lavish with an orchestra and dancing every night. The only trouble was that there were few girls to dance with, since fraternising with Germans was forbidden and the English clerks employed by the Control Commission for Germany (CCG) were not thought suitable. This did not stop one of our company commanders who had spent most of the war in command of mule transport in Burma, from sending his driver to pick up three or four of them, selecting the best to have dinner with him. Meanwhile most of the Germans were desperately short of food and shelter so that many died.

When not on duty, officers amused themselves mainly with shooting, riding horses or as the winter progressed, skiing and skating. At the start of the shooting season each regiment sent an officer to brigade headquarters where they chose an area for their battalion shoot from a map. This was then split up into company areas and those wishing to shoot merely turned up at a prearranged time and started blazing away. A Company had two small areas, one either side of a stream and one around a lake. Three or four of us usually led by Johnny Walker would set off in one of the platoon half tracks with a pack lunch and spend a few hours hunting down any game that we could find. The German Jagermeisters rated everything by weight so that to their mind the greatest prize was a roe deer and then a fox and then a hare etc. We were much more interested in pheasants, partridges and duck, but we tended to be happy with whatever turned up, except that none of us approved of shooting foxes. What Johnny approved of most was a very high-class pack lunch, which needed to be washed down with plenty of vino and concluded with a glass of port. We usually enjoyed ourselves but the bag was always pretty meagre; one or two pheasants if we were lucky with the odd hare or rabbit and perhaps a pigeon.

Despite the enjoyable social life and sporting facilities I was impatient with the lack of enthusiasm and critical of the inefficiency which resulted from it. Even though most of the people in the battalion were thinking about the end of their military service, I was looking forward to a long and satisfying future in the army and I wanted to step out along the road to fame at once. Commanding an under-strength platoon with most of the men engaged on camp duties, guards, etc. did not appeal to me much. I wanted to make my men into the most alert and best-trained platoon in the battalion.

At about this time during a very cold spell the first trainload of families arrived from England. For some reason I was sent to Osnabrück station with some riflemen to form a reception party. *The Regimental Chronicle* covered the event reporting that 'it was a great day for Frank who showed how versatile the army can be. He was seen heating and distributing water to mothers to make a brew of baby food for the younger members of their families. One harassed but grateful father was heard to remark that "that there Mr Kitson would make anyone a good wife."'

Life in A Company took a turn for the better when we went to a distant training area for three weeks. Unfortunately Colin James who had been one of the few people to understand and sympathise with my frustrations, had left the battalion to become adjutant of a TA regiment. Our new company second-in-command was John Baker who apart from being very nice, was much keener than Colin on shooting and fishing. From our camp at Haltern we set off each day under Johnny's supervision to occupy defensive positions or to attack an imaginary enemy. In the evening John Baker and I used to wander around with our guns shooting pigeons. The climax of our training came on Good Friday when Johnny decided that all the half-tracks should take part in a cross-country race to the top of a wooded hill and there brew a cup of tea for him. The first to produce a drinkable cup would be the winner. One of my section half tracks won, but there was a downside to the performance which was that about three quarters of all the company vehicles broke down because of the enthusiasm with which the drivers tackled the rough going. It took some days before we could get ourselves back to Osnabrück. During this time the company signals corporal was accidentally shot and killed. His nickname was Lucky because he had been through the war without a scratch. He was due to be married and released from the army in a few weeks time.

*   *   *

Early in the summer of 1947 I was told that I would have to leave my platoon to become the battalion signals officer, one of the three officers in battalion headquarters directly serving the colonel. Together with the adjutant and intelligence officer he manned the command vehicle. He controlled the battalion wireless net and was in charge of all the battalion signallers. In July I would go on a course to the signals school at Catterick. Meanwhile I would take instruction from the battalion signals sergeant so that I would have a basic understanding of how wireless sets worked before going there. This together with looking after my platoon and going on frequent fishing trips to the River Lippe with Johnny and John Baker kept me fully occupied.

There were about thirty people on the course at Catterick of whom perhaps six were officers and the rest signals NCOs all of whom knew far more about it than the officers. I soon paired up with an ex-Indian Army captain called Tim Creasey who had recently transferred to the Royal Norfolk Regiment. His huge frame with clipped military moustache concealed a rumbustious character determined to live life to the full. He had a plentiful store of barrack room songs and enjoyed such parties as were available within the garrison. On one occasion at a drinks party we were talking together amidst the hub-bub when a sudden silence descended upon the gathering as sometimes happens. Without a pause in what he was saying to me, Tim said in a very loud voice 'and I said to her madam, have the goodness to lie on your back', whereupon all eyes were directed at him. Tim recoiled in mock embarrassment and the chat restarted throughout the room. But there was another side to Creasey, which held that as officers we should do better than the NCOs even though they had a head start on us. As a result we worked like Trojans in the evening and at night to catch up, reading from the notes we took in the day and keeping up our records. As a result both Tim and I passed the course with a distinguished grading, the only two to achieve such a good result, and I went away feeling that I had earned it.

It was October by the time I returned to the battalion and joined Headquarters Company as the signals officer. The signal department was larger than an ordinary platoon and included a section of despatch riders with their motorcycles. I was responsible for a mass of wireless equipment, most of which was in a poor state of repair. Many of the signallers had been released from the army without replacement so that I was also under strength. I set about collecting some potential signallers from the rifle companies and ran a training course to teach them their jobs.

The big question at this time was whether I would be given a regular commission in The Rifle Brigade. I was still serving on what was termed an emergency commission. In mid-November I returned to England to attend a Regular Commissions Board, which I passed. This meant that the regiment could keep me on if it wanted to do so but there were a number of officers applying for the few vacancies available. Early in December Dick Poole went to a colonel commandants meeting in England at which the matter was discussed and on his return told me that he thought my application would be accepted, which took a weight off my mind.

*　*　*

In February 1948 the battalion moved to Minden, a horrible place on the banks of the Weser. We were surrounded by miles of flat fields, which made for dull riding and there was no game to shoot. Heaven knows who decided to send a rifle brigade battalion to such a place. But worse was to come when at the end of March Dick Poole was replaced as commanding officer by Freddy Stephens. Unlike his predecessor who had considerable ability but no desire for military preferment, Freddy, despite having successfully commanded the battalion at Alamein, appeared to have less ability but was keen to get on and was in a constant fuss that something would go wrong. He was at his worst when the battalion was out of barracks on an exercise when he often got worked up with whoever was nearest to him, usually the signallers. Luckily at the end of the year Bill Brownlow took over as adjutant and Freddy calmed down a bit.

In August 1949 I heard that after three years in the battalion I was to go as the intelligence staff officer at brigade headquarters which would bring with it promotion to captain. I felt that it was time for me to get away and see what happened beyond the confines of the regiment and I was glad that I would not have to be an aide-de-camp (ADC) to some old general which was the fate of many of my friends. I had no idea what my new job would entail and was relieved to hear that I did not have to go on a training course to find out.

*   *   *

In the three years that had elapsed since my arrival in Germany, much had changed in the world at large. Russia, which had seemed like a gallant but awkward ally in 1946, was now clearly a major threat to the West, a fact underlined in June 1948 when Russia blockaded Berlin. This caused the Western powers to mount an airlift, not only to keep their own contingents in Berlin supplied, but also to uphold the day-to-day life of the German population in those parts of the city not occupied by the Russians. It was a massive undertaking. Soon afterwards the Western European Union came into being designed to co-ordinate defence against a Russian attack and in April 1949 the United States and Canada joined the countries of Western Europe in the North Atlantic Treaty Organization (NATO).

During the same three years the composition of the British Army of the Rhine had also changed to the extent that all of the men who had fought in the war and who did not intend to make the army their career had left. They were replaced by national servicemen, conscripted for two years. These people, conscious that they did not know the business, were mostly prepared to become good soldiers however reluctant they may have been to be conscripted in the first place. This, together with the obvious Russian threat, meant that training at all levels had been greatly intensified, a fact that was very apparent from the first moment that I arrived in HQ 7th Armoured Brigade (formerly 22nd Armoured Brigade) now stationed at Bad Lippspringe near Sennelager.

The 7th Armoured Brigade consisted of four armoured regiments and a motor battalion (1 RB). A new commander had taken over the brigade about two weeks before my arrival. He was Brigadier Foote, an officer of the Royal Tank Regiment who had won a Victoria Cross in the desert. He was an expert on tank design as well as having much battle experience. He was also very fat, had a petite American wife, no children and was totally relaxed and unflappable. On the other hand, unlike most of his staff, he took no interest in horses or fishing. He sometimes appeared with a shotgun but he preferred golf. The Deputy Commander, Colonel Gregson, was very different. He was a slim and fit gunner with a good war record and he was an expert in all forms of horsemanship. He had represented England at polo before the war and was a fine amateur steeplechase jockey and trainer. He was also a keen shot and fisherman but noticeably less keen on military training having had enough of warfare in the recent conflict. He had a beautiful young wife and a small son. He soon took me under his wing determined to make a jockey of me. The brigade major was a highly competent cavalry officer and the grade 3 staff officer with whom I shared an office, was another cavalryman called Pat Howard-Dobson.

When in barracks my job had little to do with intelligence apart from the fact that I looked after the map store. What happened was that the brigade major allocated the work for which he was responsible to Pat Howard-Dobson or myself according to which one of us was least busy at the time. In the field I had two main jobs. First, it was my responsibility to ensure that the commander's map and the maps of the general staff officers were kept marked up to date. The positions of our own troops were marked red (for British) and those of the exercise enemy were marked blue (for French), the system having been developed in the nineteenth century. Not long afterwards the system changed and 'own troops' became blue (NATO) and the enemy red (Russians). It was all rather confusing. My other job was to act as the commander's ADC, which meant going with him when he left the HQ to visit units and reading the map to make sure that he got there. This was more fun than Pat's job, which confined him to the armoured command vehicle helping the brigade major. The one thing that both of us had in common was that we got very little sleep because so much preparation for the next day had to be done during the short periods of darkness at the end of each day's battle. It was invaluable training for me since it taught me how to cat-nap and thereby to get along without going to bed for days at a time.

In March brigade headquarters moved to Soltau, between Hanover and Hamburg, so as to be close to the armoured training area, which stretched for miles across the heath towards Luneburg. Divisional headquarters had already moved to Celle, some miles to the south of us. Instead of being tucked into a delightful German health spa we were in a straightforward ex-German barracks.

* * *

The increasing likelihood of war with Russia resulted in two particularly busy periods of intensive military training. First came a whole month of brigade training when the brigadier put each unit through its paces in turn. The second, a few weeks later, consisted of a vast exercise run by HQ BAOR in which several divisions took part. Most of my work on these exercises consisted of trying to ensure that the various parts of our headquarters got to the right places at the right time which was a mammoth task because, as a hangover from the war, brigade headquarters had become much too big. In addition to my other jobs I was responsible for looking after the brigadier's three tanks and his dingo and jeep. I also had a dingo and jeep of my own in which I could accompany him and of course I was responsible for the map lorry in which I slept together with the intelligence corporal who minded the maps. The tanks were a complete nuisance because they were always breaking down and the brigadier seldom used them. Indeed on the big exercise, I kept my bitch in one of them with a litter of pups which had been born the day before the exercise started. I had been unable to find someone to look after them while I was away. They would have been more comfortable in the map lorry but there was insufficient room for all of us there.

By the beginning of October the training season was deemed to be at an end. Regiments and battalions now went back to the start of the training cycle, which meant teaching individuals within units how to carry out their respective tasks. I felt that it would be a good moment to go on leave and together with an officer from the headquarters squadron we set off in my car for a three week trip through France and Spain. On my return I found the headquarters in turmoil. Two new armoured divisions were being formed in BAOR and Brigadier Foote was to command one of them as a major general. The preliminary arrangements were to be carried out at our headquarters, which meant that the brigade major would be closely involved. The GSO3 operations was going with the brigadier as his ADC and I was to take his place. Another officer was on his way to take over my job. From now on we would all be very busy. A new brigadier who was reputed to have a sharp temper, would arrive just before Christmas.

When our new brigadier arrived I went with him when he visited the regiments of the brigade and he seemed very pleasant. However our association was of short duration. The other new armoured division was being raised initially in England and as a motor battalion was needed for its armoured brigade it was decided that the KRRC would be given a second battalion. But as the KRRC did not have enough men, the Rifle Brigade would also have to contribute detachments to bring it into being. As an experienced signals officer I would be needed to get the signals going until someone else could be trained. I was not at all pleased about it, but it would be interesting setting it up from scratch and in any case I had no option. Apparently Brigadier Foote had opposed the posting with vigour on the grounds that I was needed in the headquarters but he was over ruled. In the middle of February I packed my bag and left.

*   *   *

The new battalion was forming up at the Rifle Depot in Winchester. When after ten days leave I reported to the colonel, I found that the only other officers to have arrived were the adjutant and quartermaster. Malcolm Douglas Pennant who had started life in the 60th but who was now a Rifle Brigade officer, was the colonel. In the war he had commanded a regiment of the Reconnaissance Corps and his varied career had taught him that the only way to deal with people from different regimental backgrounds was to do everything for a good reason rather than because it was the way things had always been done. He had no interest in horses but was a very keen fisherman and shot. He was no conversationalist but was friendly and pleasant. What he lacked in charisma he made up for with common sense. He was totally unfussy.

Tommy Wallis, who had been in charge of our young officers' course when I was first commissioned was the adjutant. Tommy was a different sort of person, very Irish both in terms of speech and the warmth of his character. His life revolved around the racecourse. He was a Rifle Brigade officer of great experience and despite his efforts to conceal the fact, a highly competent operator. He was also fairly recently married to Vivien an equally outgoing and friendly person. Over the next few weeks further officers arrived including another Rifle Brigade Irishman, Desmond Dunalley, as second-in-command and a high powered company commander called Tony Hunter who was a 60th officer but who had commanded 8 RB in Normandy until it was disbanded after the end of he war. I was lucky enough to get a number of my best signallers from 1 RB and also some good senior NCOs from 1 KRRC. For the rest the colonel gave me a free hand to select whoever I liked from the companies to train as signallers so that the setting up of an effective signals section was an enjoyable and satisfying experience.

* * *

Being grafted onto the Rifle Depot was an experience of a different and less pleasant kind. For one thing this organisation, officered at the time by elderly gentlemen who were looking for a quiet life was in marked contrast to the vibrant battalion that we were forming. For another thing the Depot itself was out of date and crumbling. So much was this the case that when the King decided to pay us a visit in his capacity as Colonel-in-Chief of the 60th he was told that he would have to wear a protective helmet if he came into the officers' mess because of the danger of falling plaster. In the end he was entertained in the sergeant's mess which was in a more modern part of the building. In fact the greatest danger to the officers arose from the disgusting state of the kitchen and the reluctance of the mess sergeant to put in an appearance before midday. But despite the filthy food the messing charge was many times greater than it was in any other mess in the British Army. At a mess meeting when it was proposed to raise the charge even further, I was very rude to Jeffrey Coryton, the President of the Mess Committee (PMC), who promptly made me food member and told me to get it better without any more money. I therefore refused to let the mess sergeant buy anything for a few weeks, which meant that he had to produce meals from the army rations. As this was not enough, I supplemented it by shooting rooks out of the trees round the edge of the barracks so that rook pie became a staple part of the menu much to the horror of the other officers. Our bedrooms were similarly unattractive being vast in size with little more than a bed in them. It was a cold winter and the only heating consisted of a small coal fire in each room. I shared a room with a keen Bisley shot who used religiously to lie on the floor with his rifle every night practising at a target stuck on the wall while his dog licked his face, which was often blue with cold.

When we started going out on exercises we had no half tracks so that battalion headquarters operated from the back of a three ton truck. Tommy Wallis and I sat in the back with some clerks and signallers while the documents on which we were trying to record the progress of events were frequently blown out over the tail-board. It all seemed very un-military but the general idea was getting across all right.

Much to the relief of the Depot, 2 KRRC moved out of Winchester and set up shop in Tidworth during July of 1951. Towards the end of the year my task of forming the signals section neared completion and for the first time since 1945 I was at home for Christmas.

On the 7 February, the day after the death of King George VI, I left England once more for Germany. 2 KRRC was to be the motor battalion of one of the new armoured divisions and I was part of the advance party. After ten days I heard that my father had been taken to hospital for an operation and two days later that he was dead. Although he had been a bit under the weather when I last saw him and was suffering from an irritation of the skin, there was no hint of any serious illness so I was unprepared for his departure from this world. Next day I flew back to England for his funeral.

By 8 March the battalion was complete in Oxford Barracks, Munster, and the outgoing battalion had moved away. Although the new signals officer had not yet arrived to relieve me I was made second-in-command of A company which was also awaiting the arrival of a new company commander.

From the middle of June to the end of September 1952 there were a series of intensive training exercises throughout the British Army of the Rhine with no expense spared. Having raised two extra armoured divisions, the army was determined that they should be able to function properly. These exercises certainly afforded me an opportunity to see on the ground, the problems of moving masses of tanks, guns and vehicles of all sorts along many different routes and across country. Particular attention was paid to attacking and defending a river line so that I also gained much useful experience on this subject.

On one of the exercises I acted as an umpire of a brigade trying to establish a bridgehead over the Rhine in an area defended by infantry with an armoured reserve. Assisted by two subalterns I was attached to an infantry battalion, which crossed the river in assault boats in the dark. It was interesting to see how this wonderful battalion, which had spent much of the war in Burma, worked despite the fact that only the second-in-command had been to the Staff College. The commanding officer had started the war as the regimental sergeant major at a time when most of the company commanders had been sergeants or corporals. I crossed with an elderly company commander. When our boat touched the far bank there was a cry of 'we'll get you ashore granddad' as several soldiers grabbed the company commander and carried him well up the beach. It all looked a bit cranky but the company commanders knew their stuff and worked together as they had probably done seven years earlier on the banks of the Irrawaddy. Led by these men the private soldiers most of whom were conscripts, were immensely enthusiastic. The resourceful and inspiring colonel, reacted instinctively and aggressively to all the problems posed by the defending force so that the many counter-attacks on the bridgehead were all beaten back.

Throughout these months A Company which was by then commanded by Peter Curtis functioned well. Peter had a good war record was very interested in tactics and was only too happy to leave the rest of the business to me. He never fussed or bothered about senior officers so long as the company was operating on the lines that he laid down. But by the end of the year the priority given to providing high class NCOs and men to get the battalion going in the first place had been withdrawn and replacements for those coming to the end of their time were often less good or in some cases totally lacking. A general falling off of efficiency was soon all too apparent and as the battalion became less effective it became less contented.

By the end of the year I had had more than enough of the battalion and felt that it was high time that I gained experience of the army away from the regiment and away from armoured brigades. I therefore applied for what was known as an 'extra regimental appointment' hoping to be sent to some active service theatre of operations. In the early part 1953, events followed their usual course that is to say there was a lengthy period of individual training for those new to the battalion and a series of courses designed to teach the more experienced men new skills. After this each company in turn went to a training area so that the company commanders could exercise their platoons. At the end of June, A Company found itself on the Sennelager training area some 60 miles from Munster together with its affiliated armoured regiment. Although I did not know it, my desire to get away was about to be settled in a dramatic fashion.

On the evening of Monday, 6 July I was in a leaguer area preparing to clamber into my damp sleeping bag when a despatch rider appeared with instructions for me to contact the colonel at once. I drove to the nearest telephone and eventually got through to the adjutant who told me that I had been selected to do an intelligence job in Kenya and was to return to Munster overnight and return to England on Wednesday. That gave me one day to sell my car, hand over the stables and say my goodbyes. On Thursday I was on my way. My seven years in armoured formations, almost all spent in Germany, were over.

Although spending such a long time in armoured divisions was frustrating, it had given me a thorough grounding in the nuts and bolts of the sort of soldiering which lay at the heart of the army's principal role which was to keep the Russians out of western Europe. It would be twenty-three years before I returned to command an armoured division but when I did, I found that most of what I had learnt was still relevant. Meanwhile it would be necessary for me to learn about a different sort of war.

Chapter 2

Kenya: Finding the Way 1953–1954

My departure from Germany had been rushed to say the least. Having got back to England I was instructed to get inoculated against all sorts of diseases and to get the right uniform for East Africa. From 1 August 1953 I was put at twenty-four hours notice to move and told to stay by the end of a telephone. The order did not come until 23 August, the intervening period being taken up by visits to numerous friends. I also spent a few days with some friends of Tom in Ireland and visited Tom himself at Gosport where he was based while commanding a motor torpedo boat. A telephone call to Monk's Hill each evening was enough to discover that my departure was not imminent.

It was during this period that I discovered where Kenya was in relation to the rest of the world and also a bit about the events that had been taking place there over the past year. On 24 August I set off for Kenya in a passenger version of the old Dakota transport aircraft. It took three days to get there. On the first day we got as far as Malta where my cousin, Robert de Pass, met me. He was Earl Mountbatten's flag lieutenant and he introduced me to the admiral and his wife before giving me dinner. On the second day we reached Khartoum and during the afternoon of the third we reached Nairobi. I had now arrived in an insurgency situation, to do a job for which I had no training. I would be working with a wide variety of people whose background was totally different from my own. It was exactly what I needed after my long spell in Germany.

Many regard Kenya as being one of the most beautiful countries in the world. It is not large, being roughly 600 miles long by 500 wide, but within its borders is a variation of altitude, which provides an ever changing pattern of scenery and climate. The equator passes through Mount Kenya itself which rising to over 17,000 feet, has snow on its peaks throughout the year. Within a few hundred miles lies a coastline with the Indian Ocean. In between are areas of tropical rain forest, fertile pasture and arid scrub, some of which was then inhabited by massive concentrations of game animals.

Being in a colony was like living in an old fashioned monarchy with the Governor as King, ruling through a hierarchy of Provincial Commissioners, District Commissioners, District officers, Chiefs and Headmen. All except the Chiefs and Headmen were English officers of the colonial service. Collectively they were known as the administration. The Governor was naturally obliged to take account of any instructions he might receive from London and he was of course bound to work in accordance with the law. There was a Legislative Council consisting of senior members of the colonial government and representatives from the settler community together with a few Asians and Africans, composed in such a way that new legislation was usually enacted in accordance with the wishes of the administration.

*   *   *

From time to time noisy settler politics welled up from the legislative council resulting in marches and demonstrations, well covered by the press. Some African politicians, frustrated by their lack of influence, had recently instigated and then lost control of a subversive movement known as Mau Mau, which accounted for my presence in the colony. There were around 6.5 million Africans in Kenya and an Asian population of perhaps 150,000, which was mainly concerned with commercial activities. Large areas of land were designated as native reserves in which most of the Africans lived. Of the many tribes only the Kikuyu were involved in the Mau Mau, but they were the most numerous and politically active. The rest of the land was owned by Europeans and was known as settled area. The total number of Europeans in the colony was around 40,000. Their influence far exceeded their numbers and the value of what they produced, kept the place afloat. They had been encouraged to come to the colony by the British government, which felt that it had an obligation to look after them, and indeed it did, up to a point. During my first few weeks I heard a lot about what the Europeans thought and wanted but not too much about the Africans and Asians.

To bring the Mau Mau uprising under control, a state of emergency had been declared in October 1952. This mainly affected the districts in which the Kikuyu lived together with the surrounding forests, the adjacent European settled areas and Nairobi. Government forces included the regular police of 7,000 men recruited from different tribes with British officers, backed by a part time Kenya Police Reserve (KPR) consisting of Kenya Europeans and Asians, which rose to a strength of about 12,000. There were five regiments of the King's African Rifles (KAR) consisting of Africans recruited throughout East Africa with British officers. In addition there were three British Army battalions: a further two arrived later. There was also a Territorial Army battalion manned by Kenya settlers called the Kenya Regiment which proved to be highly successful. At the time of my arrival no one had any idea how many Mau Mau members were active altogether but it was thought that there might be as many as 15,000 in the forest gangs.

After a few days being briefed in Nairobi I was sent as District Military Intelligence Officer (DMIO) Kiambu, which was the most southerly of the districts occupied by the Kikuyu and which was adjacent to Nairobi. There was also some settled area where Europeans grew coffee. The district stretched for about 50 miles from north to south and thirty from east to west. About 350,000 Kikuyu lived in Kiambu District. There were a further 65,000 Kikuyu living in Nairobi which amounted to a little over half of the city's population. I was also told to 'keep an eye' on the neighbouring district of Thika, which consisted entirely of European farms. My task as DMIO was to work in concert with the assistant superintendent of the police Special Branch, who was called Ken Goodale. I was technically on loan to the Kenya Police Reserve but I was administered by the army and was required to keep the GSO 2 Intelligence at HQ East Africa, John Holmes, in touch with my activities.

The idea of using the army to reinforce police intelligence agencies had no doubt been tried out in other colonies in the past, but the system had not formerly been used in Kenya and we were given a pretty free hand to decide how to make it work. Initially our main problem was the shortage of resources. Goodale had three or four African constables working for him spread around the district and I was supposed to have one sergeant of the Kenya Regiment, which was composed of Kenya based Europeans, working for me. There were plans to make further sergeants available, but before any of them arrived the one I did have went on leave and was accidentally shot in a pub. There was nowhere for me to live so I billeted myself on a battalion of the King's African Rifles in a tented camp near Kiambu township. Goodale invited me to share his office in the police headquarters, which was conveniently placed next door to the operations room manned by lady members of the Kenya Police Reserve.

Even now I can remember wondering what exactly I should be doing. In an attempt to get the matter straight I even tried to carry out what the army calls an appreciation of the situation, but with limited success. I did at least manage to get my aim straight. Clearly Special Branch as a whole was responsible for getting information on all matters connected with the security of the colony and I assumed that the military intelligence officers, as part of Special Branch, must be responsible for carrying out part of this commitment. Furthermore it was obvious that our part must concern the extra work that had fallen to Special Branch as a result of the rebellion. I therefore decided that my aim must be 'to provide the security forces with the information they needed to destroy Mau Mau in the area for which I was responsible' i.e. Kiambu and Thika districts. I wrote it down and kept it tucked into the fly-leaf of my bible where I could not fail to see it at regular intervals.

My appreciation was less effective at showing me how to carry out this aim. For a start, with so few resources of my own and knowing nothing of the language, it seemed wise to concentrate on making the acquaintance of as many of the District officers and police as possible. In the course of doing so I might pick up bits of information useful to the members of the District Emergency Committee which consisted of the District Commissioner, the Superintendent of Police and the commander of any army units in the district. It also enabled me to get to know my way around the countryside. This is how I occupied myself for the first few weeks.

During my travels I got a good idea of the lay out of the district. I noticed how the numerous mountain streams flowed out of the forest in the west through steep valleys of scrub and wattle and then joined together to form rivers which passed through wider areas of more fertile ground. In this part of the Kikuyu Reserve groups of round native huts were sprinkled around haphazardly amongst small areas of maize and bananas, interspersed with patches of coarse grass grazed by goats and native cattle. Further to the east as the altitude dropped, the pattern of the reserve gave way to rows of dark green coffee bushes owned by Europeans. Here the settlers lived in sizeable stone houses a short distance from the labour lines, which accommodated their estate workers. The key factor was the height of the land, which ranged from 8,000 feet in the highest part of our bit of forest, down to 4,500 feet in the settled area to the east. Height naturally determined temperature and rainfall, the lower land being the warmest and driest.

*   *   *

Kiambu District was divided into three divisions each run by a District officer who combined the functions of administrator and magistrate. There were several police stations in each division and a larger number of Kikuyu Guard posts where groups of African loyalists congregated to defend their local area from marauding Mau Mau gangs. Roads consisted of little more than tracks of dusty red murram running along the ridges and connecting one ridge with the next across the intervening valleys. Even the main road north from Nairobi to Nyeri via Thika and Fort Hall, was murram. And murram, which is dusty when dry, is extremely slippery when wet.

The most active area at the time of my arrival was around the southern tip of the forest. The District officer there was a tall and friendly man called John Cumber who was a great help to me. Amongst other people he introduced me to a stocky middle aged settler in the Kenya Police Reserve called Kitchener Morson who had been born and bred in the area. He knew more about the Africans in this part of Kenya than anyone else and he agreed to join my organisation on an unofficial, part-time basis. The nearest police station to the forest in this division was at Uplands where I soon got to know the inspector in charge, Philip Myburgh, and his right hand man, Dennis Kearney. Dennis was an 18-year-old on loan from the Kenya Regiment, who spoke fluent Kikuyu as well as Swahili. Cumber, Morson, Myburgh and Kearney between them were chiefly responsible for getting me accepted into the world of Kenya born Europeans without whom I would get nowhere. But Dennis, who looked as though butter would not melt in his mouth, was greatly addicted to practical jokes and, in my ignorance of colonial life, I was a sitting target.

In spite of trying hard to get involved in the fighting, I always seemed to arrive too late. Contacts only lasted for a brief period and unless I happened to be in the immediate vicinity when one occurred, it would be all over before I could get there. I was left with the job of passing on an account of what had happened or possibly taking a body back to the police station to get it identified. At this time, if a terrorist was killed deep in the forest his hand would be cut off and taken back for finger printing. On one occasion I was given two hands to

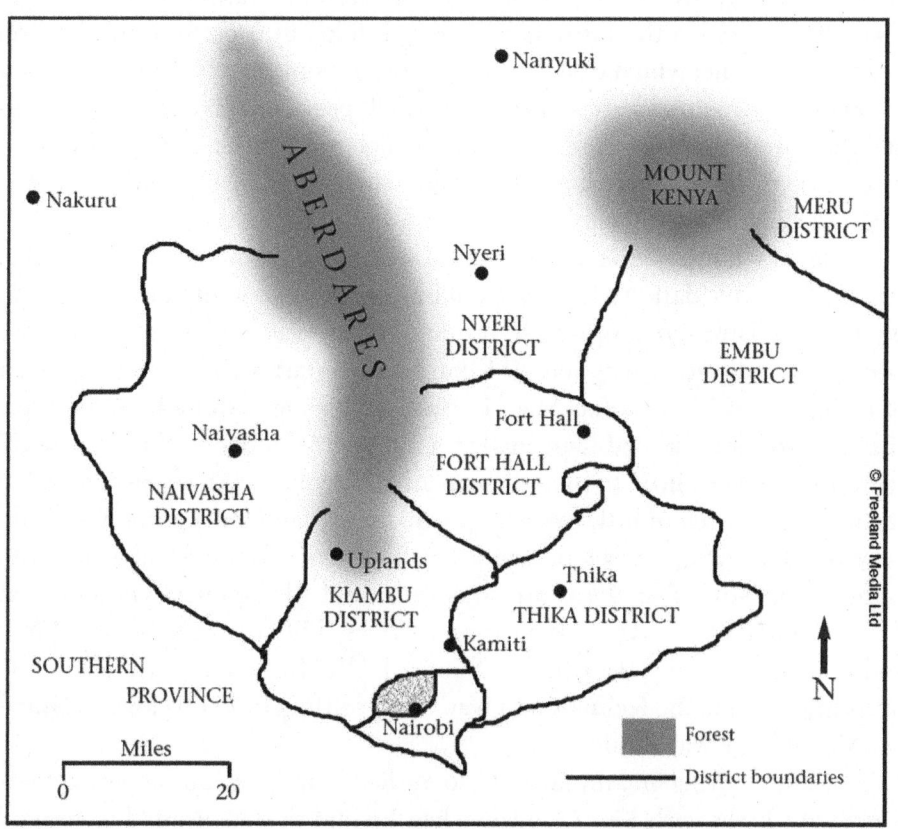

get identified and having nowhere else to put them I wrapped them in sacking and put them in my pockets. Kearney, observing this, shouted in an assumed sergeant major type voice 'Captain Kitson, get those hands out of your pockets', which raised a laugh from the bystanders. Fortunately, a few months later, the distasteful business of cutting hands off dead terrorists was stopped.

It was soon apparent that I could no longer base myself on the King's African Rifles because my movements were too uncertain to fit in with their routine. I therefore rented a house from a coffee farmer for £15 a month, which became my home for the next two years. It was in a convenient place near the village of Kamiti on the edge of the reserve and on the border between Kiambu and Thika districts. It was old by Kenya standards and was made of mud and wattle with a thatched roof. It was all on one floor and was one room wide. There was a bedroom at each end and an entrance hall in the middle, which also served as pantry and larder. Between the hall and one of the bedrooms was a bathroom and between it and the other bedroom was the dining room and sitting room. Behind the house was a hut in which the cooking was done and another for the cook. Behind that again was a long shed in which lived the house-boy, the garden-boy and, later when I got one, the driver of my Land Rover. There was a supply of water in the form of a large tank filled by a pump from the river and a smaller one, which caught water from the roof for drinking. There was an oil drum cemented onto some bricks which provided a boiler for hot water and there were three pressure lamps with which to light the house, there being no electricity. The cook, house-boy and garden-boy were each paid 50 shillings a month (£2.50) together with a sack of posho (maize meal).

By day my house seemed wonderful: I had never before had a house all to myself. But after dark with no more illumination than could be provided by my pressure lamps, one of which did not work, I was not so sure. The cook, house-boy and garden-boy were all Kikuyu and to start with I was a bit nervous of being visited by the Mau Mau. I visualised a gang coming in when I was sitting there alone, as had happened to a number of settler families. Certainly there was precious little to prevent such an eventuality, as in places the wall of the house consisted of little more than wire netting and most of the door bolts were missing. After a week or two my nervousness wore off and as October turned into November the short rains came and the country was refreshed. Bright blue blooms covered the jacaranda trees. The dry grass became green and the roses in front of my house flowered. Watching the Kenya equivalent of spring gave me the feeling that I was at last settling in to this lovely country and this strange way of life.

Soon after moving into my house I had my first taste of genuine unpleasantness. One night I was with Ken Goodale when he said that he wanted to stop off at a mortuary to see if one of his informers had found their way there. I was told to hold the torch as he rummaged around in the human wreckage. There had been a number of actions over the past few days and there must have been about eighteen bodies lying in various stages of decomposition on the floor of what was little more than a shed. The repulsive sight was only exceeded by the stench. Ken kept on talking about whatever we had been talking about before, and I realised that I could hardly make off and leave him to it. Since arriving in Kenya I had been a bit nervous of how I would react to a really disgusting sight but I soon got used to it and was relieved to find that apart from the smell it did not bother me.

In December the arrangement under which Kenya Regiment NCOs like Kearney were attached to the police, came to an end, which freed up men to reinforce the intelligence organisation. Over the next few weeks I got three for Kiambu, and two for Thika to act as Field Intelligence Assistants (FIAs). One went to each of the divisions to work alongside the District officers. I was also given one extra, just 19 years old, called Eric Holyoak, who was considered too young to go out to a division. He was to help me as an interrogator and translator.

There was seldom anyone to interrogate, but I was in dire need of a translator. Despite having picked up a few words of Swahili I was still incapable of communicating adequately with the house staff. By means of sign language and help from the odd visitor I had arranged to have steak and pineapple whenever I asked for lunch or dinner and fried eggs when I was in for breakfast, but I was getting a bit tired of this diet. I therefore installed Eric in the spare room of my house and he took on the business of running it, including ordering the meals. One morning soon after he arrived, the cook approached him in an agitated state. It seems that I had made a mistake ordering my breakfast having asked for 'malaya mbile' which means two prostitutes instead of 'myia mbile' which means two eggs. Eric guessed that it was my primitive Swahili that was at fault as opposed to my morals, but the cook took some convincing.

By this time Ken Goodale had returned to England and been replaced by Peter Dempster, who had been at Stowe and who had some experience as a race rider before joining the Kenya Police Reserve. Goodale's view was that Nairobi and Kiambu were working together as the main base for the Mau Mau movement. The large gangs, 200 or 300 strong, living in the Aberdare and Mount Kenya forests relied on this base to supply them with money, medical supplies, weapons, ammunition and recruits. In theory the major gang leaders in the Aberdares and Mount Kenya were still supposed to accept direction from the Mau Mau Central Committee in Nairobi, but by late 1953 they paid no more attention to this organisation than was necessary to ensure a continuation of supplies.

*   *   *

In Kiambu and Nairobi there was a chain of Mau Mau committees, each one backed by a strong-arm group whose purpose was to collect the money levied on those taking the Mau Mau oath and killing or mutilating those that refused. Most of the incidents that occurred in the district were either caused by bands of recruits passing between Nairobi and the forest or by these strong-arm groups operating at night to cover their nefarious activities. And for the Kikuyu who lived their lives heavily dependent on magic and the influence of the spirit world, darkness often brought terror. It was the Mau Mau Central Committee in Nairobi that had organised the spread of oathing throughout the tribal areas and it was the Mau Mau oath that had poisoned the atmosphere and spread the sort of misery throughout the land that I was just beginning to feel. It is therefore worth trying to explain its significance.

Fifty years before the start of the Kenya Emergency most of the Kikuyu had never seen animals harnessed or ridden, nor had they heard of the wheel or the plough. Misfortune was put down to malignant spirits or the anger of their god. Witch doctors tried to cure sickness by providing concoctions to counter the evil spirits and the spells thought to have caused it. Disputes were referred to tribal elders and one of the methods used to resolve them was to get those involved to take an oath verifying their stories. If the oath was administered in such a way as to persuade the person taking it that he would die if he lied, he would either tell the truth or say nothing. The oath consisted of two parts. The first part concerned the actions taken to summon the supernatural power and the second was the declaration that the person made, swearing that he had not done whatever it was, or perhaps guaranteeing to do something in the future. Those taking the Mau Mau oath swore themselves to secrecy, to obey orders and to help other members of the movement. The main difference between a Mau Mau oath and a traditional tribal one was that the methods used to summon the power of the oath were disgusting and prohibited by tribal custom. The idea was that this would push the person concerned beyond the pale and away from the influence of the tribal elders. Many of those that had taken the oath felt guilty, foul and threatened by it. Nearly all believed in its power.

Soon after Eric arrived, he got hold of one or two reliable Kikuyu to act as bodyguards. Now I felt more secure at home and when I went to areas where contacts had taken place Eric and one of his men came with me as a result of which we got a much better idea of what was going on. While I was talking to the FIA for example, Eric might be talking to the chief or a headman while his man could be chatting to members of the Kikuyu Guard or possibly to a prisoner. If it looked as if the prisoner would be of use outside the division in which he had been captured we could take him back to Kamiti where Eric or one of his men continued talking to him. If not we could leave him with the FIA concerned or hand him over at the nearest police station.

Mau Mau activity in the form of small incidents and murders increased during the last three months of 1953. Incidents seemed to come in bursts so that for two or three days at a time we would get hardly any sleep after which things settled down a bit until the next lot occurred. One of my duties was to write a weekly report, which throughout my years in Kenya took up valuable time. Often I could only fit it in by staying up all night if it was due the day after a particularly busy chain of events.

Towards the end of November an operation took place when some members of the Kenya Police Reserve spotted a large gang close to the borders of Thika and Fort Hall. Travelling to the scene I drove down a road between coffee farms. On either side stretched row upon row of green bushes 6 to 8 feet tall. Every now and then a drive would fork off from the road leading to a farm-house or African labour lines. After a while I found little pockets of Kenya Police Reservists who were cordoning off an area in which the gang was supposed to be hiding. Then I met a doctor who said that an officer of the Kenya Police Reserve had become a casualty. We pushed on together for some distance until discovering a car containing the body of a man who I recognised as Mr Lyall Shaw: I had often met him when attending meetings at Thika. He had spotted the gang when they appeared on his land and he tried to shadow it so as to be able to direct security force units in the right direction when they arrived. Unfortunately he ran into an ambush and was killed. The gang crossed the border into the Fort Hall reserve pursued by the army. From a prisoner taken from another gang in a battle near Kamiti that same day, it transpired that both gangs were part of a large-scale movement of recruits from Nairobi to the forest.

Shortly before Christmas I was driving with Eric up to our house one dark evening when we heard a burst of fire from a nearby settler's farm. We got there as fast as possible to be greeted by an appalling sight: broken windows, door knocked down and bits of clothing and other oddments littering the yard. Inside, the beams of Eric's torch revealed an even greater shambles. We all knew what it would be like to find the mutilated bodies of the inmates as we had seen pictures of similar situations. Apprehensively we made our way from room to room until we heard a little voice calling. After a few moment an old lady appeared from underneath the floor-boards which she kept loose for just such an emergency. She seemed not at all frightened.

On Christmas Eve I drove into Nairobi to dine with the Commander-in-Chief's ADC who was an old friend. It was the first time since arriving in Kenya that I had put on a dinner jacket. We had hardly started the meal when Eric rang up to say that I should return at once because a patrol of the Black

Watch had attacked a gang near Thika and the company commander, Earl Wavell, who was also the military commander for the district, had been killed. Two policemen with the patrol had been wounded. It was a dark and windy night. By the time that we arrived the gang was hiding in a patch of thick bush surrounded on one side by a railway embankment, on another side by the main Nairobi to Thika road and on the third side by a track. The whole area was no more than 300 yards long and 200 wide at the base. A cordon consisting mainly of members of the Kenya Police Reserve, the Black Watch Company and some regular police, surrounded the area. The District Commandant of the KPR called Peter Dene, had taken over command of the operation on the death of the company commander. As the enemy had refused to surrender, he planned to pour petrol from the embankment onto the scrub, set it on fire and shoot at the terrorists by the light of mortar flares.

We attached ourselves to that part of the cordon lining the track opposite the railway embankment. As the flares lit up, distances shrunk and the men on the embankment opposite were easily recognisable. As the flares faded the people receded until the embankment itself was only faintly visible in the darkness. But the petrol failed to set the wet grass alight properly. When the flares went up for the third time, the gang opened fire on the cordon. One or two shots came our way but most were directed at the men with the petrol on the embankment who, at a range of 30 to 40 yards, were nicely silhouetted against the sky. For a quarter of a minute while the flare illuminated the scene, the gang fired as many shots as they could and the men on the embankment returned the fire. But our people were firing at an area of grass while they were firing at clearly defined targets. By the time the darkness returned, four members of the cordon had fallen.

As soon as the firing stopped Eric and I ran down the track to the railway embankment to help with the casualties. One African police constable was dead and another badly wounded. Peter Dene's assistant commandant had been hit in the arm and the leg and Peter himself was hit in the stomach. We helped to carry the wounded to an ambulance. We later heard that the assistant commandant and constable would recover but Peter Dene had died which was a serious loss. After this incident it was decided that the cordon should concentrate on holding the gang until daylight at which time it could be flushed out and destroyed, but during the night they crept up to the cordon, shot two more policemen and passed through the gap, escaping into the darkness. The first thing that I saw next morning in the grey light of dawn was a wet and dishevelled Eric smiling broadly. Wondering what was so funny, I realised that I was still wearing a sodden dinner jacket and a pair of squelching patent leather shoes.

Some time later we discovered that the gang was from Fort Hall. Later still it turned out that its commander was a former corporal in the KAR, who had learnt his trade in Burma during the war. Our main problem was that we only heard about these things when it was too late. We were being helpful to the security forces but we were not achieving our aim of providing them with the information they needed in order to neutralise the gangs and the people supporting them.

* * *

Of the five FIAs who arrived during December 1953 and January 1954, two became outstandingly successful and stayed for nearly two years. Jacky Miller who looked after the southern half of Thika District, was born in England and came to Kenya at the age of 16 to farm. Glen Cottar whose father and grandfather had both been white hunters went to the southernmost division of Kiambu called Chura. They had all joined the Kenya Regiment at the start of the Kenya Emergency and trained together in Rhodesia. Most of the members of the Kenya Regiment had also been educated at the Prince of Wales School in Nairobi so that they had known each other for years. Their sisters had gone to the Kenya Girls' High School nearby, known as 'The Boma' (literally 'cattle pen') which was an additional link.

In January 1954 gang activity in Kiambu and Thika increased and my life got ever more hectic. There were gangs appearing in several different places. One debouched from the forest and attacked a settler's house in the extreme north-west corner of the district. Shortly afterwards another overran a Kikuyu Guard post just to the east of the forest opposite to the attack on the settler's house. In addition there were two contacts with a gang in the Uplands area and then another near the border with Fort Hall District. Eric and I spent much time visiting the places that had been attacked, examining bodies and talking to prisoners in an attempt to work out where the various gangs had come from and where they might be found by our troops. We kept going day and night: heat and dust by day, but cold at night near the forest edge. As we talked to prisoners during the long dark hours, scorched insects fell into the sticky mess that oozed out of the pressure lamps and the atmosphere became thick with smoke from our cigarettes. I tried to fit all the sightings and contacts together to form some sort of a coherent picture of what was happening, but could seldom get agreement from the people on the spot. What annoyed me was that although they would not agree with my ideas, they would never put forward ideas of their own, often justifying themselves by disputing some minor part of my reasoning. I had a lot to learn about collecting intelligence.

At the end of the month, after a five or six days of non-stop activity, I was creeping up to a hut near Kiambu with Kitch Morson and Dennis Kearney where the leader of one of the main Mau Mau committees was supposed to be hiding. For once we were in luck and managed to capture the person concerned but afterwards I felt pretty ill. Two days later I was in hospital with pneumonia. But this time antibiotics were available, so my stay there was not so prolonged as it had been in the hospital at Carlisle five years earlier. On being discharged I was sent to the coast at Malindi to recuperate. Ian Feild who was the DMIO of Fort Hall and who had arrived in Kenya with me, came as well. During January I had officially been made DMIO of Thika as well as Kiambu with orders to 'keep an eye on Nairobi' where there was one FIA called Bill Henning, who stood in for me while I was away.

Malindi consisted of an Arab fishing village and an area of sandy beach stretching for about a mile or so to the north of it. Along the beach from north to south were four hotels called the Eden Rock, Sinbad, Lawford's and Brady's Palm Beach (later re-named the Blue Marlin). Lawford's was frequented by the older settlers, Eden Rock by their sons most of whom were in the Kenya Regiment. The Sinbad catered mainly for expatriates such as members of the administration or the British Army and Brady's Palm Beach looked after those who could not get into anywhere else. We went to the Sinbad, which was the most comfortable and which had the best food. We did however stray up to the Eden Rock for a drink from time to time, to take a look at the owner, a peer with a dubious reputation called Lord Carberry, and his even more interesting wife, Junie, who had played a part in the events leading up to the famous Errol murder and she was reputedly the only person left who knew who did it, apart presumably from the murderer, if still alive.

We spent about ten days at Malindi and became engrossed in goggle fishing and surfing. Eric had warned me how to avoid painful jellyfish, sharp coral, sunburn and the sting of the stonefish, all of which made it sound much more dangerous than the Mau Mau. The thought of such perils helped to turn our minds away from thinking about terrorists, chiefs, district officers and policemen. With no weekly report to write we could concentrate on the hundreds of different sorts of highly coloured fish which we tried to harpoon.

But when lying on the beach I did sometimes wonder how on earth we could get the sort of information that would put the security forces in touch with the enemy, which was what they wanted. They showed little enthusiasm for the background knowledge that we were able to impart, such as the names of gang members and the places where they had operated in the past. As a start I thought that it would be a good idea if each of the FIAs built little camps in their divisions where they could keep a handful of Africans to help with interrogations and to move around the countryside planting and visiting informers. The idea caught my fancy and I visualised small clusters of mud huts surrounded by wire, with Africans pedalling in and out on bicycles. Clearly there would be difficulties since mud huts, barbed wire and bicycles do not appear out of thin air and my budget only amounted to £40 per month for everything including wages. On my return Eric said that I could leave it to him and he would consult Glen Cottar who would know exactly what to do.

Cottar did. By the end of March we had a wired in compound behind the house containing a number of mud huts thatched with banana leaves and Eric had increased the number of his bodyguard to seven men. Cottar also built himself a camp and recruited some men to help him so we now had two places where we could keep prisoners for a short time while talking to them.

While these developments were taking place, Mau Mau incidents seem to intensify particularly along the western edge of Thika District. It soon became apparent that there was a gang of Fort Hall men dividing their time between the labour lines of European farms and the Fort Hall Reserve; another gang consisting of Kiambu men was doing the same thing between European farms further south and the Kiambu Reserve. Between them these gangs were killing many loyalists. So far as we were concerned they provided the testing ground for some of the new methods that we were beginning to develop. The increased activity in Thika District enabled me to get Henning promoted to captain and appointed Assistant DMIO Thika, although I would retain responsibility for this district with him working for me. Another sergeant called Don Bush took over from Henning in Nairobi.

Building huts and developing ideas were all very well, but they were a poor substitute for involvement in active operations. It was therefore with some relish that Eric and I set off one Sunday morning for Fort Hall where a large gang had been seen not far north of our border. As we drove along one of the ridge tracks towards the forest we started to meet little groups of police and Kikuyu Guard. Once or twice we passed people whom Eric knew and he waved in their direction. He looked happy driving along in his usual khaki shirt, short shorts and a blue beret. It was our 'day off' and for once he would be free to chase a gang without having to bother about collecting prisoners or interrogating them. He might even get a shot at a terrorist and in any case he would be sure to meet friends from the Kenya Regiment. For concentrating in one place a large number of FIAs, Kikuyu Guard officers, soldiers and policemen there was nothing to beat a foray from the forest by a large gang.

In the event we had an interesting day. We soon heard that about 200 of the gang had taken up a position in a wattle plantation on the side of a steep valley after overrunning a Kikuyu Guard post and slaughtering the occupants. We were asked to observe the gang from one side while a Kikuyu Guard officer went to the other. Our job would be to direct a detachment of soldiers that was hurrying to the scene, to the right place. We clambered down our side of the valley until we could see the right flank of the enemy's position. We could hear their leaders shouting orders reinforced by bugle calls. There was a certain amount of firing but not much came in our direction. After a time the gang moved down the ridge away from the forest and we returned to our vehicle and tried to follow it. In fact we lost the enemy for a while as they moved sideways into the next valley, but we caught up with them later and had a good view of the proceedings at long range. And so the day passed. Once we got close enough to fire a few shots. From what we heard, the gang, which had started out about 500 strong, had split into several groups as it passed through the reserve. We returned to Kamiti in the evening but the operation continued for several more days before the survivors managed to get back to the forest having inflicted a number of casualties on the Kikuyu Guard but having sustained twice as many themselves, including their commander.

By early April our organisation had collected much information, including documents taken from captured and dead Mau Mau. Some of the FIAs had also managed to persuade a few low-level Mau Mau supporters to inform in return for money. Although this information was not yet of much use to the army, it was helpful to us. It was in this context that I had a bit of luck. One day I was sitting in my office with a prisoner recently taken from a small forest gang. Eric was away, so Jacky Miller had come from Thika to help me talk to the prisoner: although I now knew the difference between an egg and a prostitute, my command of the language was inadequate for interrogating prisoners. None of us had been taught how to interrogate, but it was obvious that if you knew the answers to some of your own questions, you could quickly expose a prisoner who was not telling the truth. You could then threaten to hand him over to the police to be prosecuted unless he did better, which was no idle threat at a time when so many offences carried the death penalty.

This prisoner was sitting facing us at my desk. As usual he was saying that he had been forced to join the gang and that he had only been with it for a few days before he was captured. He maintained that he did not know any of the other members of the gang or where they had been or what they had done. But I remembered that we had recently received an exercise book taken from the body of a man from the same gang a few weeks earlier. It included a list of the gang members and their weapons and it was even now sitting on the clerk's desk at the back of my office. Raising my hand, I shouted 'book' in English. The clerk threw it to me over the prisoner's head. Catching it, I thrust it before him thus giving him irrefutable proof that he had been in the gang for several months. The prisoner who had not noticed the clerk, was immensely impressed by my ability to conjure out of thin air a book that he thought to be safely in the pack of his gang leader, deep in the forest. This was magic of a powerful sort and he started to talk without more ado. For several hours he poured out truthful answers to all our questions, which gave us an unrivalled knowledge of the gang's recent doings and of the committees in the nearby reserve that were supporting it. Better still he offered to work for us in any way we wanted. He said his name was George.

George's first job was to go with Miller to see whether he could discover where the Kiambu terrorists lived when they went to Thika District. Although he was unable to do this, he did manage to identify a number of people who had been supporting them. One night Miller sent him to visit one of these people pretending that he was a terrorist who had got separated from his gang. Telling them that he wanted to get back to the forest, he was put in touch with some men who had come from the gang to collect food. George led them into an ambush. Subsequently George was lent to two other FIAs, one in Fort Hall and one in north Thika where he had further success. After his immediate use was over he came back to Kamiti and joined Eric's team of loyalists.

*   *   *

By this time there were several stories going round of members of the security forces who had managed to fool the Mau Mau into thinking that they were also members of the movement. Dennis Kearney, now a Kikuyu Guard officer had got a favourable response when some of his men visited suspected gang supporters to say that they were part of a gang in need of assistance. One of the Fort Hall FIAs with a couple of bodyguards had accidentally run into a large gang and passed themselves off as supporters thus escaping a fate worse than death. Eric reckoned that he could produce a credible gang of his own consisting of his seven loyalists and George, which he could use to penetrate supporters and their strong-arm groups. George soon taught them how to dress, talk and behave like a real gang.

At first Eric used to go out with his men and hide up nearby before they actually met the Mau Mau. But soon he found that by blacking his hands and face with a burnt cork, he could at night remain with them when they were talking to the terrorists, providing he stayed in the background and left the talking to George. The aim was always to get information, which we could give to the army or police for immediate action. In this way we were able to turn the background information which we had been collecting from informers, document and interrogations into the sort of contact information that the security forces wanted. But sometimes our little gang was confronted by a situation, which could only be dealt with by immediate action and on these occasions it was necessary to kill or capture the enemy outright.

After a while Eric took me out occasionally to see how it worked, because I had to sell the idea to my superiors in the army and police some of whom were worried by the risk of casualties or for other reasons. On these occasions I had to be very careful not to interfere because my ability to understand Swahili was so limited.

By their very nature these operations all took place in the dark and they usually involved a lot of waiting while George was talking in hushed tones to the people we had come to meet. Unlike Eric and our men who could at least understand what was said, I usually had no idea what was happening, or whether we were in the presence of supporters or of the gangsters themselves. Sometimes there were raised voices and a hostile atmosphere. More often there was friendliness and subdued laughter such being the normal reaction of Africans. Either way the outcome was totally unpredictable so far as I was concerned and all I could do was to remain as calm as possible and ready for whatever might befall.

It soon became clear that George was not the only prisoner willing to work for us. It was also apparent that we needed people from other gangs in different places in order to work effectively in those areas. Over the coming months we recruited many more like George. To use former terrorists in such delicate circumstances meant that we had to trust them and they us. Selection, which was done by Eric in conjunction with his loyalists, required great skill and care. To show how much we trusted them, they were housed in a shed built onto the side of my bedroom with a connecting door between us. From their first operation they were given a weapon to carry. In this way the so-called pseudo-gangs that played such an important role in destroying Mau Mau, began.

As time went on I was able to see how Eric selected certain specific captured Mau Mau to join our organisation and it became apparent that three conditions needed to be in place. First the man had to feel that he would gain something from doing so, for example regular food, pay, fun and a safer existence than he had enjoyed in the forest. Second, he should be made to realise that something very unsatisfactory would happen to him if he did not accept our offer, for example that he would be tried and hanged for his past activities, or at best interned. Third, he had to feel that what he was doing was for the overall good of the Kikuyu and that he would ultimately be able to persuade them of it. Carrot and stick were not enough. Self-respect was also needed. I subsequently found this to hold good in other parts of the world.

Chapter 3

Kenya: Reaping the Harvest 1954–1955

It is now necessary to say a bit about the general situation that prevailed in the colony in the spring of 1954. When General Sir George Erskine became C-in-C East Africa in June 1953, he decided that the key to putting down the insurrection lay in protecting loyal Kikuyu before Mau Mau could kill them or force them into supporting their cause. He therefore concentrated his forces in the native reserves to reinforce the Kikuyu Guard while it was building up its strength and while Mau Mau supporters were being identified and neutralised by criminal prosecutions or detention. During this period he had been unable to make much headway in the forest or in Nairobi. By early 1954 he felt that the Kikuyu reserves were secure and that he could tackle Nairobi. Once the forest gangs were cut off from the supplies they were getting from their supporters in the reserves and from Nairobi, he reckoned that they would wither on the vine and quickly succumb to military action in the forest. A large-scale operation in Nairobi would therefore be launched in April 1954 the aim of which was to remove the Mau Mau committees and strong-arm groups that were organising the collection of men and supplies for the gangs. An important aspect of the operation would be to cut Nairobi off from Kiambu District, which, with its large population, was a significant source of funding for the movement.

The development of General Erskine's plan considerably affected our organisation. My responsibility for gaining intelligence meant that I needed to meet each FIA nearly every day to keep abreast of events. I had to attend meetings in each of the districts for which I was responsible to give reports on the situation and answer questions. Each week I had to produce a formal written report for Special Branch Headquarters and HQ East Africa and I tried to brief commanding officers when they were planning operations. To achieve this I was nearly always up by 0530 and seldom went to bed before midnight even when there were no major operations in progress. To ease the pressure it was decided that officers should be appointed as DMIOs for Kiambu and Nairobi and that Henning should become fully responsible for Thika. I would now be the military intelligence officer for Nairobi area, which was a Police area covering these three districts. There was a police superintendent called Vic Aubrey who was the Special Branch officer for Nairobi area and I would now work as his opposite number. The one difficulty with this arrangement was that the administration boundaries did not fit in with the police boundaries. This was sorted out by dividing Central Province into two so that there would in future be a Central Province North based in Nyeri and a Central Province South based in Nairobi consisting of our three districts and Fort Hall for intelligence purposes only. Tony Swann who had been the District Commissioner in Kiambu, became our Provincial Commissioner and a Provincial Committee was formed to meet at regular intervals. I was the Provincial MIO and attended these meetings but I no longer had to attend the district meetings. Furthermore it was no longer necessary for me to visit each FIA on a daily basis as they were now being looked after by their own District MIOs.

In May I received a DMIO for Nairobi called Norman Coleman. He was a captain in the Royal Army Service Corps who was immensely resourceful as a result of the varied posts that he had held in the past: in the war he had even been in the Royal Navy. He knew no more about intelligence than I did when I arrived in Kenya but he was a quick learner. At the same time I received a captain from the Kenya Regiment called Walter Gash to be DMIO Kiambu.

Gash was older than most of the FIAs, being about the same age as myself, but he was a second-generation Kenya man from the Prince of Wales School. He had a clear brain and huge determination and he was not prepared to take anything for granted. He therefore wanted to test for himself all our ideas about the use of informers, interrogation and the use of pseudo-gangs, as they were now known. He was argumentative and direct in his approach, so that I had to spend long hours with him before I could get him to do what I wanted. But the longer he stayed the more I appreciated his immense value. It was Holyoak, Miller, Cottar and the other FIAs in the divisions who had got the show on the road over the past few months. Now Gash worked out how to organise the way their information could be assembled and put to best use. In particular he devised a system whereby each FIA recorded all the information that he was getting in such a way that he could find it quickly when wanted and disseminate it to those in need of it. He even made sure that his FIAs did what they were told in this respect which was in some ways foreign to the natural inclinations of the young Kenyan born members of our organisation. I ensured that the system became standard throughout Nairobi area.

No sooner had the new system relieved me of some of my work than I found myself saddled with a number of extra problems. The first was to get official approval for the pseudo-gangs. For this purpose General Erskine visited our house at Kamiti with the head of Special Branch in order to hear about it direct from Eric Holyoak and to see some of the captured terrorists. Unfortunately the guard of honour consisting of ex-terrorists that Eric organised to greet him, faded away just before his arrival. Having decided that there was no more than an acceptable level of risk and that our operations were consistent with the emergency legislation, he agreed that they should continue and that additional resources should be made available to us. Complying with the emergency regulations was not always as simple as it sounds. For example in order to carry conviction as Mau Mau gangsters, our pseudo-gangs sometimes had to administer the Mau Mau oath, but this was against the law. To get round the problem we had to devise an oath that was slightly different from a Mau Mau oath and considerably less disgusting, but which carried conviction with those taking it. Luckily administering non-Mau Mau oaths was widely practised by the Kikuyu and there was even a band of official oath administrators who regularly held cleansing session for those who regretted taking the Mau Mau oath.

Soon after General Erskine's visit I was required to explain our methods to MIOs from other parts of the colony. I was also told that I should set up a small training centre near Kamiti where FIAs from outside my area together with all new FIAs could come, four at a time, and spend a few days discussing and learning about the methods we had developed. Whenever possible Eric would take them out with a pseudo-gang to visit supporters and see how it worked. Two Kenya Regiment sergeants would be sent to run the training centre, but I would be responsible for what was being taught.

As if that was not enough I was also made the Provincial MIO of Southern Province as well as Central Province, South. In theory there should have been no Mau Mau operating in Southern Province because it was inhabited by tribes other than the Kikuyu, but in one of the districts occupied by the Masai called Narok there was some Mau Mau activity. Over the years Masai from this area had married Kikuyu wives so that there existed a colony of half-castes who were sympathetic to gangs from the west edge of Kiambu District. When under too much pressure from the security forces, these gangs would seek refuge in Narok and by the middle of 1954 the situation needed attention. A Kenya Regiment officer called Perry Verlaque was appointed DMIO and Glen Cottar who had many contacts in the Masai country was sent to work there with him. Because of the distances involved, visiting Verlaque and Cottar took up a lot of time, but it was great fun and together with Eric and some of his team we had some interesting journeys through the tsetse fly areas between Narok township and the Mara river.

*　*　*

While all this was going on it was difficult for me to keep in touch with day-to-day events but I still managed to get involved in some of the action. Very early one morning, shortly before General Erskine's visit, I had been taken by Bill Henning to the scene of a contact he had had with one of the Thika gangs the night before. Two had been killed and their bodies lay where they had fallen and Henning was sure that others had been hit. While the FIA went off to get some troops to sweep the area we cast around and found some spots of blood. For some time we followed the trail crawling along under rows of coffee bushes conscious of the fact that a wounded terrorist hiding up, could easily get off a shot or two at us before we spotted him. Luckily I saw him first and we were able to capture him without any shooting. From speaking to him we discovered that all twelve of the Mau Mau in the ambush had been hit and over the next few days they were all rounded up. It was the end of a particularly vicious gang, which had killed between sixty and seventy loyalists including some Europeans during recent months.

On another occasion soon afterwards I was talking to Peter Dempster in Kiambu when we got a call from one of Eric's men called Chebere asking me to return to Kamiti at once as something important had cropped up and Eric was away on a job. As my Swahili was still pretty rudimentary Peter came with me to make sure that I understood what the man was saying. On our arrival we found three of Eric's men one of whom had borrowed a rifle from my driver. Chebere said that he had discovered where a senior Mau Mau with his bodyguard was resting in a coffee planter's labour lines a few yards from a swamp in which they could hide if need be. He also said that the gang was about to move away so that if we wanted to do anything we would have to do it at once: there was no time to get reinforcements.

Apparently there were twelve men in the gang, but they only had six weapons between them. There was a sentry on the edge of the swamp and the rest were in one of the huts.

We had between the five of us one rifle, two pistols, three simis (short swords) and a hand grenade and we reckoned that if we could surprise the gang in the hut we should be able to overcome resistance. A difficulty would arise if the gang was already on the move when we arrived, or if the sentry spotted us in time to get the gang out of the hut in a position to repel our attack. We drove for a few miles and then made our way quickly through a coffee plantation until we could see some huts ahead of us. Chebere explained that the gang was in a hut hidden in a fold in the ground just beyond the ones we could see, the door being on the far side facing the swamp. We crept through the coffee bushes and then ran as fast as we could across about 20 yards of open ground to the hut. Leaving two of our men by the window at the rear, Peter and I went round to the door. With a racing heart I pushed the door open and could see in the darkness a number of people inside. At this moment the sentry fired at us from the marsh and Chebere who had the rifle fired back. The gang supposing that they were surrounded by troops, decided to surrender and came out with their hands up while Chebere set off in pursuit of the sentry who, having fired five shots at us without effect, was making off as fast as he could go. He succeeded in escaping but we had captured the gang leader with ten of his bodyguard and five weapons.

This represented a good morning's work, thanks to the daring of Chebere who, having heard from one of his informers of the gang's whereabouts, had gone by himself to talk to them under the pretence of being from a neighbouring strong arm group. Unfortunately a few weeks later he unsuccessfully tried a similar deception and was killed. When he failed to return to our camp I searched for him and discovered his mutilated body in the mortuary at Kiambu, which was a great sadness to our team.

*   *   *

The breaking up of the Mau Mau organisation in Nairobi that came about as a result of General Erskine's big operation in April, not only disrupted their organisation in the city, but also resulted in a number of the Nairobi strong arm groups moving out of the city into Kiambu District. Some of these coalesced into a strong, well-armed gang, which wreaked havoc in the settled area for some months, before being brought to book. Once on arriving at a Kikuyu Guard post that had been overrun, I was taken to view the result. The whole post had been reduced to hot stinking ashes amongst which were the bodies of some of the defenders. At first I did not even recognise them as bodies. They were so badly burnt that only the trunks were left together with a few stumps indicating where the arms, legs and heads had once been. On another occasion when Eric and I had been at a farewell party in Kiambu, we heard that a nearby African labour lines had been attacked. On hurrying to the scene we found burnt huts, the body of an old man and a little girl who had received a slicing blow from a simi (native slashing sword) that had cut off a slice of skull exposing her brain. I clapped the bit of skull back securing it in place with my tie before sending her off to the hospital.

Although the Mau Mau were taking more offensive action in Kiambu and Thika than had formerly been the case, we were much better placed to provide information to the army and police than we had been six months earlier. This was largely because our pseudo-gangs were in a position to develop the information we were receiving from informers and interrogations into information that they could use to make contact with the gangs and their supporters. But it was the informer network that the FIAs were building up using their loyalists and as time went by their ex-terrorists that underpinned all else because this constituted the background information that was being developed. Throughout our organisation everyone was engaged in collecting information by any and every means. In this way they all had a thorough idea of what was going on, which enabled them to operate effectively as pseudo-gangsters or as informer handlers or interrogators.

Another method of exploiting the background information that we were developing at this time was the use of hooded men. This involved collecting together a number of ex-terrorists and informers, clothing them from head to foot in long white hoods with slits for seeing and breathing and then sitting them in a row. The army or police would cordon off an area and march the inhabitants past the hooded men each of whom would have an FIA standing with him. If the hooded man recognised a Mau Mau supporter, or even on occasion a forest gangster visiting the area, he would tell the FIA who would then stop the person concerned. If only one of the hooded men recognised him, it might well be no more than paying off old scores, but if a number did, there was a good chance that there was something in it, and the identified man would be taken off for questioning. Much damage was done to the Mau Mau infrastructure in this way, especially in Nairobi and Kiambu and I spent many hours in the early morning watching these operations take place.

*   *   *

As the summer of 1954 wore on my organisation steadily increased. A year after arriving in Kenya it consisted of 6 officers, 13 sergeants and a large number of loyal Africans, and ex-terrorists amounting to perhaps 200 all told, not counting informers. Much of my time was spent in offices and at meetings, visiting security force commanders and briefing them or administering my force. I also spent time working out what we should teach on our courses and discussing with FIAs from other parts, the methods that had borne fruit in their areas. On one occasion I flew over the Mount Kenya forest in a Lincoln bomber to get an idea of the problems that the Royal Air Force had to overcome when striking at the gangs. After taking part in a raid it was pretty obvious that there was little likelihood of them doing much more than frightening the enemy, but this in itself, had its uses at a time when the army was busy in the reserves or Nairobi.

In September my extra responsibilities were recognised by my being promoted to major. Life was certainly hectic but also enjoyable. Occasionally I went with Eric to Nairobi for a visit to the cinema followed by supper at the Halcyon Restaurant: curried prawns and ice cream. On one such occasion we saw *Calamity Jane* which, forever after, has been my favourite film. On another we saw *Mogambo*, a particularly ridiculous story of a white hunter's flirtations with his susceptible clients. At one stage the hunter takes his party to a piece of high ground overlooking an expanse of forest and says 'Gorilla Country'. At this the whole audience rose to their feet with howls of laughter as the viewpoint was easily recognisable, being about 15 miles from Nairobi on the main road to Naivasha. The nearest Gorilla would have been several hundred miles away in the Belgian Congo.

Despite the lack of Gorillas in our area, there were plenty of other large animals such as elephant and buffalo that we occasionally came across in the forest. Although they could be troublesome, the tracks they made were of great assistance when it came to moving around. In addition to these massive creatures, we sometimes saw giraffe and many different sorts of antelope and gazelle in the lower lying areas of Thika. Leopards, though seldom seen were scattered around in the reserves and settled areas and occasionally one would get caught in the headlights as we drove around at night.

By this time there was a teeming community in the compound behind our house consisting of our loyalists, many ex-terrorists and a number of attendant females, one or two of which would sometimes go out with our pseudo-gangs since there were plenty of women in the real gangs. To house these people we had built three round huts and a longer straight one, all surrounded by a barbed wire fence which also enclosed my house. There were sandbagged parapets in convenient places and slit trenches from which we could engage any gang that tried to attack us.

Nearly all the occupants were young and when not engaged on operations of one sort or another took great delight in playing games, wrestling and generally ragging around. Eric with his extensive understanding of the Kikuyu and their language controlled matters by spending long hours talking to them and above all by letting them all have their say in accordance with their tribal custom. From him I learnt a lot about Kenya and Africans as a result of which my outlook had changed a great deal. When I first arrived I had thought of Kenya merely as part of the Empire and existing primarily for the good of England. Now I saw it as a country in its own right, existing for its own good. To start with I had thought of the Africans as strange people who either supported the colonial authorities, good Africans, or opposed it, bad Africans. Now I could see that the Empire, the Colonial government and the settlers were of much less importance to the Africans than their relationships with each other.

In addition to the men, we kept chickens and a few turkeys who lived under the shade of a massive avocado tree, straying in and out of the house leaving fleas and feathers in their wake. A small terrier, inappropriately called Wambogo (son of a buffalo), was also part of our extended family.

* * *

An added complication entered my life at this time relating to the fact that in February 1955 I would have to sit the Staff College entrance exam, which consisted of seven separate papers. It was necessary to get 50 per cent in all papers and an overall score of at least 60 per cent to pass. Officers in England or Germany would be given several weeks off in which to prepare and courses were run for them by the Army Education Corps. As it was not possible for me to take time off, I enrolled in a correspondence course, which resulted in my being bombarded with reading material and written questions. The time spent doing the reading and writing out the answers added at least an hour to my working day at a time when I was already well occupied. It was lucky that during my lengthy stay in Germany I had learnt to do with very little sleep.

By the late summer of 1954, the gangs in the Fort Hall and Nyeri forests were becoming less active because of the erosion of the support they had been receiving from the adjacent reserve and from Nairobi. When under severe pressure, one crossed into Kiambu, it was broken up by the army and a prisoner sent to us at Kamiti. He had the long plaited hair of the hardcore forest terrorist but he was emaciated and covered in sores. We badly needed a Fort Hall man for our pseudo-gangs so Eric decided to keep him. Unlike most captured terrorists he did not boast of his exploits but was quiet and willing to join in with our men. He had a good sense of humour and seemed anxious to help. He even seemed to understand my primitive Swahili and, by talking to me slowly and distinctly, made it possible for me to get the gist of what he was saying. His name was Kamau and I adopted him as my personal bodyguard and attendant. He kept his hair long for use when impersonating Mau Mau, but tucked it into a large tweed cap for the rest of the time so as not to attract attention. Under his guidance my Swahili rapidly improved as did my understanding of the ways of his people.

At the time of Kamau's arrival, the Nairobi gangs were still very active in our area. On one day alone there were eight separate Mau Mau inspired incidents. Although they were doing damage, there were some advantages from our point of view in that they provided opportunities for the courses that we were instructing, to practice on a live enemy. It was at about this time that Philip Myburgh was killed in a battle with a gang in the nearby reserve, greatly missed by Eric and myself.

Shortly afterwards, taking advantage of a dark and windy night, a gang attacked our post at Kamiti. The sentry was probably asleep when a terrorist with a can of petrol started to climb the perimeter fence in an attempt to set light to one of the huts, but Wambogo gave the alarm after which all hell broke lose. The sentry fired at the gang, which was lying under the coffee bushes beyond the wire. The gang fired back. I was woken by the noise and ran out through the hut where the ex-terrorists were sleeping, to find Eric pouring a stream of bullets into the coffee bushes. The terrorists fled. We suffered no casualties but it was an alarming experience. Waking up in the dark to the accompaniment of gunfire and shouting does not rate as fun.

A few days later I was having breakfast with Eric on the veranda of our house. It had been a wet night but the clouds had passed and the sun was shining brightly. The air was intensely clear in a way that can only be understood by people who have lived in East Africa. A few hundred yards away three or four kites circled hopefully over the dukka where an African was skinning a goat. We were discussing ways of making our camp more secure but we did not get far because we did not have enough men to post sentries in pairs and when we posted them singly they always went to sleep; hence our reliance on the dog. Over the next year Mau Mau gangs had five more goes at us, but all were beaten off, largely thanks to the speed with which Eric got from his bed to his firing position, usually without bothering to put on any clothes.

* * *

By this time the operational company of the Kenya Regiment which had been sent to look after the western edge of Kiambu District quickly became successful at rooting out the gangs there. Amongst their officers were Bill Woodley, Francis Erskine and Stan Bleazard all of whom were well known to Eric and Gash. They soon started using Africans disguised as Mau Mau to get close enough to the gangs they were chasing in order to engage them successfully. They developed close links with our organisation and we exchanged ex-terrorists and information. I was much involved in co-ordinating matters with their commanding officer, Lieutenant Colonel Guy Campbell and his adjutant, Roly Guy, both of whom were Green Jackets: also with the company commander, Tony Veitch.

Despite the disruption caused to the Mau Mau in Nairobi, one last bunch of recruits was despatched to Mount Kenya in October. A police patrol bumped into them by chance and an army battalion hurried to the area encircling the gang, which took refuge in an area of rushes as darkness fell. One or two stragglers had been captured during the day and by talking to them overnight we discovered that the gang, estimated to be about eighty strong, was being taken along by one of the Mount Kenya leaders. This man had arrived in Nairobi a few weeks earlier together with some of his followers. Next day the army assisted by some Kikuyu Guards killed or captured almost all of the gang. The gang leader who spent some days with us, was typical of the better sort of young terrorist. He had a great sense of humour and had joined the gangs in search of excitement. He had gained promotion on account of his personality and daring. He was as callous as most of his tribe which we discovered when we found a member of his gang who had been punished for some crime by having his fingers cut off and his eyes gouged out. Before the troubles, he had been a great friend of Chebere and one of Eric's loyalists, so we had no difficulty in getting him to tell us all he knew. This enabled us to arrest some of his supporters in Nairobi. It was the last time any organised gang of recruits left Nairobi for the forest.

In November 1954, Kenya benefited from a further infusion of riflemen in the form of 1 RB which after three weeks of acclimatisation, started operating in the settled area north of Nyeri from its base at Naro Moru. Commanded by Dick Fyffe, they were a much happier and more efficient battalion than they had been in Germany. Over the coming months I was able to renew contact with a number of old friends such as David Alexander Sinclair who was now adjutant.

In the latter part of the year my eyes gave up, probably because of too much reading and writing by the light of a pressure lamp. Luckily Kitch Morson recommended an excellent oculist in Nairobi who prescribed exercises rather than spectacles, but it meant total eye rest for six weeks at a most inconvenient time so far as the Staff College exam was concerned. There was however a long-term advantage in that in doing the exercises I learnt to cross my eyes, which can raise a laugh from children, especially if done at the same time as waggling the ears. Also by placing two identical photographs next to each other and looking at them cross-wise it is possible to get one three-dimensional image.

One of my most enduring and least pleasant recollections of 1954 is of the endless investigations carried out by the police into the activities of various members of the security forces. No doubt cases of misconduct by individual soldiers and policemen took place, but they were relatively rare. Complaints made by people in sympathy with Mau Mau, for the purpose of getting rid of individuals who were proving too successful, were far more common. Following up these allegations wasted a huge amount of time. Despite the fact that our FIAs were unlikely to abuse prisoners whose whole-hearted help they wished to obtain, they were sometimes attacked in this way. To forestall these assaults I wrote a leaflet pointing out the absolute necessity of behaving properly and within the law, which I persuaded General Erskine to sign. This was distributed to all my DMIOs and FIAs and also to those attending our training courses. Once when explaining to Colonel Mike Carver, the officer responsible for discipline, how much time was wasted in dealing with complaints, he pointed out that unless they were investigated, we would have no defence against them, which was very true. Certainly General Erskine himself took a strong line, not only in making sure that all ranks behaved properly, but also in attacking those making false complaints, with particular reference to the missionaries. None of our people was ever proved to have erred in this respect, I am glad to say.

* * *

Towards the end of the year I took part in a pseudo operation in the course of which I actually managed to make myself useful. One night our gang was visiting some supporters inside an African's hut when a security force patrol was heard to be approaching. This was the one thing that we tried hard to avoid. If the patrol mistook us for terrorists we would be shot. If we told them who we were, our cover would be blown so far as the Mau Mau were concerned and a warning would swiftly be passed around making further pseudo operations in the area unworkable. In this case there was just time for me to wash off the black actor's make-up which we now used instead of burnt cork, crawl towards the patrol and call out quietly in English to tell them who I was. My excuse for being alone in a native area at night convinced the officer in charge, but did nothing for my reputation: at that time any hint that a white man was consorting with a black woman was considered highly discreditable. While we were talking our pseudo-gang crept away.

By the end of 1954 the tide was flowing strongly against the Mau Mau. The gangs that had been debouching into the native reserve from the Aberdares and Mount Kenya were now pretty well confined to the forest. In the reserve itself the population had been concentrated into villages protected by the Kikuyu Guard which made it difficult for the gangs either to collect food or terrorise the people into supporting them. The link between the forest gangs and Nairobi was broken so that recruits and supplies could no longer get through.

The downside to these developments was that the gangs which could no longer get support from their friends in the reserve tended to spend more time raiding European farms to the west of the Aberdares for their supplies. Also in Kiambu where the population had not been put into villages because the Mau Mau had deliberately kept the district free of forest gangs, the situation was less favourable. Although the gangs that had been formed from the old Nairobi strong-arm groups had been weakened, they were still operating in the south and east of Kiambu District. In addition new gangs brought together by a Kiambu leader called Waruingi Kurier were basing themselves in the forest to the west of the district. Thus whereas in 1953 and the first half of 1954 most of the Mau Mau activity was in the north of the emergency area, it was now in the south.

* * *

The 1955 New Year Honours List came as a pleasant surprise. Jacky Miller was awarded the Distinguished Conduct Medal, the highest award possible for a soldier after the Victoria Cross. He had undertaken an act of great gallantry when trying to rescue a wounded police askari in a large-scale engagement near Thika and he had also been involved in some fairly hazardous actions in the early stages of the development of pseudo-gangs. Eric Holyoak got the Military Medal, which he richly deserved, as he had been the person mainly concerned with the development of the pseudo-gang idea, in the course of which he had been pressing into unknown territory at great risk to himself. By dint of much quiet discussion with his people, he persuaded them to try out one thing after another which none of them would have considered for a moment on their own. Bearing in mind that he was still under 20 years old it was quite remarkable. Both Miller and Holyoak had also been promoted to warrant officer earlier in the year. I got the Military Cross. Although the Mau Mau were not very dangerous opponents in open fight, they posed a considerable threat to our little groups, particularly in the early stages when the Kikuyu as a whole still took the Mau Mau oath seriously and thought that they were gaining ground. At this time there was a risk that those working with us might desert us for their former friends, damaging us in the process. As time went by and it became obvious that the Mau Mau were going to be defeated, the risk receded almost to nil. I can remember being uneasy about some of the ex-terrorists living next door to my bedroom when we started, but by the end of 1954 I looked on them all as friends and had no worries about them.

Early in 1955 I retired to Malindi for a further bout of surfing and goggle fishing. Once I went deep-sea fishing and caught a large tunny weighing 50 lbs. On my return I spent a week at Naro Moru with 1 RB where Dick Fyffe tried to make good the deficiency in my preparation for the Staff College exam. I took Kamau with me as batman. He excited some interest and even disapproval to start with along the lines of 'what does Kitson think he's doing bringing this flea ridden terrorist here.' But Kamau soon made himself useful by finding various sorts of edible fungus in the nearby woodland, which he brought back in his capacious cap and presented to the officers and sergeants messes. By the end of the week he was very popular. Soon afterward I sat the exam itself in Nairobi.

In the early months of 1955 General Erskine was satisfied that, with the loyalists safe in the reserves and Nairobi neutered, the gangs were ripe for attack in the forest. He therefore launched a major operation in the north Aberdare Forest followed by a second one in Mount Kenya. Neither was particularly productive in terms of Mau Mau killed or captured, but they had the effect of breaking up the large gangs into small groups intent on survival. Indeed throughout the colony Mau Mau was very much on the defensive.

From the point of view of my organisation, we had now developed operating procedures well suited to the business of hunting down the strong-arm groups remaining in the reserve and the gangs hiding in the forest. Our main difficulty was that many of our best men were coming to the end of their two years service and were returning to civilian life. The first to go was Bill Henning who was replaced as DMIO in Thika by Don Bush. Soon afterwards Walter Gash was replaced in Kiambu by Peter Hewett and Norman Coleman was replaced in Nairobi by Derek Prophet. Ian Feild also left Fort Hall to be replaced by Bob Martin. Many of the FIAs also changed during the first six months of the year. Although the new men were almost all first class, they had to learn the job from scratch, which involved me in spending much time with them during their first few months. Not only that. Having spent long hours under all sorts of conditions with their predecessors, I found that I greatly missed them.

In March Eric, accompanied by me and Kamau, captured a man who was high up in the Mau Mau command structure in Nairobi and the border area between Kiambu and Thika around Kahawa. After a lengthy talk during which I played him at drafts while Eric was getting some food, he decided to give us his whole-hearted support. Realising that we were likely to be making a large number of arrests over the next few weeks, I set up a special team to deal with the operation in a row of disused shops a few miles mile outside Kiambu. Don Bush who had a good knowledge of the situation in Nairobi and Thika took charge and the police lent us a Special Branch inspector and a CID inspector to process the prisoners. Dennis Kearney with a section of Kikuyu Guard also joined us to look after the security of the new camp and the prisoners.

Over the next three weeks we were able to round up most of the remnants of the old Nairobi Central Committee and its satellite groups in the surrounding area. When we eventually picked up the chairman we were in for a big surprise. He was a man well known to us as the respected foreman of a large coffee estate, leader of an African Christian group and also of the local farm guard. Faced by our other prisoners, he made no attempt to deny his activities. The odd thing was that he seemed to be utterly sincere in all his different roles and was genuinely upset to think that he had betrayed the trust of his European employer. He immediately offered to help us and encouraged the others to do so as well. As a result, by the end of three weeks we had destroyed all that was left of the Mau Mau infrastructure in and around Nairobi.

In the course of doing this, we discovered that there were three dangerous gangs working for these committees which proved more elusive than the committees themselves. One of these consisted of men from Naivasha living in Nairobi, one of Fort Hall men living there and the third was resident in Thika District. Eventually Prophet got a lead on the Naivasha men. That evening I joined Prophet and his FIAs in Nairobi and after supper, disguised as Mau Mau, six of us set off to find the hut some way outside the city where the gang was supposed to be hiding. After moving through a coffee plantation, we passed some disused sheds and then walked along the edge of some maize. It was a light night and we had little difficulty in finding the way but as we got nearer to our destination I became a bit nervous. My recipe for avoiding the ill effects of fear has always been to think of other things until it is too late to avoid the consequences. Suddenly the hut was there in front of us and one of our pseudos was whispering to the sentry who was evidently satisfied, as he opened the door to let our man in. Yelling abuse, Prophet rushed past and we all piled in behind him shouting loudly. Soon we had the gang pinned against the wall. There were nine of them but they were half asleep and far more frightened than I had been a few moments earlier. None of then tried to bolt which was lucky for them, because we had our weapons ready. We had not only captured the leader and seven men of the Naivasha gang but also the leader and second-in-command of the Fort Hall gang who had joined them for a meeting. They were a tough bunch as we later discovered when talking to them.

Shortly afterwards Miller carried out a pseudo operation backed up by a police striking force that destroyed the Thika gang, two of whom were killed and 15 taken prisoner. Altogether these operations resulted in the killing or capturing of well over 100 assorted gangsters and committee men, a higher tally than either of the big forest operations that had taken place in the early part of the year.

*   *   *

In May 1955 General Erskine handed over command to Lieutenant General Lathbury. By this time the Mau Mau had been greatly reduced in strength and it was apparent to the tribe as a whole that further progress could best be achieved in conjunction with the colonial government and not by insurrection. This meant that nearly all terrorists who surrendered or were captured, were prepared to help the security forces. On the other hand there were still many small groups dotted around the forest and hiding in the reserves. The army and police would have employment for many months to come in searching them out and destroying them. General Lathbury was quick to see that the time for large operations was over and the future lay with smaller specialised forces such as tracker/combat teams manned by the army and pseudo-gangs operating largely in the forest.

It was against this background that the police in Special Branch started to feel uneasy about the extent and influence of its military element. Bearing in mind that the soldiers were certain to be withdrawn at some stage, it made sense that policemen should take over some of its functions. As a start all the DMIOs and FIAs who were members of the Kenya Regiment called up for two years of active service, were released and then re-employed on a civilian contract doing the same jobs, but now called DIOs or FIOs instead of DMIOs and FIAs. This made little actual difference except that the police administrative arrangements were less effective than those of the army.

Having disposed of the Mau Mau organisation in Nairobi and the nearby rural areas, most of our effort was now directed against the forest gangs in the west of the district. These, having absorbed many of the Mau Mau formerly active in the reserve, were now small but numerous. Their activities were co-ordinated by Waruingi Kurier, who had been particularly murderous in and around that district ever since I could remember. Dedan Kimathi who was now the most prominent terrorist in the Aberdares had for some time been trying to get Waruingi to accept his overall leadership, sending him presents and addressing him as Field Marshal, but Waruingi had consistently maintained his independence.

At this time Eric started taking pseudo-gangs into the forest, often going in for several days, using methods developed a few months earlier in Fort Hall by Ian Feild and one of his FIAs called Pritchard. After a time Eric even allowed me to accompany him to get a feel for the business. It was certainly very different from the one-night jobs, which we did in the reserve, which usually took place in the dark. In the forest it was necessary to behave like Mau Mau the whole time in case one was being observed. This particularly applied to how we made fires to cook and what we eat, preceded by the ritual of saying prayers as darkness fell. For this ceremony we formed up two abreast facing Mount Kenya, the dwelling place of the Kikuyu God called Ngai. We then took a handful of earth in the left hand raising our simis in a threatening manner in the right hand. At this point our gang leader would say a few payers at the end of which we all said 'Thai' a few times meaning praise rather than amen.

Quite apart from the way we behaved, the forest was a different world to the one in which we normally lived. On entering it everything seems strange for a time, after which it is memories of the outside world that seem strange. The forest is different in the way that the heavy canopy causes much of the light to emanate from ground level rather than from the sky. The horizon is often no more than a few yards distant and movement is restricted by vegetation and the steepness of the valleys and ridges. The forest smells different from the outside world because of the layer upon layer of rotting vegetation that covers so much of the ground. All of this I knew from the many occasions that I had been in it for short periods over the past two years, but it impinged on my consciousness more forcibly after spending a few days and nights there pretending to be a Mau Mau gang member.

* * *

In June it was decided that as over the past ten months, all the DIOs and FIOs had passed through my Training Centre, it should now be closed down which reduced my workload to a considerable extent. In July the last of the big army operations took place in our bit of forest and we were kept busy trying to keep tags on what the soldiers found out. There were a few prisoners to be interrogated and documents to be translated. The results had to be put together and the information distributed to the brigade and battalion commanders. For three weeks either Peter Hewett or myself visited each unit on a daily basis for this purpose. As with the other big operations the results were disappointing in terms of tangible results but the gangs were further fragmented and harassed. The disadvantage was that we could not send our own patrols into the forest and so lost touch with where the gangs were. When the operation finished we returned with our pseudo-gangs.

In July also, thought was given to the idea of centralising the pseudo-gangs under an Assistant Commissioner of Police for special forces who would release them to districts as required. There were some advantages to this arrangement but it raised problems. Up to this point those of our people working in the pseudo-gangs were not solely used in this way. They were also used to find informers for us and then to keep in contact with them. They were present when new prisoners came in and took a part in interrogating them. They were often the best people to get them to change sides and become members of pseudo-gangs themselves. They therefore had a wide general knowledge of the gangs that we were trying to penetrate and of the men in them. If the pseudo-gangs were centralised and therefore separated from the local intelligence organisation, they would mainly be reduced to providing a way of getting disguised men into real gangs for the purpose of engaging them at close quarters. This is something that the Operations Company of the Kenya Regiment had been doing since the summer of 1954. They would be less good for getting detailed information about the gangs and their supporters. Although the decision was made to go down this route, it did not happen until the end of 1955, by which time I had left the colony.

In August 1955 one of the district officers had a bright idea. As it was difficult to find gangs in the forest, perhaps he could surround a particular bit of it in which we knew there was a gang, with Kikuyu Guards. He would then collect hundreds of women with pangas (agricultural type choppers) and cut down all the undergrowth and small trees thereby exposing the gang. Everyone laughed at this idea, but he tried it in a very restricted area. As luck would have it there was a small group of terrorists there and as they became exposed, the Kikuyu Guard shot them. The only trouble was that as soon as they were down the girls fell upon them with their pangas and cut them into tiny pieces so that they were unrecognisable. Soon afterwards the District Commissioner decided that if we could identify an area where one or more gangs were lying up, he would arrange for a massive population sweep to take place.

In the middle of August using a pseudo-gang we identified a suitable area at the southern tip of the forest in which we thought that a number of terrorists had taken refuge during the major military operation of the previous month and a sweep was organised. In the morning the whole area was surrounded by Kikuyu Guard and Tribal Police after which no less than 15,000 women were assembled from the nearby reserve. This time they moved inwards from the edge with the Kikuyu Guard following close behind the line of cutters. This great mass of women, mostly wearing colourful dresses with their pangas flashing in the sun, was an amazing sight. We had concentrated as many FIOs as we could muster and spread them throughout the line with instructions to get to any Mau Mau shot down by the Kikuyu Guard before the women could hack them to pieces. We wanted identifications, weapons, documents and if possible some prisoners capable of telling us who was where.

After hearing some shots Eric and I found a badly hacked but recognisable corpse, which Eric identified as one of Waruingi's couriers. Later, as the girls reached a clearing, a terrorist fired at the line. The cutters fell to the ground to give the Kikuyu Guard a free field of fire. We saw two men fall and ran towards them, reaching them ahead of the women. One was a well-known gang leader and the other a member of his gang. Trying to protect the bodies I feared we might get minced, but luckily another terrorist jumped up and the women transferred their attention to the newcomer. By this time we were bloody and sweating from our exertions. And so it went on for several hours before the superintendent of police who was running the operation, called a halt. There was no more undergrowth to cut and no more terrorists left inside the cordon. It had been a great success.

By the time the bodies had been identified we realised that Waruingi's gangs were no longer in a position to do much harm. The final reward for the day's work came when one of the terrorists killed was identified as Waruingi himself. It would take time to assemble and translate all the documents, but with this man gone it seemed unlikely that centralised control of the Kiambu gangs would ever be re-established. I well remember realising as we made a start to assess the contents of the documents taken that day, that everything that was likely to happen afterwards would be a bit of an anti-climax compared to the operations of the past two years. I started to wonder how I should best occupy my time during the three months remaining of my tour in Kenya. Now that the training centre was gone and the pseudo-gangs were to be centralised elsewhere, there was little left for Eric's men to do. Furthermore Eric's two years would soon be up so there was no point in retaining the post at Kamiti. At the end of August we closed it down and moved in with Peter Hewett and his men who had taken over some houses as a base about a mile outside Kiambu.

In the week before Eric left to work in his cousin's saw mill, we went on a prolonged visit to Narok with two of his favourite men and Kamau. We combined business with pleasure and had a great time looking at game and shooting guinea fowl and lesser bustard together with a Thompson's Gazelle and an Impala for the pot. The night after we got the Impala, we put it on the ground between our two camp beds to prevent it being taken by a lion. We hung a pressure light suspended from a forked stick over it. At some stage I woke up for no apparent reason. I remember thinking that it could not be too late because otherwise the pressure lamp would have gone out. And then I realised that what had woken me up was the noise of fang crunching bone. Not 6 feet from my bed was a leopard straddling the Impala illuminated by the light. I was alarmed to say the least but dared not move or utter a sound. After about ten minutes the leopard dragged the Impala off into some nearby bushes and after a further bout of snuffling and crunching, took it further away. Eric whose bed had been even nearer to the leopard than mine, then reckoned that we could afford to sit up and light a fag to calm our nerves.

At about this time we also lost the services of Don Bush and Jacky Miller. Miller wanted to join the regular police but they only recruited from England. Although he was an Englishman from Derbyshire they made him fly home at his own expense where he was duly recruited and returned to Kenya: typical of the bureaucratic attitude of the Colonial Office and the Kenya Police Reserve.

There were still a couple of months left before I was due to return to England in order to attend the Staff College. During this time Hewett's men were busy rounding up the remnants of Waruingi's gangs. I still had plenty to do writing reports, briefing committees and looking after our men in the districts. A further trip to Malindi preceded a lengthy hand-over to my successor. On 26 November I left for England, seen off at the airport by Kamau.

*   *   *

Looking back on my time in Kenya two things stand out. The first concerns the extent to which the army element in Special Branch was successful or otherwise. It is clear that in a short space of time we collected a lot of information about the gangs and their supporters by talking to people involved in events, by interrogation and by the collection of information from informers. But this was not what the police and military needed to contact Mau Mau gangs. So over a period of months, we discovered ways of developing this background information we were collecting into contact information using special methods such as pseudo-gangs and hooded men. This greatly helped to bring the Kenya Emergency to an end, but for the future what was needed, was a system that would enable ordinary soldiers and police to develop background information into contact information. I left Kenya knowing that only by working this out, could maximum use be made of conventional forces in an insurgency situation.

The second thing that stands out in my mind is the tremendous amount that was achieved by the very young men of the Kenya Regiment. It was the DMIOs and FIAs who developed by trial and error the system initially worked out by Eric Holyoak to get the sort of information that the army and police wanted. Although they included men like Walter Gash and Bill Henning in their mid-twenties, they were mostly aged between 19 and 21. And it is worth remembering that other Kenya Regiment men of the same vintage, were operating with the Kikuyu Guard, regular British battalions and battalions of the King's African Rifles. Knowing each other so well, they achieved a great deal by passing useful ideas between these different parts of the security forces.

In a general sense people seem to have difficulty in understanding that the Kenya Emergency was not a national uprising against the colonial power, but a civil war within one of the many tribal groups. On one side were those who wanted to increase the political influence of the African population in step with the colonial government and on the other side were those who wanted to force the government's hand by violence. Although the government naturally supported the first group, most of the people in it were Africans and therefore most of the 2,000 plus loyalists killed, were Africans, either in the army, police, Kikuyu Guard or as civilians supporting these organisations. It is massively offensive to read the work of some authors, who insist on comparing the ten to fifteen thousand Mau Mau killed with the hundred or so Europeans killed or even with the thirty to forty settlers murdered on their farms. Such comparison undermines the sacrifices made by those acting on behalf of the government and the responsible members of the Kikuyu tribe. Certainly when we lost an African member of our team, we were just as sad as we would have been had he been a European.

From a personal point of view, I had gained two years and three months of fairly intense operational experience and an introduction to counter-insurgency warfare that would stand me in good stead over the coming years. I had endured considerable fatigue, endless stomach upsets in the early days until I got used to Kamiti cooking, a fair bit of asthma especially when the grass grew long after the rains and I hope I had learnt to control the fear I inevitably felt from time to time.

Chapter 4

Malaya 1955–1957

On 27 November 1955 my mother and brother met me at Blackbush Airport and I started the process of acclimatising myself to life in polite society: no easy task. The Staff College course was not due to start until 21 January which gave me nearly two months in which to catch up with friends and to renew contact with such people as Colin James, Dick Poole and Tommy and Vivien Wallis.

At just 29 years old I was the youngest student at the Staff College. The oldest was probably 34 and the rest were in between. This meant that about two thirds had served as officers during the war. It was Staff College policy to work the students hard in the first term, which dealt with the detailed preparation of letters, minutes, appreciations and orders, so as to get them into the habit of thinking that unbridled mental energy was essential to success. As most were keen to get on in the army, they buried themselves in paper and scarcely surfaced from a social point of view until Easter. Having pushed myself fairly hard in Kenya and in Germany I was not particularly worried by the workload, but could not get it done any quicker than anyone else. My problem was compounded by the fact that the commandant thought it would be a good idea if I wrote a paper outlining the way in which the army could be made ready to deal with future Colonial emergencies, which he would then send to the War Office. This coming on top of my normal work, restricted my social life for some time to come.

There were two packs of hounds kennelled together at Camberley; the Sandhurst Foxhounds and the Staff College Draghounds. Shortly before the end of the first term I was asked whether I would take on the job of whipping-in to the Staff College Drag for the coming season. This seemed to be a good idea, but I would need a horse. My attention was directed to a Colonel Spencer, then serving in the War Office but living in Camberley, who was thought to have one for sale.

The colonel's 17-year-old daughter, home for the weekend from a finishing school, was told to trot Gremlin (the horse's name), up for me. I got the impression that the girl, called Elizabeth, wanted to keep Gremlin and accordingly looked unfavourably on me. Nonetheless I bought him for £135 and a few weeks later I took Elizabeth to see him and I do remember hoping that we would meet again. Indeed on later occasions Elizabeth came out with the Drag and when the Hunt Ball took place I went to it with her and her parents.

*   *   *

As the summer wore on the work became more interesting and we spent much time out of doors discussing tactical problems. In August the Staff College removed itself to Normandy to tour the battlefields and to have selected operations described on the ground by some of the British and German officers who had taken part. Towards the end of the course the workload eased off and we spent most of the time listening to lectures given by prominent people from outside the college. Amongst these a summary of the world situation by Field Marshal Montgomery was particularly memorable. His speech was clarity itself and it was made plain that anyone who held a different view regarding any of the complex issues of the day was quite simply wrong. His reply to questions paid no regard to the feelings of the audience, which included many Arabs. When asked whether he thought that we should use an atomic weapon on Nasser's Egyptians he replied 'You don't waste atom bombs on savages, you stamp on the swabs.' When an American officer asked him what he thought of Eisenhower's strategy after D-Day, he replied that 'he had never said that Ike was wrong: just that he disagreed with him.' This was put across in such a way as to imply that so far as strategy was concerned, Eisenhower was a non-starter. Talks by other notables such as the First Sea Lord (Mountbatten) and the Chief of the Imperial General Staff (Templer) were more relevant, but less amusing.

The course ended on 13 December. There is no doubt that it had been worthwhile. Although disappointed by many of my fellow students, I had become well acquainted with some interesting people such as the German student Hans Hinrichs who had been on Rommel's staff in the Desert and with Manstein in Russia. I became friendly with Jim Chichester-Clark who was certainly the least ambitious person at Camberley. As soon as the commandant announced that everyone who had not already been thrown out had passed, Jim requested an interview and said that he wished to retire from the army. He said he would have done so earlier had it not been for the fact that he did not want people to think that he was leaving because he could not pass the course. Predictably the commandant reminded him that having passed, he could not retire for five years. So poor old Jim had to soldier on.

The Directing Staff were more progressive in their views than most of the students whose determination to say nothing that might prejudice their future, led them into being be assertively conservative. By contrast the paper I wrote for the commandant proved to be too unconventional for him to send to the

War Office. Instead he decided that it should be discussed by the syndicates within the college. Realising that my ideas represented some departure from accepted military practice, I decided to prepare the minds of my fellow students by anonymously circulating a leaflet to them and to the directing staff ahead of the discussion. My leaflet purported to be a Staff College publication written 100 years later, i.e. in October 2056. It described the way in which warfare had developed in the century following the end of the Second World War. It pointed out that the communists were the first to see that nuclear weapons made the old sort of war impracticable and that the best way to wreck their opponents was by a mixture of people's uprisings and economic chicanery, keeping their armies as a threat to finish off the work of partisans when no risk attached to their employment. My leaflet pointed out that it took the West a long time to realise that this was not some sort of peripheral war but the real war. It finished by saying that eventually daylight dawned and that what had started in 1945 as a collection of odds and ends known as special forces eventually turned into the main offensive and defensive weapon of the Western world. The leaflet evidently did not carry conviction and when my paper was discussed it was naturally widely savaged by the student body who thought that it might lead to a proliferation of private armies such as the Chindits or the SAS which it was then the fashion to decry.

Having been away from regimental duty for the past three and a half years it was arranged that I should return to 1 RB, now in Malaya, as a company commander, although I would not be leaving England until the end of January. It was on the 26th of that month that I left England for my new posting.

*   *   *

By 1957 Malaya consisted of a federation of nine states and two settlements, which equated roughly with the provinces of an African colony and there was a High Commissioner who fulfilled the function of a governor. A complication arose from the fact that almost half the population were Chinese or Indians, these people having come to the country to work in the rubber plantations and tin mines which the Malays did not like doing. During the war when the Japanese occupied the country, they had been particularly unpleasant to the Chinese, forcing many to become squatters along the edge of the jungle. At this time an anti-Japanese army consisting mainly of Chinese aided by the British, was built up in the jungle. After the war it disbanded, but soon afterwards reformed as an anti-British Army. Its intention was to take over the country for the communists, thus thwarting Britain's plan of giving the country independence as a monarchy within the Commonwealth, each of the state Sultans taking it in turns to be King. Unlike the Kenya Emergency which happened by accident when certain Kikuyu politicians seeking redress of perceived grievances lost control of their followers, the Malayan Emergency resulted from the deliberate action of Chinese communists intent on pursuing their own political interest.

By the time that an emergency was declared in 1948, a chain of communist committees for state, districts and branches had been set up. The members of these committees mainly lived within the Chinese squatter communities along the edge of the jungle while gangs of so called communist terrorists (CTs) lived nearby within the jungle. The aim was to coerce or persuade the population into supporting the communists and to damage the British interest. As the Malayan Emergency progressed these gangs were worn down and the squatter communities were concentrated into villages where they could be controlled by Home Guard and largely prevented from providing food to the gangs. As the committees could not function in these villages, they joined the gangs in the jungle and in effect became part of them. From the start, the uprising had little chance of success providing the government acted with good sense. The fighting was less intense than in Kenya where at least 15,000 people were killed over a period of three-and-a-half years in an area 150 miles long by 100 wide. In Malaya a smaller number were killed over a period of ten years in an area 500 miles long by 250 wide. Nonetheless the insurgency had to be rooted out and this required careful organisation and much hard work by the security forces.

My journey from England to 1 RB involved a lengthy flight with night stops at Brindisi, Karachi and Bangkok followed by a train journey from Singapore to Kuala Lumpur and thence by car to Kuala Kubu Bahru. I was destined to take over support company composed of the 3-inch mortar platoon, the medium machine gun platoon and the draft training platoon. The company lived with battalion headquarters at Kuala Kubu Bahru, the rifle companies being spread round the battalion area. Although the mortars and MMGs sometimes fired into the jungle for training purposes their chief value was providing extra patrols for the use of the rifle companies. It was disappointing to have no operational role, as my experience of fighting terrorists in Kenya would have been helpful.

The battalion seemed to be in good shape despite the fact that the army's operational procedures, which might have been effective years earlier when there were heavier concentrations of CTs to attack, were hugely cumbersome when applied to the elimination of small fugitive gangs. The only odd thing immediately detectable was that Paddy Boden, who was now the colonel, was greatly disliked by the company commanders. I had known him since Osnabrück days when he was a company commander and had always found him helpful and charming although more concerned with detail than most, which his platoon commanders found irksome. But when visiting the battalion in Kenya to be coached by Dick Fyffe for the Staff College exam, I distinctly remember noticing that he was relaxed and apparently ready to decentralise to a considerable extent. I was therefore surprised by the company commanders' hostility especially as Alan Cowan, Peter Hudson and Ralph Stewart Wilson were all easy-going and highly competent.

For the next four months the battalion remained at Kuala Kubu Bahru during which time S Company functioned as described above. Soon after my arrival I went out with a platoon of I company commanded by Mark Scrase-Dickens to see how men were expected to work in the jungle. We walked for some distance through rubber plantations and then up a steep track into the jungle, all the while weighed down by a massive rucksack containing dry clothes, a ground sheet, a hammock, and the standard five days rations. When we reached a suitable place we set up a base camp. Mark then sent out two patrols, each with orders to search a set area looking for tracks or signs of a CT camp. When the patrols returned we cooked a meal, put on dry clothes and settled down for the night in our hammocks under small bashas made from ground sheets slung between two trees. In the morning two more patrols went out to carry out further searches. After a few days Mark reckoned that he had covered the area given to him, so the camp was broken up and we returned to the road where we were picked up by transport. If it was considered necessary to continue an operation beyond five days, further rations could be dropped into the base camp from aircraft by parachute, or a re-supply party could carry them in on foot.

The jungle in this area was different to the Kenya forest. Trees, foliage and steep gradients were similar but it remained warm during the night as well as the day. Probably for this reason the general smell of decomposing vegetation was stronger and we had more trouble from leeches which penetrated ones boots and crept up ones legs to suck blood from the most unfortunate places. Another important difference was that there were few large animals such as rhino, buffalo and elephants as a result of which there were no well-worn animal tracks to assist movement which, tended to be direct along a compass bearing. This involved going straight regardless of contours and cutting through whatever was in the way. It thus took longer. Night movement was considered virtually impossible.

After a few weeks I was becoming highly critical of the way in which the army was tackling the problems facing it. Although Special Branch was providing a certain amount of background information on the gangs, it was accepted that they would only occasionally be able to produce contact information. Army policy was therefore to flood one region after another with troops so that sooner or later they would make contact with the enemy. If every battalion managed to kill one CT per month in this way, it would eventually be possible to clear a given area of CTs after which the troops could move and flood another area until that was clear. It was hopelessly uneconomical and by moving troops from one place to another it prevented a company commander getting to know his area well enough to develop such background information as Special Branch might provide. The system also led to a hidebound adoption of procedures such as everyone carrying vast quantities of equipment around with them and only operating by daylight on the grounds that young conscripts could not be expected to exist in the jungle in any other way.

While the new drafts were being trained to operate in the approved manner, I decided to carry out some experiments. To start with I went into the jungle with two riflemen called Russell and Handley, taking no more than we could carry wrapped up in a ground sheet slung on our belts. My feeling was that as it was so warm at night, it was unnecessary to take a change of clothes in which to sleep as a bit of parachute silk would do. We certainly did not need a hammock. The silk and some individual ration packs containing mainly dried food and condensed milk could be wrapped in a ground sheet attached to the belt. By my reckoning a patrol equipped in this way should be able to live for four or five days. Thus equipped we spent the day watching the recruits doing their training but when they returned to their base camp for the night we pooled our ground sheets and made a basha nearby. We again spent the day watching the draft training, moving around comfortably with all our kit. When they went into their little camp for the night we marched in the dark on a compass bearing for some hours to a pre-selected area before settling down until it got light. Next morning we discovered that we were within 100 yards of where we intended to be, which showed that some night movement in the jungle was possible.

Russell and Handley were both from the East End of London and their conversation carried out in the jungle in a hoarse whisper was vintage cockney. They had no special feelings about the jungle and certainly did not regard it as eerie or sinister. They merely lumped it together with everywhere other than London as being thoroughly unsatisfactory and looked forward to getting back to their birds and families as soon as their period of National Service was over. When the draft training course finished I took a man called Pascoe from it as my batman and the three of them stayed with me as a team for the rest of our time Malaya.

* * *

At the end of May the battalion was due to move to a new area some 150 miles to the south in order to take part in another operation designed to flood a certain area with troops. Battalion headquarters was to be in the town of Gemas and the companies were allotted permanent camps in and around the new operational area. This time S Company was to share one of these camps with B Company, now commanded by Dick Worsley, although we would continue as before to conduct draft training and use the mortar and machine gun platoons to reinforce rifle companies as required, which did not suit me. Towards the end of May companies sent advance parties to the new camps. On the night of 28 May a rubber planter was attacked by CTs a few miles away from our new camp just outside the battalion's operational area. As soon as I heard, I set off under the pretext of taking additional ammunition to our advance party. Arriving during the evening of 29 May I was told that the brigadier under who we would be serving, Henry Alexander, intended to hold a meeting next day with the local district officer and the police. This meeting was to help him decide whether he could afford to keep all his troops concentrated for the big operation or whether he should detach some troops to chase the CTs outside the operational area. I invited myself to the meeting.

At the meeting we heard that within the operational area allocated to 1 RB there was only one gang of twelve CTs based on one of the old communist branch committees. But outside the operational area, near the B and S Company camp, were seven run down gangs representing the remains of one of the old state committees, two old district committees and four branch committees; a total of around thirty-six CTs. Because government policy was to flood one area at a time the Brigadier was under pressure not to dissipate his force, but the administration and police were insistent that they should not be left unprotected in the face of the threat to their security. Reluctantly the Brigadier decided that although B Company must operate within the main battalion area, S Company should be given the task of containing the other gangs. He also agreed that up to one platoon of B Company could be lent to us if not otherwise engaged.

This would give me a chance to discover whether it was possible to develop background information into contact information using normal troops as opposed to special forces. But being concerned that Paddy Boden might object to the way in which the brigadier had tasked his companies without consulting him, I suggested that I should at once return so as to explain the way in which the situation had developed. The brigadier agreed and provided me with a light aircraft so that I could do this and get back as quickly as possible.

Having got Paddy's agreement I flew back and the same day drove the 29 miles to the district officer's headquarters at Muar to meet him. Not wanting to waste the time it would take to get my vehicle across the mouth of the River Muar on a ferry, I crossed in a boat and completed the journey in the sidecar of a bicycle pedalled by a particularly scruffy native of indeterminate origin. This, as I later discovered got me off to a bad start with the district officer, Mr Moloney, an elderly member of the colonial service whose rank equated to that of a District

Commissioner in Kenya. It took him some days to accept me with any degree of enthusiasm as a member of his District War Emergency Committee (DWEC). After seeing him I spent some time with the Special Branch officer who was Chinese, collecting a great deal of background information about the gangs in my new area. In the usual way my operational area did not fit comfortably into one administrative district, part of it being in another one. Consequently after leaving Muar I had to drive another 45 miles to this headquarters which was at Segamat, to meet the DO, police superintendent and Special Branch officer there. The two Special Branch officers, Inspector Boey at Muar and Inspector Cheong at Segamat, became my inseparable companions over the coming months and thanks to them I was lent a recently surrendered CT called Ah Meng, who came to live with us at Bukit Serampang.

It was late by the time I got back to Bukit Serampang. I immediately set about putting up maps and making an appreciation of the situation so that we could start operations as soon as our main party arrived. The new B and S Company camp was in and around the requisitioned house of a rubber planter. I selected a large room to be my company office and it was here that I set to work. Helping me with the maps was Acting Corporal Gillard, the very well built company clerk, together with Russell and Handley. On the floor my driver and Pascoe were cooking a meal on a hexamine cooker. Try as I might to concentrate on my appreciation, the constant flow of banter passing between the men made it almost impossible until eventually they fell asleep.

The area allotted to S Company was about 40 miles from north to south and 25 miles from east to west. It consisted of jungle, swamp and rubber plantations and a few small villages. It was bordered on the east by the River Muar, navigable by motor launches and smaller craft. Bukit Serampang was in the middle of our area, a short distance from the only major road, which passed from the coast at Muar to Segamat. To the west of our camp was a sizeable jungle clad hill called Mount Ophir. To the east was low lying jungle running down to the River Muar. Strips of rubber trees bordered the various tracts of jungle and there were also areas of vegetable cultivation particularly to the north and to the south of Bukit Serampang, between the rubber and the low lying jungle.

It was obvious that the number of five-day jungle patrols that the force at my disposal could maintain in this large area would be unlikely to find or even inconvenience the opposition, even if assisted by a platoon of B Company. In S Company, excluding the draft training platoon commanded by Andrew Palmer, I had the mortar platoon commanded by Jonathan Peel and the machine-gun platoon which had no officer for the time being although subalterns were sometimes attached to S Company for short periods when not needed elsewhere. Each platoon had a good regular sergeant. There were one or two

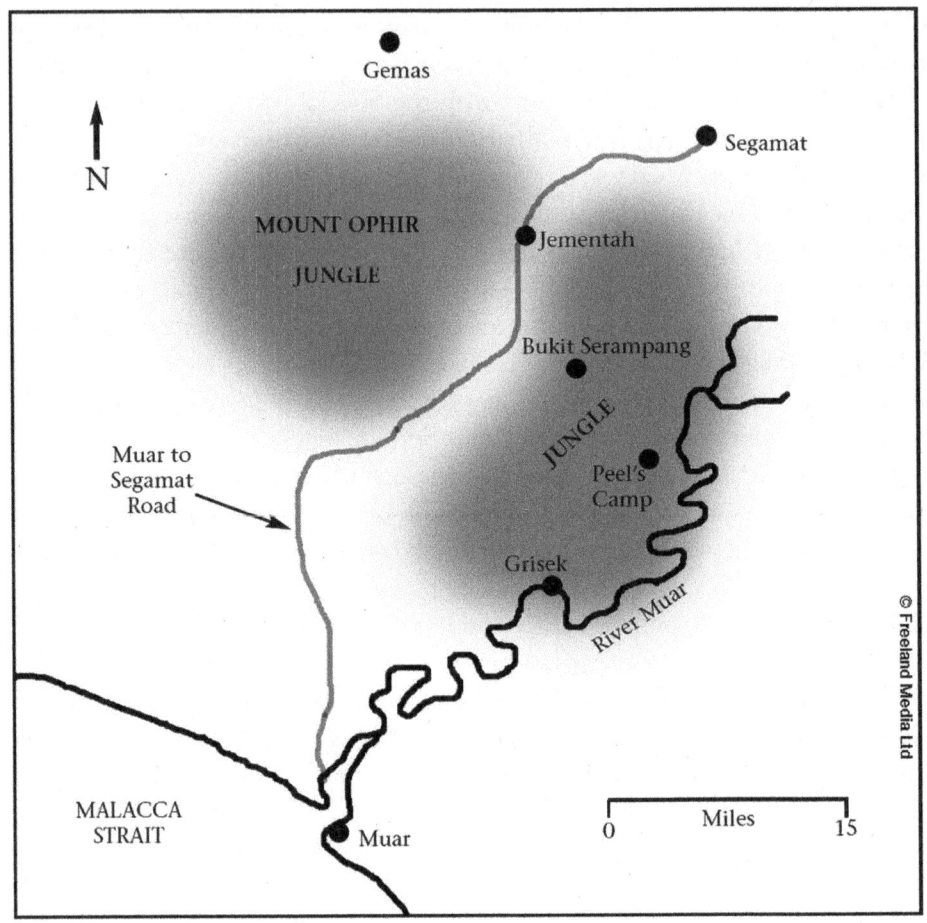

regular corporals and a number of national service corporals most of whom were excellent. Nearly all the acting corporals and riflemen were national servicemen aged between 18 and 20 years old, mostly from the East End of London. By contrast B Company had a full complement of officers including Paul Greenwood as second-in-command and three officer platoon commanders all of whom took a full part in our operations whenever possible.

From Inspectors Boey and Cheong I got photographs of most of the CTs, together with an outline of their life histories and from Ah Meng I had a fairly detailed knowledge of the way in which they lived. I also knew where jungle camps had been found over recent years. The enemy's Achilles' heel was that the CTs could not just sit in the jungle doing nothing. Parties had to emerge to contact their supporters amongst the civilian population in order to ensure that they was no backsliding in their adherence to communism or in their desire to assist their fighters. CTs also had to come out to get food, either by collecting it from the villagers or by digging it out of areas of cultivation.

Having examined the area from a topographical point of view, I decided to start by concentrating on the Kebun Bahru Branch gang living on Mount Ophir, which was led by the District Committee Secretary. This man was in charge of three of the five branch gangs in our area. If I could discover the exact position of his jungle hideout, it might be worth trying to attack it, but until then I would leave the deep jungle alone. It was no part of my plan to alarm the CTs, thereby causing them to change their pattern of living and operating, just as I was building up a picture of their likely movements and the places where they might be visiting to contact their supporters. At the same time we needed to be ready to take advantage of any pinpoint information that Special Branch might provide whether on Mount Ophir or elsewhere.

The supporters of the Mount Ophir gang were mostly rubber tappers from the local village, that is to say men who collected latex from the rubber trees every morning. From time to time CTs would leave their jungle hideout during the night and move around amongst the tappers when they were working. But without knowing the position of their hideout it would be difficult to intercept them on the way to the rubber. On the other hand it would be hard for tappers to get food out of their village to give the CTs because of gate checks mounted by the police and village guards. This meant that when they needed food, the CTs would have to go right through the rubber and cross the Muar to Segamat road in order to get to the cultivations from where they could steal it. There were dozens of tracks going from the road into the rubber, only a few of which would continue as logging tracks into the mountain and these would be the ones the CTs would use to get from their hideout to the rubber. Fewer still would lead to a road-crossing place that would take them to the cultivations.

On the arrival of the main party I arranged for a stand-by patrol to be held at immediate readiness to react to any Special Branch information which often included sightings of CTs passed to them by their informers. Inspector Boey also said that he might hear when CTs were planning to enter a village called Grisek on the banks of the Muar to pick up food. Although these CTs were not from the Mount Ophir gang, we would obviously want to make use of this pin point information if we could. Accordingly Sergeant Bagley of the mortar platoon, Russell, Handley and I carried out a water-born reconnaissance of the village from a police launch. A few days later we went into the village by night through a gap in the perimeter fence, which Boey thought that the gang was using, to pick out possible ambush positions.

While this was going on we sent out patrols to follow tracks leading from the road into the rubber and to plot on a map those that went on into the jungle. They could then follow these tracks back to the road and see which went over it and join up with tracks leading to the cultivations. In this way we discovered that there were about eight tracks that went all the way from the jungle, through the rubber, across the road and on to the plantations. When in possession of this information I examined each crossing and worked out how it could be ambushed, taking photographs of the ambush positions for use in briefing those selected to man the ambush when the time came. Other patrols were sent onto the lower slopes of Mount Ophir to see whether they could find signs of enemy movement through the jungle, which would indicate the general location of their jungle hideout. Any men not out on patrol or at immediate stand-by, were subjected to an intense programme of firing on the jungle range by day and, using flares, by night. If we ever did manage to contact the enemy, we intended to be capable of taking full advantage of the situation. I also arranged for each man in the company to be given a set of photographs of all the CTs in the area and a brief outline of their former activities so that they could, in a way, get to know them on a personal basis.

After a few weeks we had narrowed down where we might contact the enemy in terms of space. It would also be necessary to do the same in terms of time. From Ah Meng we learned that the CTs liked moonlight when they were moving through the jungle, but darkness when they were crossing the road and raiding the cultivations. It was not difficult to work out when there would be a moon, which set at around midnight. By now it seemed likely that the CT's camp was in one of two general areas of the jungle and that they were going to one of two possible areas of cultivation. From this it was possible to see that if we ambushed four of the crossing points for the six days in the month when the moon was right, we stood a good chance of success. In other words I had taken the background information provided by Special Branch and Ah Meng and used our own troops to develop it by looking to see which of many tracks were most likely to be used by the CTs when raiding the cultivations.

Based on these calculations I set the ambushes and on the fifth night struck lucky. It was exactly one month after the company had arrived at Bukit Serampang. Only one CT was killed but he turned out to be the District Committee Secretary called Leong Tek Chai. As soon as it got light next morning I went to the scene of the ambush to discover whether the follow up patrol had found anything. A wounded CT, or an abandoned weapon, or at least some tracks showing the direction in which the survivors of the ambush had gone, would have helped me to decide on our next move, but there was nothing. Congratulations together with the suggestion that we should 'strike while the iron was hot', came in from the colonel and brigadier.

But we knew no more than before and I had no desire to frighten the CTs into changing their pattern of life. Also there was a possibility that if a gang member had got separated from his comrades during the firing, he might take the opportunity to surrender providing that the area was kept quiet for a day or two. Next day one did surrender but he was not from the party that had been ambushed. This man who was a young recruit had been left in the hideout with a more experienced CT when the group which we had ambushed went to collect food. He said that another group went at about the same time to visit supporters elsewhere. Hearing the firing and finding that the members of the food party failed to return during the night, he reckoned that something had gone wrong. Next day he decided to surrender. Knowing that his companion, who was asleep, would not want to do so, he bashed his brains out with a lump of wood. Making his way to the road, he got himself taken to the police who speedily handed him over to us. We now had someone who knew where the enemy's hideout was and who was prepared to take us there. He also knew how we could approach and surround the camp without blundering into the sentry. Under these circumstances there was a good chance of eliminating the gang.

That same afternoon Jonathan Peel and Sergeant Bagley set off with the surrendered CT and a patrol from the mortar platoon with every expectation of reaching the camp before dark. On several occasions the surrendered CT thought that the camp was just over the next ridge but each time it turned out to be a false alarm, much to his and the patrol's disappointment. Eventually they settled down for the night, confident of finding the camp next morning. This went on for the next two days but on the third day they did at last find the enemy camp. It was unoccupied except for the bloated body of the man whose brains had been knocked out. By this time the patrol, which had set off with light scales of equipment, was almost out of food. But Jonathan decided to ambush the place in the hope that one at least of the two groups that had left the camp would return. He found odd bits of food left by the CTs and by putting the men on half rations felt that he could stay for about another four days. On the third morning a CT appeared and was killed. He turned out to be from the group that had been visiting supporters. At this point Andrew Palmer took in another patrol to remove the dead man and re-supply the patrol. Jonathan was to stay for a further two days in case anyone else came back, but we felt that there was little likelihood of the gang, which had now lost four of its members, returning to that part of the jungle.

Five days later Inspector Boey said that the food party was due to visit Grisek the following evening. Next night those of us that had done the reconnaissance set off with high hopes of making a contact. We travelled in a van that took a cinema show into the village to entertain the villagers. The van dropped us about a quarter of a mile outside and under cover of darkness we crept through the gap in the perimeter fence and set up our ambushes behind a drain. Each of us had a flare, which we would set off when the CTs approached so as to be able to see to shoot. We expected that they would arrive within the hour. Lying by the evil smelling drain, tormented by mosquitoes, I hoped that we would not have to wait that long. But we waited and waited. Suddenly after several hours Sergeant Bagley's flare went off and every second we expected to hear him open fire. But nothing happened and after a few minutes Bagley crept up to say that his flare had gone off by itself. Supposing that our cover was blown and that there was no point in waiting any longer we withdrew the way we had come, highly embarrassed to have made such a mess of the one bit of contact information supplied by Special Branch. Had it been anyone but the highly experienced Bagley who said that his flare had gone off by itself, no one would have believed him, but we subsequently discovered that it was possible for this to happen if damp got into the firing mechanism. I trembled to think what Paddy Boden, the brigadier and the district officer would say. But next morning the first person to appear was Moloney, who did his best to assure me on behalf of the District War Executive Committee that they all knew how easy it was for such things to happen. He said that he was sure that we would soon be successful again after all the trouble we had taken over the last few weeks. Neither Paddy nor the brigadier seemed much bothered.

*   *   *

It might take some time to discover what had happened to the survivors of the Kebun Bahru Branch gang on Mount Ophir and re-establish their pattern of activity so I decided to turn my attention to the next biggest gang which was the one getting food from Grisek. It operated in the swampy bit of jungle between Bukit Serampang and the River Muar and consisted of nine men commanded by Seet Ho Ching. This time the jungle ran right down to the River Muar although there were three small rubber enclaves backing on the river. The tappers arrived in these enclaves by boats from a village that was across the river.

I decided that we would have to set up a small base camp in the jungle near the central enclave from where patrols could try to intercept CTs going between their hideout in the deep jungle and the tappers. But to get to such a camp would involve a 6-mile trek across the cultivations and through the jungle from Bukit Serampang, or the men would have to go in by boat like the tappers. Clearly we could not hope for our camp to remain a secret from the CTs or the tappers if we kept moving men in and out of it, so it would be necessary for two platoons to go in and stay in until the gang was destroyed.

This raised the problem of re-supply which could not be done from the air as the sight of numerous highly coloured parachutes descending on the jungle would immediately give the game away. There were only two possible ways of re-supplying the camp. The first was through the jungle from Bukit Serampang by night. It would be just possible to get in and return during darkness using logging tracks for much of the distance. If bicycles could be provided to act as wheelbarrows, fewer men would be needed, as a man pushing a bicycle could take much more than if he was carrying it on his back. The second way was by boat during the night when the villagers were kept in by the Home Guard, but this could only be done occasionally as the sound of repeated boat trips would be noticed in the villages backing onto the river.

The first thing to be done was to find a suitable place for the camp so I set off on a reconnaissance into the jungle with Russell, Handley and Pascoe. We travelled as far as we could on the first day and when it got dark lay down under a great tree on our groundsheets. The day had been unusually hot and sticky even for Malaya and thunder was rumbling around in the distance when we went to sleep. After a few hours I woke and realised that a storm of epic proportions was heading our way. Soon the rain was lashing down and the thunder deafening. Much to my amusement Russell was still sleeping although Handley and Pascoe were awake. Suddenly there was a blinding flash as lightning hit a tree close beside us. The whole top of the tree broke off and came crashing down into some bamboo, which made a noise like a burst of machine gun fire. At this Russell woke up and leaping to his feet, grabbed his rifle and took up a firing position. He evidently thought that we were being attacked by the enemy. He quickly realised his mistake and after a while, though soaked to the skin, we settled down again. Next morning we resumed our search and after another night in the jungle found a suitable place for the camp.

It later transpired that, unbeknownst to us, a detachment of the Grisek gang were spending the night at one of their staging camps nearby. An occupational hazard of moving around in the jungle was that one side could unexpectedly bump into the other at any time, in which case the advantage would lie with the one that heard the other first. In this case they only discovered our presence when they found our tracks after we had gone.

Jonathan Peel who had recently celebrated his twentieth birthday, would command the two platoons going in to the jungle. John Starkey who now commanded the machine gun platoon, went with him. The only problem was that my simple request for a few bicycles for the re-supply party was instantly turned down on the grounds that no one had ever wanted bicycles before. Had I asked for the support of the whole of the Far East Air Force I would not have aroused so much opposition. Luckily B and S Companies were to be visited next day by General Sir Roger Bower who was the Director of Operations for Malaya. On his arrival I briefed him on our operations to date and on our future plans which seemed to interest him greatly. When told of my difficulty in getting bicycles, he assured me that they would be forthcoming. He also said that the whole of B Company should be released from the big operation to work in our area.

A few days later on 4 August, Jonathan Peel took his two platoons into the jungle. Almost immediately a patrol led by John Starkey had a chance contact with some CTs but without success. Soon afterwards I did a further reconnaissance inside Grisek village with Inspector Boey to pinpoint the actual houses visited by the CTs when they came for food.

*   *   *

Even while our operations around Mount Ophir had been going on I had been trying to build up a picture by research and discussion with Special Branch, of the movements of the gang commanded by the other District Committee Secretary called It Hiong. He had by then lost all his Branch Committees and was moving around in the south-west part of the Mount Ophir Jungle that is to say on the opposite side of the mountain to Bukit Serampang. He only had six followers but it was important to destroy the gang, since if it was left alone its experienced leader might be able to rebuild a network of committees and gangs and I had on six occasions sent in patrols to build up information on their movements. Soon after General Bower's visit I despatched one of the B Company platoons, newly available to me, to intercept this gang which my calculations indicated would be in a particular area. A few days later the patrol led by Sergeant Cassidy and Corporal Cooke, made a contact and killed three CTs including It Hiong. My only regret was that a follow up operation that was supposed to be carried out by a Malay Police Field Force Platoon seemed to make no real effort at all so that the survivors of the engagement got away.

Having the extra B Company platoons was a great help but there was a snag. Dick Worsley was senior to me and should therefore be in command of the operations, but I had been running them so far, had done all the planning and had gained the confidence of the police and administration. At first Paddy Boden said I should continue, but Dick objected so Paddy produced a hopeless compromise under which I remained the contact with the outside world but Dick was in overall command. We tried to make this work but we both soon realised that it would not. After a while, conscious that there must be absolute clarity in everybody's mind as to who was in command, I suggested that Dick should do the whole thing. But, as I afterwards discovered, the brigadier would not let this happen so Paddy had to give me operational command of both companies, which was the only sensible answer. This issue rumbled on for several weeks and greatly interfered with the efficiency of us all. Because I was working flat out, I got edgy and difficult to live with. Entirely thanks to Dick, we remained good friends.

A few days later there was a further source of aggravation when the brigadier decided to draw a line through the middle of Mount Ophir giving one half to a Gurkha battalion and leaving the other half to us. This was a half-witted idea because it meant splitting the area in which the gang lived in the jungle from the area in which it visited its supporters and from which it got its food. It would therefore make it impossible to work out where to patrol or ambush in the way I had done in order to get the contacts we had been making. I made a big fuss as a result of which the brigadier appeared at Bukit Serampang. On explaining my objections he cancelled the arrangement saying he had only thought of it to give the Gurkhas something to do. Like the command business it had wasted time that I could not afford and had me biting my fingers with annoyance. At the risk of stating the obvious, I did not then know that our operations were going to finish up as well as they did. I had been working on a different system to that taught by the army and realised that there were people who would have been happy to see it discredited. I was getting edgy and had a rash in my mouth and a poisoned arm. I was gradually learning that all military operations involve endless frustrations brought about by trying to accommodate the views of people whose ideas differ. I don't suppose that I was very good company.

We did not have to wait long for our next success as an elderly CT who had been Leong Tek Chai's second-in-command, surrendered within a week of the brigadier's visit. He was a revolting specimen but he said that he was very keen to help us get rid of his former comrades who he claimed to dislike and despise, so we sent him to work with patrols in different parts of the area. In every case his detailed recommendations for action proved abortive. He entertained the men by singing anti-Japanese songs and on one occasion managed to purloin and drink the patrol's rum ration, thereafter rolling around drunk. A few days later he mistook the patrol's insect repellent for gin and got badly burnt. After a while, having learnt nothing from him, we handed him over to the police. He was either very cunning or mad.

Meanwhile Jonathan Peel's force continued to develop their operations. Every so often a re-supply party led by the company sergeant major, Lobby Lunn, picked their way through the jungle pushing the bicycles that we had acquired with such difficulty. With them went their precious cargo of composite rations supplemented by oranges and raw onions, which I obtained in an attempt to prevent the men from getting diseased. With them on their first run also went

Lieutenant Colonel Clutterbuck who I had met when he was one of the directing staff at Camberley. He was now working as General Bower's chief operational staff officer at Kuala Lumpur and he had come to spend a weekend with me in order to discuss my methods which seemed to be producing unusually good results. In addition to our talks he asked me to let him go with a re-supply party in order to get first hand experience of the jungle. The programme for his visit would have exhausted most people, but his thirst for knowledge was unquenchable.

I kept in close touch with Peel by wireless, letter, or by visiting his camp so as to pass on any information about the Grisek gang that I had picked up from Inspector Boey or elsewhere. Each of the men with Jonathan had a complete set of photographs of the CTs and they constantly discussed among themselves the characteristics of the members of their opposing team. By this time we had unearthed a great deal of information about these people and most of the riflemen knew as much about their history, tastes and habits as they did about each other. An indication of the amount of information which they had picked up was brought home to us when they found some old bits of rag which a female had used in connection with one of her monthly periods. They were unearthed in a temporary camp, which had been used by a detachment of the Grisek gang. There were two women in this gang, one of whom was Seet Ho Ching's wife and the other the wife of one of the gang members called Wu Kuay. It was known that Wu Kuay's woman was pregnant and therefore the gang must have included Seet Ho Ching's wife and therefore probably Seet Ho Ching himself. This deduction added to the calculations that Jonathan had made to work out the areas in which the CTs were living and the routes that they were taking to get food and visit the tappers, led to our next contact at the end of August.

On this occasion a patrol led by Sergeant Bagley was fired on by a number of CTs close to the edge of the rubber and in the ensuing skirmish one of the CTs was killed. He turned out to be one of the Grisek gang's officers. The rest made off through the jungle pursued by Sergeant Bagley's patrol. Next day, taking advantage of the fact that the enemy must know that we were in the area, I went to see Jonathan by boat taking with me a lot of extra rations. On my arrival it turned out that Bagley had caught up with the gang and killed two more CTs, one of whom was the gang leader's wife and the other a member of the old Kebun Bahru gang. This was interesting as it confirmed our suspicion that this gang had broken up, with its survivors joining other gangs in the area. It was also likely that the only CT to have escaped the encounter was Seet Ho Ching himself, which was confirmed by the fact that the magazine of a Thompson sub-machine gun belonging to him was found at the scene.

For some time before this incident I was being subjected to pressure from outside the company to withdraw the two platoons from the jungle on the grounds that conscripts without specialist training could not be expected to stay there for long periods without risk to their physical and mental well being. In fact the men were in good shape and enjoying themselves but after Sergeant Bagley's two contacts and the sight of bodies being brought out by boat it was obvious that the enemy would know that there were troops in the area. I therefore decided to withdraw most of the men ostentatiously by boat via the nearest village so as to give the impression that we were leaving the area, a fact that would rapidly be passed on to the CTs. After a short rest at Bukit Serampang they returned quietly by night.

It was at about this time that Malaya received its independence and the great moment, known as Merdeka Day, was supposed to be the focus for unbridled enthusiasm on the part of the Malays. There was a ceremony in Kuala Lumpur when the Duke of Gloucester formally handed over sovereignty and all villages and towns were supposed to put up decorations and organise festivities. But there were few signs of rejoicing. At the ceremony in Kuala Lumpur the stadium was half-empty and in our local village no one could be found to erect the Merdeka Arch so we sent a few men round to do it. The Duke as Colonel-in-Chief of the Rifle Brigade, visited the battalion at Gemas on his way home. I had assumed that my presence would not be required but on coming out of the jungle early one morning all covered in sweat, I received a message to report at once to Gemas. I duly arrived clean and smelling as sweet as possible to discover that I was destined to sit next to the Duke at lunch. All went well until we got to the savoury, which consisted of a cheese omelette with a dab of jam on top. By this time he was smoking a cigarette and had probably had all he wanted in the way of food. Turning to me he asked what it was that had appeared on his plate. Reading from the menu I announced that it was an 'omelette surprise'. 'Bloody awful "surprise" if you ask me' he said, as he stubbed out his cigarette in the jam.

For some time I had been concerned about the way in which Special Branch worked. Despite the great co-operation I was getting from Inspectors Boey and Cheong, it seemed to me that the system operating in Malaya was not what we needed. Special Branch was as usual concentrating on providing a few good agents at the expense of a widespread informer network. I had discussed this with Paddy Boden on many occasions pointing out that what I mainly needed from Special Branch could be obtained from a low-grade informer network. Paddy strongly agreed. Now Richard Clutterbuck invited me to stay with him at Kuala Lumpur for a night to continue the talks we had had when he visited us. The evening before going to see him I paid a lightning visit to Jonathan's base camp accompanied by Gillard and Pascoe. Leaving an hour after dark we rode bicycles by the light of the moon for some of the way along a logging track and then hid them and made our way through the jungle on a compass bearing. After about an hour we returned in the same way. Inevitably we had some falls and in one case Pascoe skidded into a disgusting muddy pool covered in algae. But we got back in time for me to wash and change before leaving for Segamat where I was picked up by a light aircraft for the journey to Kuala Lumpur.

Operational methods and the organisation of Special Branch occupied our attention for the rest of the day. In the evening we were joined for dinner in Richard Clutterbuck's house by General Bower and we went on talking into the early hours. Next morning I was handed over to the police officer in Special Branch Headquarters responsible for getting operational information, for further discussions. That afternoon I flew back to Segamat. In Kenya General Erskine had made a sound plan for getting the situation under control. When he left, General Lathbury had reassessed the situation and made new arrangements to suit the mopping up period. In Malaya General Templer had put into effect a good plan, but no one had noticed that some years later alterations were needed to exploit its success. A few days after my visit to Kuala Lumpur Tom, whose ship was in Singapore, came for a short visit.

Towards the end of the following week an ambush manned by members of the mortar platoon killed a CT visiting tappers in the rubber enclave near Jonathan's base camp. The CT was of no particular importance being a rank and file member of the seven man entourage of the State Committee Secretary, Ah Chien, but it indicated that these people must now be living with the Grisek Branch. In other words the Grisek Branch would have to be feeding an extra seven people which would involve them in more visits to Grisek village with the possibility of us pulling off a successful ambush there.

This thought had also occurred to one of the last remaining officers of the gang called Tay Boon Hui who was responsible for getting food from Grisek village. I knew about this from Inspector Boey who told me that, together with his contact in the village, he was working on a plan to get Tay Boon Hui to surrender. On 28 September, Boey rang up to say that Tay Boon Hui would like to meet me that evening at a certain place on a jungle track near the village. The difficulty was that he would be accompanied by another CT, who would not know about his intention to surrender. My plan was to leave Boey who was accompanied by a senior officer of the Johore Special Branch, with Pascoe and my driver a short distance from the meeting place. I would then go on with the contact man in time to meet Tay Boon Hui. I thought that it would be sensible to get to the meeting place well before the CTs arrived to make sure that they were not preparing an ambush, so I set off about twenty minutes before the time of the meeting. I carried no weapon but had a hammer wrapped in sacking in my pocket in case Tay Boon Hui needed help in persuading his escort to surrender. Leaving Boey and the others nearby, I went forward but before getting to the rendezvous I ran into a CT coming down the track in the opposite direction. Tay Boon Hui was as surprised as I was. Whereas he was in the wrong place, I was much too early. All the same we could hardly disengage and start again and it was clear that neither of us was bent on ambushing the other, so I held out my hand and said good evening. He handed over his rifle. Inspector Boey now appeared and discovered that Tay Boon Hui had left his escort about 100 yards away because he did not want any trouble when surrendering, but that he would now go back and persuade him to surrender. For what seemed like a long time we sat by the track hoping that we had not been foolish in letting Tay Boon Hui go. Although I knew from past experience that it would take the other CT time to get used to the idea of surrender, the two Special Branch officers became impatient. In the end I sent Boey's contact man to see what was happening. After a further delay I decided to go myself. Almost immediately I again experienced the unusual sensation of confronting an armed terrorist in the middle of the track. This time it was Kam San who shook me by the hand and gave me his rifle.

We now had about 2 miles to walk to reach our vehicle and I used the time to get the two CTs into a co-operative frame of mind. From the start I treated Tay Boon Hui as if he was an officer from a nearby unit visiting my company and I gave them both back their rifles to show that we they we trusted them. I also chatted away about the members of the Grisek branch and Ah Chien's people to show that we knew a great deal about them. In this way I hoped that when Boey started interrogating them, no time would be wasted winkling out a lot of information that we knew already. On arrival at Bukit Serampang I installed our guests in my bedroom where Boey and I could talk to them without their presence becoming known. We soon discovered that they would not be able to lead us to their camp as the gang had left for a new camp at the same time as Tay Boon Hui and Kam San had left for Grisek. The arrangement was that Seet Ho Ching and another CT would meet them at a pre-arranged spot in the jungle next evening and lead them back to the new camp. We decided that Tay Boon Hui should go to the rendezvous, kill his former leader and capture the other CT who would then be able to take us back to the new camp. Tay Boon Hui was adamant that Seet Ho Ching would never surrender and would have to be killed. We would lie in an ambush position around the meeting place and set off flares as soon as Seet Ho Ching was shot in order to demonstrate to his companion that escape was impossible. I then sent word by wireless to Jonathan to bring ten men to Bukit Serampang to form the ambush party. If successful they could accompany the prisoner back to the enemy camp and with luck destroy the gang.

I was not too happy with our plan because it was complicated: even the simplest plans never turn out as one expects. But I could not think of anything better. Next day while waiting for Jonathan's party to arrive I took Tay Boon Hui down to the 30 yards range and lay down with him under the targets. Some riflemen then shot at the targets to give him a feel for what it might be like if we had to shoot close to him during the ambush. We also got his own rifle which was filthy and clogged up with dirt into working order so that he could carry out his part of the plan when the time came. By 7 pm we were manning the ambush surrounding Tay Boon Hui who was sitting on a fallen tree at the meeting place. The meeting was due to take place at 8 pm by which time it would be dark.

For the first half an hour I was uncomfortable, but hopeful of a great result. Gradually the discomfort and the hope wore off as I sank into a well-remembered numbness of waiting. Ever since my youth I seem to have been waiting when trying to shoot things. Sometimes I am waiting in the corner of a wood for pigeons to fly within range: at other times crouching in the rushes by a pond hoping for a shot at a duck. Or perhaps I am waiting for my ferret to reappear from a rabbit hole after it has killed below ground and had a good feed. In Kenya we spent hours waiting silently in the dark for a contact to show up, or possibly for some enemy to attack. The fact is that hunting birds, animals, or people often involves long periods of waiting. In novels and films people are always rushing around. In real life they spend much time waiting.

At 11.30 we were still in position. What had happened was that Seet Ho Ching decided not to come but to send two other CTs instead. They did not know the exact spot and had been waiting 200 yards away. Eventually they found Tay Boon Hui who now had to decide what to do in the very different circumstances to those envisaged. He decided to separate them and took one of them out of the ambush to talk to him privately and persuade him to surrender. He then returned and tried to do the same with the other man. Naturally we did not know what was going on. Having seen one man taken out of the ambush in one direction and then seeing the other disappear in the opposite direction we thought that we might lose them both. Flares were fired and Tay Boon Hui ran like a stag along a prearranged escape route. The other man was hit and sank to the ground.

After sitting silently for nearly five hours the flares and the shooting resulted in a great release of tension and it was a job to get the men to cease firing. Eventually calm was restored and John Starkey ran forward to the CT who was moaning on the ground. Finding a wound in his leg he rapidly applied a tourniquet. But from the hoarse wheezing that he was emitting I guessed that the leg wound was only part of the problem. Shining my torch on his face it was easy to see the hole in his forehead. The man was dead. Although we had killed one terrorist who turned out to be another member of Ah Chien's entourage, the man who had come with him was nowhere to be found. We therefore had no one to lead us to the gang's new camp. Tay Boon Hui now re-appeared and said that the other CT was Wu Kuay and that he would certainly surrender within the next few days. But by then the gang might have moved again as they would probably have heard the firing and would certainly be worried by the non-appearance of the men sent to meet Tay Boon Hui.

Next day Boey's contact man in Grisek said that Wu Kuay was ready to surrender and I picked him up at a prearranged point on the jungle edge. He was keen to lead us back to the gang as he hoped by so doing to recover his heavily pregnant wife who was still with them. But he had only been to the place once, in the dark and was not sure whether he would be able to find it again. By now Jonathan had returned to his base camp with his detachment, taking Tay Boon Hui and Kam San with him so that they could show him the various places where the Grisek gang used to meet tappers and get stores. I took Wu Kuay and some men from Bukit Serampang to try and find the enemy camp. We sweated our way through the jungle for some hours before Wu Kuay said that he thought we were very close. We made a quick plan and put in an attack, but there was no camp there. Later in the day he found the right place and once more we put in an attack but the birds had flown. Soon afterwards we settled down for the night and next day joined Jonathan in his base camp.

*　　*　　*

I returned to Bukit Serampang on 2 October. Tay Boon Hui and his friends were left with Jonathan and became integrated into the company under names given to them by the riflemen. Tay Boon Hui, because of his officer status, became Mr Wong, Kam San became Chopper Gleasby and Wu Kuay, as a result of an unfortunate mistake when sleeping near one of the Iban trackers whom he mistook for his wife, became the Ponce. They wore British uniforms and carried rifles. The riflemen treated them well, Rifleman Neale even teaching the Ponce a few words of English. His best effort was to get him to reply to 'Good Morning' by clenching his fist and saying 'Bunch of Five, f**k yer.' When they all came out of the jungle, Neale tried to persuade visitors to Bukit Serampang to say 'Good Morning' to Wu Kuay in order to raise a laugh.

For the next three weeks Jonathan's patrols, accompanied by the surrendered CTs, scoured the area finding food dumps, dead letter boxes and Seet Ho

Ching's Tommy gun which was no good without the lost magazine. After a while it became clear that the remains of Ah Chien's entourage and the Grisek gang had abandoned the area. This was confirmed shortly afterwards when a patrol of B Company searching for the last remaining gang in the northern part of our area had a contact. They were unlucky not to get a kill but they found documents and clothing in a nearby camp, which proved that these two groups had joined up with the small resident gang.

By now our time in Malaya was nearly up. On 19 October, Peel and Starkey brought their two platoons out of the jungle where they had been for two and a half months despite the prevailing wisdom that national servicemen could not normally manage more than five or ten days there.

Two days later I handed over responsibility for my area to the Cheshire Regiment. In little over five months we had completely disrupted the enemy's organisation in our area. We had killed or captured sixteen CTs, a further fifteen surrendering over the next two months. They included Ah Chien and all the officers. Thereafter there were no more terrorist incidents. Mr Moloney who had been a stalwart ally throughout my time on the District War Executive Committee wrote a letter to the colonel when we left which included the following. 'Of all the Security Forces who at different times have operated in the area, The Rifle Brigade was far and away the best. Their operations were more carefully planned; they were better led; they shot straight; they patrolled more quietly and they hung on more tenaciously than anyone else.'

A few days before we left by troopship for England, the company held a party which was paid for by the police out of money we had found on killed and surrendered terrorists. The riflemen were in terrific form and made all the officers and senior NCOs sing a song, the filthier the better so far as they were concerned. At the end I said a few words to thank them for their splendid efforts at which point one of the riflemen stood up and said that as the party had been paid for by our opponents he would like to propose the health of Ah Chien who, he reckoned, had given us a good run for our money. The toast was drunk with great good humour although our recent recruits, Mr Wong, Chopper Gleasby and the Ponce looked a bit surprised.

At the end of the day it was the riflemen who were chiefly responsible for our success. By now I knew them all, almost as well as I knew the terrorists who I had studied so carefully. From talking to them and from hearing about them from each other I knew what jobs they had held between leaving school at 15 and joining the army two or three years later and what they hoped to do when they were de-mobbed. They all knew about each others' birds and a popular pass-time was betting on who would next get a 'Dear John', that is to say a letter saying that the relationship was over. Some of them having been out of England since they joined up, may not have seen their girl for a couple of years and in which case she might well have taken on a new man. The imminent return of the company to England resulted in a flood of 'Dear Johns', which caused much hilarity and a certain amount of apprehension on the part of those wondering whether theirs was in the post. I had often noticed that senior officers spoke with concern about the effect of a three-year overseas tour on married men, but in many ways single men were more vulnerable to infidelity. At any rate that was what they were thinking as they went aboard the *Empire Orwell* for the return trip to England.

For myself, I just leant over the rail to watch as we left the harbour. At first Singapore and hundreds of ships and smaller craft made up the view, but soon they occupied no more than one corner of the canvas. Before long the all-pervading impression was of a vast expanse of dark green jungle under a streaming grey sky. Later still the land became partly obscured by black thunderclouds which seemed to rise out of the sea itself and spiral up to meet the heavy banks above.

Eventually the land disappeared altogether and I realised that another chapter in my military life was over. From a personal point of view I felt that, building on my experiences in Kenya, I had worked out one way of turning background information into contact information using ordinary soldiers rather than special forces which is what I had been hoping to do. It would ultimately prove to be the basis for my whole approach to dealing with insurgencies and peacekeeping activities. Since moving to Bukit Serampang I had again been working flat out, but for a much shorter time than in Kenya and in less blood-soaked surroundings. All the same, despite the freedom to experiment that Paddy Boden had given me, the climate together with the frustrations of working in a militarily regulated environment had taken their toll. I was quite ready for a break.

Chapter 5

Widening Horizons:
War Office and Oman 1958–1961

We had not been long at sea before I realised that life on a troopship did not suit me. Accordingly, with Paddy Boden's permission, I disembarked at Aden with Jonathan Peel and together we made our way to Kenya. We stayed there for three weeks, which included one week at Malindi in a house belonging to Kitch Morson. Whilst in Kenya I looked up as many of my former associates as possible including Holyoak, Miller, Gash, Hewett, John Cumber and of course the Morsons. I also managed to find Kamau and one or two other members of our Kamiti community. We got back to England at almost the same time as the battalion after which we all went on leave until the end of January 1958.

The battalion re-assembled at Tidworth at the beginning of February in the same barracks that 2 KRRC had occupied in 1951. Support Company had amalgamated with I Company, which I commanded with Adrian Arthur as my second-in-command. There were a number of subalterns including Mark Scrase-Dickens from the old I Company and Jonathan Peel from S Company. Soon afterwards Tony Mellor replaced Paddy Boden as commanding officer. Paddy had certainly been a better colonel than one or two of his predecessors and he was always good to me. He had a strong will but slightly lacked the personality to make himself acceptable to most of his company commanders. At Tidworth the battalion was part of 1st Division commanded by Peter Gregson who I was delighted to see again. General Erskine was the Commander-in-Chief, living a few miles away at Bulford Manor.

My task was now to make the company ready for war in Europe. I was particularly anxious to ensure that the regular subalterns should make a serious study of their profession to compensate for what they had missed while chasing terrorists in Kenya and Malaya. Obviously they would be more interested in studying the social scene in London and the sporting facilities available, but I gave them a series of little talks while their men were otherwise occupied. These covered subjects ranging from minor tactics and appreciations to the fundamentals of leadership and the principles of war. I also got them to read a book on a military subject, which we discussed together after they had all read it.

When time allowed it I went in the evening to the opera or ballet in London. In March the regiment held a ball at the Ironmonger's Hall and I took Elizabeth Spencer, now often in my thoughts, as my guest and also Tom and his girlfriend.

Later that month I happened to meet the publisher Tony Samuel, who suggested I write a book about my time in Kenya. He offered an advance against royalties of £500 and, somewhat rashly I agreed. A day or two later I heard that I had been posted to a job in the War Office and would be leaving the battalion in about a month's time. But I still had a book to write, a fact of which I was reminded when Tony Samuel took me to lunch at the Savoy shortly afterwards. Over the next two weeks, working like a demon, I drafted the first ten chapters.

Before I left the battalion we had another visit from the Duke of Gloucester who was accompanied by General Stopford, our colonel commandant and by General Erskine. After visiting the companies on the training area he had dinner in the mess and, as was his custom, spent a long time afterwards leaning up against the fireplace chatting away with a glass in his hand. Until he withdrew no one could go to bed, which caused General Erskine to suggest that I should produce my photograph albums covering my time in Kenya. They were duly laid out in the billiards room and over the period that the Duke spent studying the pictures and discussing the operations with General Erskine, the officers were able to slip away to their rooms.

A few days later Dick Worsley rang up to congratulate me on getting a bar to my military cross which had apparently been published in *The London Gazette* a week earlier. It was nice of him to ring, but I was surprised that no one had told me about it earlier: so few of ones friends take *The London Gazette* on a regular basis. Apparently Sergeant Bagley got the Distinguished Conduct Medal and several other members of the battalion were 'Mentioned in Despatches.' Jonathan Peel had been given the Military Cross before we left Malaya. Although the system for determining who should get awards is well organised, the business of distributing them thereafter is pretty chancy. For example my Kenya MC got lost and it was nearly two years before I received it from the Queen at Buckingham Palace.

* * *

I reported for work at the War Office on 21 June 1958. At this time there were still nearly half a million men in the army, never mind the other two services. Each service had its own secretary of state and ministry, known in our case as the War Office. Unconnected with the War Office was a separate Minister for Defence and a serving officer known as the Chief of the Defence Staff and these two people together with a small planning and briefing staff lived in Storeys Gate just beyond the Foreign Office. The War Office consisted of the General Staff, and the staffs of respectively the Adjutant General who dealt with personnel matters, the Quartermaster General who dealt with logistics and the Master General of the Ordnance who dealt with procurement. The professional head of the army was the Chief of the Imperial General Staff, General Sir Gerald Templer of Malaya fame and a national figure in his own right. By contrast the young Secretary of State for War, who was a former captain in the Coldstream Guards called Christopher Soames, was at this time only known for being Churchill's son-in-law. He was looked after by the Permanent Undersecretary and some Civil Servants.

The General Staff in the War Office consisted of several directorates, each run by a major general. I was posted to the Directorate of Military Operations, which was divided into a number of branches. Mine was the branch that dealt with the Middle East and East Africa, known as MO 4. The branch was headed by Colonel Tony Hunter, formerly of 2 KRRC, and in it were two majors, Tony Lewis who looked after the Mediterranean, the Levant and Iraq and myself who looked after Aden, the Persian Gulf and East Africa. We each had two captains to help us.

My predecessor was David Pontifex of the Rifle Brigade, an experienced perfectionist whose hand-over notes were my bible for weeks to come. My main job consisted of corresponding with the two overseas headquarters in my area, acting as the War Office link with other Whitehall ministries such as the Foreign Office and the Colonial Office and writing briefs for the Chief of the Imperial General Staff to use at meetings of the Chiefs of Staffs Committee. What I did not immediately understand was that the Military Operations Directorate dealt with the formulation of policy and the making of plans. Its business did not lie in the execution of policies and plans once these had been agreed. This was the function of what was misleadingly called the Directorate of Staff Duties (SD) and in particular of SD2, a branch run by Lieutenant Colonel Harry Tuzo.

The first thing to strike me on arriving in MO 4 was the unsatisfactory conditions in which we worked. Although Tony Hunter had his own office, the six of us were crammed together in one room, each with one or more telephones: sometimes all of us were talking at the same time. It was also apparent that everything was done in a rush and that virtually no one was able to take a decision on his own account so that nearly everything had to be referred to a committee which ultimately wasted a lot of time. Another thing that struck me was that I was the youngest officer in the whole of the Military Operations Directorate, which included my own two captains. Some of the other majors were as much as eight years older.

What bothered me most was that this life had little in common with anything that I had previously experienced in the army. I had always thought that performance was directly related to leadership and that leadership meant, at the least, involvement with one's men to the extent necessary for producing an outlook that would enable them to give of their best. I took it for granted that a soldier's main concern was for his unit and that other connections such as his family were of minor importance. Here everything was different. People turned up in the morning and went home in the evening and no one knew or cared what they thought or did when not in the office provided that the work got done. The army as a way of life had given way to routine office work between certain hours on five days a week. The sharp distinction between being a soldier and being something else such as a businessman, politician or Civil Servant was blurred. It was disturbing and unpleasant at the time, although as the years passed I discovered that lots of other parts of the army were like this as well. Later, when married, I was obliged to adjust my own priorities to some extent.

* * *

About three weeks after my arrival the regularity of my existence was dispelled when the King of Iraq was murdered and we were required to produce several briefs for an emergency meeting of the Chiefs of Staff at record speed. There was concern for the large British garrison in Iraq and also for the security of Kuwait for which we were responsible. Most of the states in the Persian Gulf at this time were under British Protection, which meant that they each had a British Resident whose advice the ruler was required to accept. In our office all the telephones were ringing and the racket caused by the bells and everyone talking at once, had to be experienced to be believed: it was more like travelling on a fire engine than sitting in an office. To make matters worse we were in the middle of a heat-wave and the sun poured through the windows of our first floor office overlooking Whitehall. Outside a man was digging up the road with a pneumatic drill.

Day after day the hubbub continued as more and more plans were made to cover every conceivable contingency. At every level officers were working out what they would suggest if some new circumstance arose: they were not prepared to wait until it did, because by doing it in advance they might save valuable time in a crisis. And so we worked on and on. Sometimes we missed lunch and sometimes we did not leave the office until late at night. We abandoned the Whitehall weekend in favour of getting one day off each week; if we were lucky. Although my working hours were as nothing compared to Kenya or Malaya, they seemed far longer because of the frustration of most of the work and the foulness of the surroundings. I soon came to hate London as a whole and the War Office in particular. I was certainly unhappy and probably a bit depressed.

After about six weeks of this, things started to ease off. Nothing happened in Iraq after our garrison was withdrawn and the danger of Iraq invading Kuwait receded. Soon afterwards I went to Buckingham Palace to get the bar to my Military Cross in company with a good collection of Rifle Brigade officers who were getting awards of one sort or another.

There was now time to discover what was going on in other parts of my area. There were two main places of interest. First, Aden itself where there was unrest in the Protectorate instigated largely from the neighbouring Yemen and in the colony where subversive elements were beginning to think about dislodging the British. As the military headquarters for the area was in Aden, this was distinctly relevant. Realising that there was no system for co-ordinating the actions of the army, police and administration I circulated a paper advocating the establishment of an internal security headquarters together with a military intelligence officer. Somewhat to my surprise the suggestion was agreed.

The second area of interest was the Sultanate of Muscat and Oman, now just called Oman. This country was not formally under our protection but we had a number of treaties with the Sultan, which made it difficult for us to refuse, should he call on us for assistance. The country of Oman consists of 1,300 miles of the Arabian coastline and the mountainous land lying between it and the uninhabitable desert behind, known as the Empty Quarter. The Sultan's problem derived from the fact that two tribes living on a vast mountain in the north of the country called the Jebal Akhdar, were defying his authority.

The spiritual leader of these tribes was the Imam Ghalib, but the revolt was the doing of his brother and military commander, Talib, and the tribal leader of the Bani Riyam called Sulaiman. Two separate influences were working on these three men. First was the Arab nationalism of the Egyptian leader Nasser who was busily attacking Western influence wherever it presented itself in the wake of the Suez fiasco of 1956. The second was the enmity that existed between the ruler of Saudi Arabia and the Sultan of Oman as a result of conflicting interests with regard to the Buraimi Oasis and because of rivalry regarding the exploitation of newly discovered oil reserves. Talib's problem was that for the revolt to succeed, his brother, a leader of the Ibadi sect, had to ally himself with a Saudi ruler whose religious beliefs were anathema to him. Likewise the Saudi ruler who had much in common with the autocratic Sultan of Oman, had to exploit the left wing republicanism of Nasser in order to defeat the Sultan's interests around the Buraimi Oasis. In practice, although some of the rebels were probably disturbed by these considerations, most were content to think that they were forwarding their own material interests.

In 1957, the British had tried to put down the revolt by sending a brigade group from the strategic reserve stationed in Kenya to assist the Sultan's forces. But all they succeeded in doing before the hot weather brought operations to a halt, was to turn the rebels out of the villages round the base of the Jebal: they then retreated to reinforce those living on the top. The average height of the Jebal Akhdar, which was 12 miles north to south and 18 miles east to west, was 6,500 feet, but it was surrounded by a ring of mountain peaks some of which rose to 10,000 feet. The problem was to force the passes through these mountains, which would be beyond the power of the Sultan's army for some time to come. Earlier in 1958, the Commander British Forces Arabian Peninsula recommended that further troops should be sent to help storm the Jebal, but by now Nasser's propaganda was such that the Foreign Office were strongly opposed to the proposal. The government therefore refused to sanction the use of troops for this purpose. Instead it decided to honour its obligations to the Sultan by providing him with arms and equipment and by sending a contingent of regular officers on secondment, including a colonel to command his armed forces, so that in the fullness of time they could carry out the attack for themselves.

By the time I started to take an interest in Oman the reinforcements were beginning to arrive, but Talib was mining the roads and tracks around the base of the Jebal and attacking isolated outposts of the Sultan's army. It was apparent that something would have to be done to hold the situation until the Sultan's army could be made capable of looking after itself. In mid-September Tony Hunter asked me to see what further help might be given to the Sultan based on the government's ruling that no reinforcement by formed bodies of troops would be allowed. After talking to as many people who knew the country as I could find, I suggested that a special operation directed at neutralising the leaders of the revolt had a chance of working.

The plan I put forward was that four or five carefully selected officers should be established in posts around the base of the Jebal, each to be provided with a tidy sum of money and a few strong and resourceful soldiers to act as guards and escorts. Each would also need a reliable English speaking Arab to act as an interpreter and a number of trackers. The first thing to be done would be for the officers, using the money supplied, to establish informers in nearby villages whose job would be to discover when and where groups of the Beni Riyam coming down from the plateau might be contacted. The next thing would be to ambush and capture some of these people. With careful handling a proportion of them would almost certainly change their allegiance and work for us. We would then get first hand knowledge of how the revolt was being organised, where pickets guarding the passes were posted and where the leaders lived. The next stage would be to form patrols of our men together with co-operative prisoners who could approach the pickets in disguise and either be waived through or, if necessary, overcome it and then pass through. Once through they would go for the leaders, doing as much damage to Talib's irregulars as possible. I reckoned that the number of troops required would be no more than forty and that the financial backing needed would be £15,000, say £170,000 in modern terms. At the time I was convinced that this plan would work providing the right people were chosen to lead the teams.

Both Tony Hunter and the Director of Military Operations, Major General Hamilton, thought that, given the limitations imposed by the Foreign Office, the plan was worth backing. In October a working party was set up under the chairmanship of a senior Foreign Office diplomat to decide whether it should be put to the government. General Hamilton was a member of the working party and I accompanied him to the Foreign Office for the meetings. The Foreign Office was a peculiar place, which combined the squalor of the War Office with a sort of musty, nineteenth century cartoon like atmosphere. On arrival one was conducted by an ancient man in a frock coat down long dimly lit corridors full of junk such as chairs without legs and disused lockers until the desired destination was found.

My ideas were naturally greeted with a certain amount of scepticism but the very fact that my operation could be put into effect without being noticed by the outside world and at a very small cost compared with the use of a brigade from Kenya, worked in its favour. The Muscat Working Party decided that I should be sent to Aden and that if the Commander British Forces Arabian Peninsula and the Political Resident in the Persian Gulf and the Commander of the Sultan's Forces agreed with it, then they might be prepared to recommend it to the government. I was delighted at the prospect of getting away from the War Office but concerned that the manning branches seemed unable to find suitable officers to run the teams or soldiers to support them. When voicing my worries to General Hamilton he said that he would put on the pressure regarding the officers and that he would get the soldiers by the simple expedient of diverting a squadron of 22nd SAS Regiment (22 SAS) which was shortly due to return to England from Malaya, to Muscat. As I was leaving I heard that the commanding officer would meet me in Aden.

*   *   *

The Special Air Service (SAS) had been founded in the desert during the Second World War to conduct fighting patrols a long way behind enemy lines. Subsequently the SAS expanded and was widely used in Europe. Soon after the end of the war its regular regiments were disbanded but one SAS Regiment was retained in the Territorial Army. Two years after the start of the Malayan Emergency an organisation called the Malayan Scouts was raised to carry out long range jungle patrols. Its first commanding officer was Mike Calvert who had commanded one of Wingate's columns in Burma during the war before becoming the SAS brigade commander in Europe. In 1951 the Malayan Scouts were re-named as 22 SAS. When in Malaya, I had met the then commanding officer who asked me to become one of the squadron commanders, but as I had been away from 1 RB for some years and was anyhow fully employed on operations, I was not able to do so. Their new commanding officer who I duly met in Aden, was Tony Deane-Drummond.

Deane-Drummond was an inspiring character with much operational experience which included several days hiding in a cupboard to avoid capture at Arnhem and having a sizeable hole knocked in his head by rioters in Cyprus some years later. He arrived in Aden knowing little of the background to the revolt in Oman and nothing about my ideas for dealing with it. Naturally when he discovered the details he was not particularly happy, so my first job was to explain the political and diplomatic restraints under which we were obliged to work. There was one good aspect from his point of view, which was that it would at least get one of his squadrons into an operational theatre at a time when there was a move to disband 22 SAS now that its job in Malaya was over. Probably he hoped that once his men arrived, it would be possible to amend the plan to make it more to his liking, but for the time being the important thing was that we should work together to get it agreed by the relevant commanders. I could also see that if good enough officers from England were not forthcoming, it would be sensible to see what the SAS could achieve using their own officers and their own methods.

After discussions with the commander and staff at Aden we had a tour round the Arabian Peninsula. Flying in a bomber to Sharjah we changed into a smaller twin engine plane for the flight over the Jebal Akhdar to the headquarters of the Sultan's army outside the town of Muscat. The mountain looked even more formidable than I had imagined it to be. We spent the night in the headquarters officers' mess, which fully reflected the fact that the Sultan's army was being built up at a great rate.

The washing arrangements, consisting of a shower made from an old oil drum, did just about work but the lavatories were indescribably revolting and I could see why so many of the officers we were sending from England were soon back with serious internal disorders.

Next day we met the Commander of the Sultan's armed forces called David Smiley. His last post had been the military attaché in Stockholm, but in the war he had worked with partisans in the Balkans, where he gained experience of irregular warfare in mountainous areas. On his arrival he had found the two battalions of the Sultan's army to be in poor shape but the equipment now arriving from England together with the seconded officers were improving their capabilities. He reckoned that further training and aggressive patrolling carried out at the same time as extensive bombing and a blockade of the tribes on the Jebal, would eventually dispose of the threat. But as this might take several years, he had favoured the idea of getting a brigade from the strategic reserve to do the job at once. He now reluctantly accepted the British government's reasons for not sending the brigade and was ready to accept a lower level of assistance provided that any reinforcement would be unreservedly under his command and would put no extra demands on his already over-stretched administrative resources. He also reckoned that conditions were too rugged for the successful use of young national servicemen. Luckily our plan met all of these provisos.

After seeing him we set off for a look around the base of the Jebal. Deane-Drummond was principally interested in seeing the ground at close quarters whilst I was keen to get an idea of the problems involved in obtaining intelligence and Arab support for our teams. Accordingly I made my way to Nizwa, which was the so-called capital of the interior and where there was an ancient fort in which resided Said Tariq, the Sultan's brother, who was his representative for the area. He turned out to be an impressive man who in the course of our discussions showed me a deep dungeon in which were incarcerated one or two captured rebels. He seemed to think that his people would be able to assist with the implementation of our plan in various ways. In the evening we returned to Muscat.

At first light next morning we set off with David Smiley to supervise the unloading of a ship-load of donkeys that had been sent from Somaliland at the prompting of Earl Mountbatten, to act as pack animals should the brigade operation be authorised. Smiley was very angry. Smiley considered that although they would be unreservedly under his command, they would grossly overload his administrative resources and would be even less capable than national servicemen of operating in the conditions prevailing on the Jebal Akhdar, which were so different from those existing in the donkeys' native land. Furthermore there was a healthy population of large native donkeys that were well suited to providing any animal transport that he might require, so what use were these rather small and weedy creatures from Somaliland? Nonetheless, as an officer from a household cavalry regiment, he felt it his duty to ensure that they were properly put ashore.

The donkeys had arrived in a ship owned by the War Department, designed to carry tanks in an amphibious operation. A motorboat took us to this vessel which was anchored across the harbour. As we chugged through the water in the early light of dawn the port of Muscat looked picturesque and even romantic, especially the fort at the entrance to the harbour and the impressive British Consulate. Soon after our arrival, unloading commenced. This consisted of the donkeys being hoisted over the side in nets and lowered into waiting Arab craft, which took them to the beach. When David Smiley had seen enough we got into one of the boats with a number of donkeys and got deposited in the surf.

Next day we had a final talk with Colonel Smiley. He said that he agreed the plan providing that the officers to lead the teams and the money arrived from England ahead of the SAS. If not, the SAS could hardly sit around doing nothing and would be invited to start deep patrolling under their own troop commanders. If the officers from England arrived subsequently, they would start working from selected centres in close touch with the SAS, either providing them with intelligence or using the SAS to get intelligence according to how the situation developed. In other words he approved the London plan if London produced what it promised in time. If not, he would obviously be obliged to modify it.

We now had to go to Bahrein to get the agreement of the Military Co-ordinating Committee (Persian Gulf), which consisted of the land, naval and air force commanders for the area, chaired by the political resident. As we left David Smiley thrust into my hands a number of letters to various people in Whitehall at the same time saying that he would set about finding suitable Arab trackers to work with the teams which was an essential part of my plan. I said I would return as soon as the government gave the go ahead. In Bahrein we had no trouble getting the necessary approval. Deane-Drummond then set off for Malaya and I returned to England after gleaning as much information about Talib's links with Saudi Arabia as I could get from the intelligence section in Bahrein.

It took the authorities in London two whole weeks to get government approval. On my first day back I saw General Hamilton and Parliamentary Undersecretary for War Julian Amery who had been in the Balkans with Smiley during the war. Then there was a meeting at the Foreign Office. The next hurdle was a meeting of the Chiefs of Staff who agreed to recommend the plan to the government only if the Foreign Office would relax a restriction they had put on some other operation elsewhere in the Arab world, i.e. a bit of blackmail. This took several days to iron out. I was then told that, as the founder of the plan, I would have to explain it to Prime Minister Harold Macmillan to prepare him for a meeting with the relevant ministers. At the last minute this was changed and I was told to brief the Chief of the Defence Staff, a marshal of the Royal Air Force, who would talk to the Prime Minister. This fellow was not particularly pleasant, making a number of sarcastic remarks and asking a few questions. I got the impression that he had enjoyed too good a lunch, but was told that he was often like that, asking just the sort of questions that he thought the Prime Minister might ask him. At any rate it seemed to do the trick as a few days later the government gave the go ahead. By mid-November I was back in Oman, arriving a few hours ahead of Deane-Drummond and D Squadron SAS commanded by John Watts. We had now reinforced Oman with a formed body of seventy very tough soldiers instead of the forty individuals to which we had originally been restricted.

In London I had been told that I would be lucky to see any of the officers from England in less than a fortnight. I therefore decided that the most useful thing I could do was to set up an intelligence organisation capable of supporting the SAS with particular reference to getting a line on the supply route between the Jebal and Saudi Arabia. At the same time I would set up a direct link to Bahrein and London through the British Consulate in Muscat to hasten the supply of intelligence available from outside British sources and indeed anything else that might be urgently needed such as the £15,000 that had still not arrived.

*   *   *

During the next ten days I made several trips to Nizwa in the course of which I discovered from the colonel of the Northern Frontier Regiment that an officer of the Sultan's army had discovered an unguarded route onto the plateau from Awabi on the northern side of the Jebal. The colonel was now planning an operation using his own regiment to capture the Jebal Akhdar. He also said that Talib had offered to call off the rebellion subject to the Sultan accepting his terms. In Bahrein this offer was regarded as an indication that the rebels could not stand the RAF bombing. David Smiley thought that it might have been due to his blockade. In Nizwa Said Tariq and the colonel thought it was no more than a trick. In any case the Sultan would have none of it and the war would go on. A week after arriving in the country the SAS were ready and armed with what information I could give them, they deployed two troops to Awabi to the north of the Jebal and two to Nizwa to the south and started to patrol. At this point Deane-Drummond returned to Malaya.

A few days later the first of the officers from England arrived. He was in fact an ex-officer of the Sudan Camel Corps who had in recent years been working closely with the Foreign Office. He was a forceful optimist and had access to various sources of information that were not available to me. No better choice could have been made. We decided that for the duration of the campaign he should be a lieutenant colonel and I provided him with suitable embellishments for his khaki shirt. I then handed over to him the running of the intelligence organisation and the responsibility for taking on other officers as they arrived. He would have to adapt the plan according to events, as I had not got the authority to absent myself indefinitely from the War Office. Indeed I had recently received a picture postcard from Tony Hunter, sent from Waterloo station on his way home one evening, saying that my two assistants were getting tired of doing my work. He also said that unless I had plans to return in the not too distant future, he would have to get someone else to do my job.

There was however one loose end that needed tying up. David Smiley had been unable to find good Arab trackers and he thought that it might be worth looking for some Africans from the Northern Frontier Province of Kenya where the terrain was similar to the country around the Jebal Akhdar. As I had experience of tracking, a working knowledge of Kenya and direct access to the relevant Ministries in Whitehall, he thought that I would be best suited to overcoming the many difficulties that were likely to be raised.

On my way to Kenya I was obliged to spend a day in Aden. Having been instrumental in getting Whitehall's agreement to the setting up of an Internal Security Headquarters in Aden, I called on the commissioner of Police to see how it was getting on. He was enthusiastic about the new headquarters, showing me round with some satisfaction.

Arriving in Nairobi next day I visited the General and his Chief of Staff before calling on the Minister of Defence whose permission I would need in order to take African trackers out of the country. The minister agreed on condition that they were accompanied by a Kenya European to look after them. My next call was on the chief game warden whose assistance would be invaluable in finding trackers. He advised me to visit George Adamson, the warden in the Northern Frontier District to whom he sent a signal. All this was accomplished in the course of the morning.

Obviously the first thing to do was to find a suitable European so after lunch I set off to see Eric Holyoak. I hoped that he would either go himself or think of someone else who might be available. Borrowing a Land Rover from the Kenya Regiment, I found Eric at his cousin's sawmill on the Kinangop but he could not get away. He recommended Stan Bleazard who he expected to be at a party in Nairobi that evening. When found, Bleazard asked to think about it overnight. When we met next day he agreed, provided that I could arrange for him to be reinstalled in his job with the Post Office at the end of the assignment without loss of pension rights. Unfortunately the Post Office was not an agency of the Kenya government but came under the East African High Commission so my next call was on the High Commissioner who handed me over to the postmaster general. By teatime all was arranged and we set about collecting camping equipment and rations. At 2 am next morning we were on our way to Isiolo.

We drove on a wet and windy night past Thika, Nyeri and Nanyuki. As it got light we started to descend to the flat arid country of the Northern Frontier Province and as we did so the sun came out and the windscreen steamed up. Half way down we stopped where a stream ran under the road to shave and cook some breakfast. At 8 am we arrived outside Adamson's house only to discover that he was away with his wife visiting a pet lioness called Elsa that they had recently released many miles away. His assistant warden, having received the signal from Nairobi, had spread the word that we were looking for trackers and said that there might be some to test later in the day. With a morning to spare I decided to call on the Provincial Commissioner and police superintendent to discuss the subject of Somali ambitions and incursions into Kenya. Although always a matter of concern to the Colonial Office, it was now considered more pressing because it was expected that Italian Somaliland would become independent within the next few years. The trackers that we saw later in the day were useless. Next morning George Adamson re-appeared and said that if Bleazard returned in a week he might be able to find some worthwhile trackers, but that in the meantime it would be worth going to see Rodney Eliot who was the warden at Maralal. We reached him that evening and his advice was the same: come back in a week. We returned to Nairobi next day and spent what was left of it dealing with the administrative arrangements such as pay, clothes, food, arms, passports and an aircraft to take them to Oman. That evening I went to the general's house to report on our journey and to discuss the Somali question. Next day I set off to return to Muscat.

There was another delay in Aden while I arranged to hitch a lift in a Beverley transport aircraft taking tents to Bahrein. By dint of a certain amount of persuasion on my part the pilot diverted so far as to drop me off at an airstrip near Nizwa but I still had to travel back to Muscat. Apparently both the aircraft belonging to the Sultan's air force were broken down but there was a squadron of the Life Guards based at Nizwa whose job was to keep the tracks around the Jebal and the road to Muscat open. One of their troops was planning to travel the 80 miles to Muscat next day and would take me along. Meanwhile I set off to find the SAS troop camping in the desert nearby. Peter de la Billiere was the troop commander and he told me about some of the patrols that he had carried out over the past two weeks. Clearly the terrain was very exacting, but despite it, he had met with much success, having killed a number of Talib's men but losing one of his corporals in the process. I spent the night with the colonel of the Northern Frontier Regiment who was annoyed that his plan to capture the Jebal had been turned down because the headquarters in Aden refused to provide the necessary air force backing.

Next day we heard that two scout cars belonging to the Life Guards had blown up on mines that morning but luckily there had been no casualties because the mines being used were small and the floors of the scout cars were well sandbagged. All the same I was apprehensive when we set off that afternoon. For most of the way we crossed empty desert but every time we came to one of the many dry river-beds we were canalised onto a well worn track as was also the case when we passed through the villages that surrounded the occasional oasis. After a time the leading scout car hit a mine. No one was hurt and the crews of this car and the one following it dismounted and took up fire positions in case of attack. Soon afterwards the troop commander was told to send me on to Muscat with one half of the troop while the other half waited for the recovery wagon. We reached Muscat well after dark and I moved into the SAS camp near the headquarters of the Sultan's army.

John Watts not only confirmed what Peter de la Billiere had said about the patrolling to the south and west of the Jebal, but he also described further successes achieved by the troops operating from Awabi. At the present rate of attrition it seemed to me and to the officer from England who was running the intelligence set up, that the SAS squadron would be able to bring the rebellion to an end reasonably soon by deep patrolling. On the other hand Watts was not so sure. He was worried by his own casualties and he may have felt that his men would have difficulty in maintaining the present pressure for long enough because of the extremely exacting conditions prevailing on the Jebal and the strength of the opposition. David Smiley's view was that Watts would not be able to complete the job before the onset of the hot weather which would curtail his operations. He felt that the rebellion must be finished by then particularly because of the damage being done by the mining campaign. His view was that he should be given a second squadron of SAS as soon as possible. Soon afterwards the Political Resident, Persian Gulf, arrived and endorsed Smiley's request. I would now have to sell the idea in London, which would certainly lead to accusations by the Foreign Office that my original proposal had been a trick to get their agreement to a course of action that was contrary to the country's interest.

The journey back to England via Bahrein and Malta took five days because of defective aircraft and bad weather. I arrived at the flat late in the evening of 17 December at an inconvenient moment so far as Colin James was concerned. Indeed I had been away for so long that he may even have forgotten that I was his lodger.

Despite accusations of bad faith and loud cries of annoyance from the Foreign Office, the Chiefs of Staff backed Smiley's request for a second SAS squadron and the government agreed the next day. Deane-Drummond arrived with it soon after Christmas and Smiley gave him tactical control of all the British troops and the Sultan's two battalions with instructions to bring the rebellion to an end as soon as possible. This he did by a combined assault on the Jebal backed by the RAF and spearheaded by the SAS on 29 January. By this time Bleazard had arrived with his trackers who proved effective at following tracks from a mining incident to a specific house in a nearby village. When the Jebal was secured it turned out that Smiley's blockade had been so effective that the tribes living there were on the verge of starvation. As a magnanimous gesture by the Sultan the Somali donkeys were driven onto the plateau and slaughtered for food. Talib, Ghalib and Sulaiman escaped to Saudi Arabia.

*   *   *

My own part in the business came to an abrupt end once the government agreed to the sending of the second SAS squadron. From my personal point of view it had got me out of the dreaded War Office for over two months and had greatly widened my experience. In British run Kenya and Malaya our operations had taken place within an established framework which included machinery for co-ordinating the various government agencies, a single intelligence organisation, a comprehensive legal system and means of influencing public opinion. In Oman where we were operating as an ally in a foreign country, much of this framework had to be put together as we went along. Apparently my superiors thought my contribution had been valuable, because I was made a Member of the Order of the British Empire (MBE) soon afterwards. I now had to give a hand to my two long-suffering assistants in the day-to-day conduct of MO 4's business.

In fact, day-to-day business had changed to some extent in my absence because General Templer had been succeeded as Chief of the Imperial General Staff by General Frankie Festing of the Rifle Brigade. No two people could have been more different. Templer was hugely energetic and meticulous. His briefs for each item on the Chiefs of Staff agenda were usually several pages long supplemented by copious side-flags often running from A-Z and then starting again at AA onwards. They took hours to prepare and it was not unusual for a junior staff officer to be sent for to explain some point of detail. On these occasions an exhausted Templer could be sharp and aggressive. But he had a heart of gold and if he thought that he had been unfair he would, some days later, find a pretext for the officer concerned to bring some papers to his house and then thank him for coming round and give him a glass of sherry. One of my assistants not only got a glass of sherry but also an omelette cooked and dished up by the general with a towel over his arm like a waiter.

On his arrival General Festing called his briefing staff together and said that he seldom read his briefs and in any case no brief was to be more than one page long and there must be no more than three side-flags. A later edict arrived saying that the labels on the side-flags should be stuck on with gum rather than pins because pins pricked his fingers. It turned out that he meant what he said which caused consternation among senior officers who felt that he might miss a trick or two at the Chiefs of Staff meetings, but it greatly reduced our workload.

The process for preparing papers for these meetings is of some interest. When it became necessary for a new plan to be prepared, such as happened when there was a danger of Iraq invading Kuwait, the Chiefs of Staff would issue terms of reference to the Joint Planning Staff. A team of the joint planners consisting of an army major and an equivalent naval and air force officer would then be allocated to the task. These three would visit the appropriate branch of the War Office, Admiralty or Air Ministry to get the basic facts relative to their own service. For example in the case of the threat to Kuwait, Major Roly Gibbs of the planners, a KRRC officer, would come to Major Kitson's desk in the War Office to get some basic facts and figures, after which the planners would prepare a preliminary draft. Major Kitson would circulate this to other War Office branches and to the overseas headquarters by signal, in order to formulate a War Office view, which then went back to the planners. The planners at a more senior level would then produce a draft, which would accommodate the single service views as far as possible and this would then be circulated. Comments at this level would form the basis for the final version of the paper prepared by the one star (brigadier or equivalent) Director of Plans and this would be the paper taken by the Chiefs of Staff. When writing the brief for the meeting it would be our job to ensure that the Chief of the Imperial General Staff knew which bits of the final paper ran counter to the army's views as presented to the planners. In a real emergency the whole process could be completed, with much rushing around and telephoning, in a very short time, but normally it would be spread over a week or so. This was the bread and butter of my job and in the course of time I became well acquainted with the planners of all three services and the briefing officers of each of the service chiefs. My opposite number as briefer to the Chief of the Defence Staff was another KRRC officer, David House.

My trip to Oman had also brought me into contact with various exalted persons. On one occasion I had to give Julian Amery who had by now moved to the Colonial Office, an account of events and this was followed by a similar visit to his successor in the War Office, Hugh Fraser. The Deputy CIGS whose son was in the Life Guard Squadron in Oman and the Adjutant General also wanted to hear about it, as did General Lathbury, now the Director General of Military Training.

* * *

Early in 1959, I was reunited with Elizabeth Spencer and a few weeks later stayed with her at her parents' house at Bovington. She was now 21 years old and very attractive, but soon afterwards she went to Canada to teach riding and I did not see her again for a long time.

* * *

On occasion, while serving as General Staff duty officer at the weekend, I had to sleep in the War Office and the following Monday mornings were taken up telling various people what had happened. Often the first person to appear was the Director of Plans, Brigadier Mike Carver, who would breeze in and sit on the corner of the desk to discuss events that were of interest to him. He was always cheerful and seemed impervious to the tension that so often affected officers preparing for meetings of the Chiefs of Staff committee. Indeed he seemed to make a point of chatting about trivialities such as the progress of his painting classes when so many others were running up and down the corridors with piles of paper wondering what to do next.

* * *

At this time I often thought about Oman and wondered whether my Special Operation could have been made to work if the government had stuck to its original ruling that no formed bodies of men could be sent to the country. In retrospect I felt that there was nothing wrong with my original idea. What was impracticable was getting the right men and some money into the country sufficiently quickly. It was apparent that we could only have done this if an organisation had existed in advance, capable of moving there at short notice with the ability to collect background information and develop it into contact information. This was the subject of my paper written for the commandant of the Staff College three years earlier and it now seemed a good moment to resurrect it. Realising that there was little chance of getting a new unit raised from scratch, I thought it might be worth giving the role to the SAS. I therefore wrote a new paper along these lines and circulated it as an official document. As a result it received more attention than my earlier one had done. In due course Deane-Drummond was asked for his opinion and he said that if the SAS could be enlarged to include an element to carry out this task and retain squadrons organised for deep patrolling, then there might be some merit in the idea. If the regiment had to be restricted to one role, then the present one was more important. In fact there was no question of enlarging the SAS so my idea was shelved, but the way in which the SAS had handled the job in Oman ensured that it was not disbanded.

Although rebuffed, the Oman campaign and the discussions about the SAS had raised interest in counter-insurgency. In an effort to exploit this I wondered whether it would be possible to get company commanders taught how to collect background information and turn it into contact information as we had done in Malaya. The subject was not taught at any of the army schools and although some officers picked it up by trial and error, most did not. By dint of a good deal of agitation on my part, it was agreed that courses should be run for this purpose. On the face of it they should take place at the School of Infantry as this is where tactics gets taught. But there was an intelligence side to the business because much of the background information would come from intelligence agencies. There was therefore a case for running the courses at the intelligence centre at Maresfield which, being nearer to London, was more accessible to the sort of people who could talk about it. I was consulted on the preparation of the syllabus and visited Maresfield once or twice to lecture.

I was pleased to think that the army had adopted one of my ideas, but it did not last long because commanding officers, thinking that their people were being taught intelligence rather than tactics, were reluctant to send them on the course. Twelve years later when I was commandant of the School of Infantry, I inserted the subject into the platoon and company commanders' courses.

*   *   *

By the middle of September it was time for me to visit Aden and East Africa to keep in touch with our overseas headquarters. This time I went first to Aden and then on to British Somaliland to meet the commander of the Somaliland Scouts. I also called on the Governor and the Commissioner of Police who was very pleased with the military intelligence officer that we had sent to help his Special Branch. I then visited an outpost of the Somaliland Scouts near the Ethiopian border, which was commanded by David Stileman. He lived in a Beau Geste fort together with his wife and young children. We went riding through the desert-like scrub on small ponies. Nairobi was the next stop where I had talks with the Chief of Staff and the Minister of Defence, Tony Swann. Amongst other things I had been told to get some more trackers for Oman. The ones that had gone with Bleazard had returned, but now Colonel Smiley wanted some more as there had been a resurgence of mining. Bleazard was no longer available so it was agreed that Pete Nicholas and Gilfrid Powys would take them instead. The main issue in Kenya at this time was Somali incursions in the Northern Frontier Province. To find out about this I visited the brigade commander in Nanyuki who was Miles Fitzalan-Howard and the Special Branch officer for the area who was none other than my old colleague Ken Goodale. This was followed by discussions with the commander of the Strategic Reserve in Kahawa, Brigadier Myers.

On my return to England I was faced with the business of getting my book ready for the printers and at the beginning of April *Gangs and Counter Gangs* was published. I was then called for by the Secretary of State, Christopher Soames, who said that some people were not entirely happy about the book, but that he saw no harm in it. He hoped that if interviewed by the BBC, I would not be too critical of the way in which the campaign had been run. He was very relaxed, wished me luck and said that it was just the sort of story that his father-in-law (Winston Churchill) would relish.

Throughout the time that I had been writing the book, Tony Samuel had been very supportive. Tony had not been in the army but had spent the war in the Special Operations Executive stirring up trouble in the occupied countries of Europe.

*   *   *

In May the Italian Ministry of Defence decided that as both British and Italian Somaliland were about to become independent and joined together, there should be a meeting to decide on how we should organise their new army. I was deputed to represent the United Kingdom. On arrival the British military attaché took me to his house outside Rome where I was to stay for the duration of the conference. He was surprised to find that I had been given no instructions as to the line I was to take which also surprised me. On arriving at the Italian Ministry of Defence next morning with the military attaché, we got stuck in the lift with an Italian admiral and a general. They turned out to be Italy's principal delegates to the meeting being their Chief of the Defence Staff and the Chief of the General Staff. We felt a bit under-gunned. The meeting itself dealt with such matters as who would advise and train the new army and where they should get their equipment. It was very hot and stuffy and we both laboured to get the meeting over as soon as possible. As a result I agreed to each of their proposals as soon as they made them, but then they all argued with each other. The conference lasted three days. Luckily we only worked in the morning which meant that the afternoons and evenings were free and the military attaché was wonderful at showing me the sights of Rome. It was most enjoyable. On my return I asked why a more senior officer had not been sent and was told that Chief of the Imperial General Staff regarded the whole thing as a waste of time. Apparently he felt that when the Somalis became independent they would turn to the Russians for help and equipment, which is exactly what happened.

* * *

With a sigh of relief I left the War Office at the end of 1960. My next job was to be the army representative at the Royal Naval College at Greenwich. Many courses were run there and I was supposed to be available to give lectures about the army when required. In addition I was to be a member of the directing staff of the new lieutenants' Greenwich course. It was designed to extend the general education of young lieutenants, to consider the historical background to modern strategy, to improve their ability to express themselves verbally and in writing and to provide a study of leadership in depth. There were to be three courses a year and the students were formed into syndicates of eight. Each syndicate had a serving officer and a member of the academic staff as joint syndicate leaders. It was intended that I would stay for three courses.

The Royal Naval College had been designed by Sir Christopher Wren as a hospital for disabled seamen on the site of a disused royal palace. In 1873 the Royal Navy took it over as a college and the famous Painted Hall became the officers' mess. The college together with a number of ancillary schools, was presided over by Rear Admiral Earl Cairns whose father and brother had both been in the Rifle Brigade and who had two sisters married to Rifle Brigade officers. Commander Farquharson-Roberts was in charge of the lieutenants' course. As it was the first course of its kind, there was quite a lot of preparation necessary to get it going. Each of us was given two or three subjects to sponsor, that is to say we did the research and prepared lecture notes. I was given subjects that were common to all three services such as leadership, the principles of war and joint planning and was able to base much of it on the work I had done preparing for the talks that I gave to my company officers on return from Malaya. Luckily the tempo at Greenwich was more relaxed than it was in MO 4 or at the Staff College so I had no trouble in preparing my notes. Work stopped altogether at midday on Friday and did not start again until midday Monday.

* * *

During this time I often found myself thinking of Elizabeth Spencer to whom I had sent a copy of my book. One day when looking at pictures in the Royal Academy I saw Colonel Spencer and asked him for news. He said that she was returning to England via Australia on a liner, which would shortly arrive at Gibraltar. I immediately sent a letter to her at Gibraltar asking her to come and stay for the Staff College Hunt Ball which was due to take place a short time after her return. As soon as she arrived at Monk's Hill I knew that I very much wanted her to be my wife. On the day after the ball I proposed. She said that my proposal was rather sudden and although I might think I had been courting her for nearly six years, she reckoned that we had only met about six times. But she would consider it. I made the point that I was due to go to America on a course at the end of January and that if she could let me know before I went, it would be helpful. This she promised to do.

At the end of 1961, I said goodbye to the Royal Navy and returned to Monk's Hill for some leave before departing for America. I had enjoyed Greenwich immensely.

Meanwhile Elizabeth kept me waiting. She later said that she did not wish to appear unduly keen. In the end I got a letter a few days before I was due to sail saying that she would like to marry me on my return from America in the summer. Though overjoyed at her decision there were obviously a number of loose ends. We decided to meet in Scott's Restaurant in London to clear some of them up and we covered as much of the ground as possible. As there was not time for me to see her father, I would have to write and ask his permission. Elizabeth had just taken a new job as chief instructor at a riding school and did not want our engagement to be made public before April. I could not get her an engagement ring so she would have to find one for herself. And so on. Two days later I sailed in the *Queen Mary*. On the way to Southampton I told my mother that I was engaged which pleased her greatly.

*   *   *

The four years that had elapsed since my return from Malaya had been educational to say the least. I had gained a much wider understanding of the way in which the army worked at the higher levels. I had been in constant contact with the Colonial Office with regard to our responsibilities for the colonial forces maintained in the area for which I was responsible, notably the King's African Rifles, the Somaliland Scouts, the Aden Protectorate Levies and the Trucial Oman Scouts. My involvement with events in Muscat and Oman resulted in links with the Foreign Office. This campaign highlighted many aspects of managing an insurgency that had not formerly been my concern, such as coping with the political limitations that had so greatly influenced the way in which the campaign developed. It had also shown up the inability of the War Office to provide what was needed to implement a workable plan at a reasonable speed. Had it proved impossible to adjust the political limitations, the operation would have fallen through. In the event political adjustments were made which enabled a different sort of operation to produce the desired result.

In terms of my private life the four years spent in and around London had been equally valuable, as it gave me the opportunity to develop a circle of friends, both male and female, outside the army. This was something that I had never before managed, because of having spent so much time in Germany, Kenya and Malaya. Learning to fit in with these people had not always been easy, but without the experience I would have been unprepared for the next major development in my life, that is to say marriage.

Chapter 6

America, Cyprus and the Ministry of Defence 1962–1967

On board the *Queen Mary* crossing the Atlantic, was another officer of the British Army heading for the US Armed Forces Staff College, Norfolk, Virginia. He was Tony Aylmer of the Irish Guards who had been on the same Camberley course as me in 1956. He had recently been married and his new wife, Shaunagh, was going to join him after a few weeks when he could find somewhere to live. Meanwhile we would both be living in the bachelor officers' quarters which is what the Americans call the mess. There were many interesting and often amusing incidents in relation to the differences between our accustomed military disciplines. In short we had an enlightening period of adjusting to the ways of our gallant allies.

Our American fellow students were lieutenant colonels, or of equivalent rank in the other services as a result of which we had been promoted to temporary unpaid lieutenant colonels for the duration of the course. There were British officers from the Royal Navy and Royal Air Force with us and various other foreign students including a very cheerful French major who had spent many years in Algeria and Indo-China. As at Camberley we were split into syndicates. There were a number of classroom exercises and some lectures given by a variety of distinguished officers and civilians. The lectures all started with the speaker telling a joke or two after which they read politically correct speeches from a prepared script. Only when it came to the question period did one get any indication of their own views or personalities and even then they stuck pretty rigidly to the party line. Ostensibly the subjects that we discussed in syndicate and the problems set for us to work out, might vary from the Russians attacking in Germany (total war) to a landing by an army corps at the southern tip of Vietnam (counter-insurgency). By contrast the procedure for tackling the problems always involved collecting information from pamphlets and writing down the answers. Right or wrong was decided by whether the information had been correctly transposed from the pamphlet to the answer. Thinking of ways to deal with the problems played no part because 'the way' was laid down in the book. As for concepts, there was only one, which was 'to get there firstest with the mostest.' Obviously this is a bit unfair, but it is how it struck us at the time.

The other indisputable fact was that the Americans were amazingly friendly and hospitable. We were constantly being asked out to meals, sometimes in their houses but more often at the chemist (drug store) where one sat on stools by the counter, eating rather surprising, ready cooked stuff which was often served in cardboard boxes.

In addition to our work at the college we were taken on a series of interesting visits to service installations and ships at different locations along the eastern side of the country. It soon became clear that in terms of quantity and the technical quality of their equipment the US armed forces were in a league of their own. It was also apparent that in the eyes of most Americans, their Navy and Marine Corps were considered a cut above the US Air Force and several cuts above the US Army.

One notable difference in the way in which work was conducted, concerned the time spent carrying it out. For example at Camberley if a syndicate was given a problem, the members of it would do the business as quick as possible so as to get away from the classroom to study or take part in sport or to be with their families. At the Armed Forces Staff College, working through the problem was made to fit the time allotted to it in the programme.

*   *   *

Invariably the Americans were hugely kind and hospitable, particularly the family with whom I stayed. After a few weeks Tony Aylmer's wife arrived and they set up house together in a married quarter in the grounds of the college. He was a year older than me and had become conscious of the fact that getting accustomed to his new wife was not as easy as he had supposed it would be before they got married. Hearing that I had only met Elizabeth a few times and that we were going to join 1 RB in Cyprus soon after the wedding, he wondered whether it would be helpful for his wife to ask her to stay so that I could get to know her better. This was obviously sensible and also utterly desirable from my point of view, so it was arranged that Elizabeth would come to Norfolk for a month from the middle of May. Meanwhile I soon found that I had more to do than I had bargained for.

The trouble arose from the fact that the Americans, who had been allowed to keep a few hundred advisors in South Vietnam since the time when that country had become divided, were finding themselves obliged to increase the number rapidly in the face of hostile action by North Vietnam. By the end of 1961 the number had gone up to around 3,000 and by the end of 1962 it would reach 11,000 and still rising. Not only were US reinforcements pouring into South Vietnam, but within America itself there was a greatly increased awareness of the problems of counter-insurgency warfare. Furthermore President Kennedy had decreed that officers of all the armed services should study the matter as a matter of urgency. Not long after our arrival the President appeared in person at the Armed Forces Staff College for a discussion with senior officers. Although the students were not involved, we saw him arrive. He did not look much like his pictures. His face was very round and his colour looked none too good. About this time he asked the Rand Corporation to conduct a Symposium. Its stated aim was to 'draw on the knowledge of men of recent and direct experience in counter-insurgency, with a view to assembling a large body of detailed information and judgement on the multifarious aspects of this inadequately explored form of conflict.'

Naturally the United Kingdom government was asked to provide delegates to the Symposium who could speak about the British experience, particularly in Malaya and Kenya. As I was 'over there' so to speak and could be got to the scene at little extra expense and as, providentially, I had been in both Kenya and Malaya, I found myself nominated as one of the British delegates. I soon found myself sitting with a motley collection of people in the Rand Corporation building in mid-April.

The business itself was conducted effectively and efficiently. Indeed I was amazed at the extent to which delegates from France, the Philippines, Australia, Britain and the United States, discussing a number of different situations, so often reached the same conclusions. The Symposium Report when finally issued, was a valuable document, which I have often found useful over the years.

As a result of my attendance at Symposium I was asked to give a lecture on counter-insurgency to the staff at the headquarters of the US Continental America Command (CONARC). On arrival I was ushered into a large hall full of officers including no less than fourteen generals, most of who would probably have preferred to be doing something else. The presidential decree was clearly having an effect. Soon afterwards I was sent to the Special Forces Center at Fort Bragg where I not only had to lecture to a large number of younger officers, but was also engaged in talks with various commanders.

*   *   *

By the time Elizabeth arrived I was more than ready for a break. Retrieving her from the airport at Norfolk, we went for a walk in the nearby park ablaze with colour from a mass of flowering shrubs. Apart from our brief meeting at Scott's Restaurant in London, this was the first time that I had seen my fiancée since we had become engaged. She looked even better than I had been imagining her over the past four months, during which time we had written to each other on a daily basis. She soon settled in with Tony Aylmer and Shaunagh who was by now heavily pregnant.

Soon after her arrival, as good luck would have it, the Armed Forces Staff College settled down to a whole week studying nuclear warfare. Much to the embarrassment of the directing staff, all allied officers on the course were excluded on security grounds. This gave Elizabeth and I some time to ourselves and to tour the American South, many of them battleground states of the Civil War. Unlike British battlefields, these were all laid out with monuments, visitor centres, cannons etc. so that the progress of events could be clearly followed. Also in getting to and from them, we passed through much lovely country at a particularly beautiful time of year. Above all we had a perfect opportunity to get to know each other and it is no exaggeration to say that the American Civil War was not uppermost in our minds all the time. It was like a pre-wedding honeymoon; up to a point. However, our month together soon passed and Elizabeth had to return to England.

Our course ended in mid-July. For someone such as myself who had no previous experience of Americans, it was immensely valuable in terms of learning how they approach military problems. In many ways their outlook was very different to ours because they depended so greatly on their technological superiority and on their ability to concentrate vast numbers of men and equipment wherever they felt it to be advantageous. There is little doubt that in most conventional operations this system is highly effective as US forces demonstrated so thoroughly in the war and in Korea.

On the other hand in their recently chosen field of counter-insurgency, commanders need to develop a state of mind that enables them to look at each individual situation on its merits. Doctrine that can be taken from a pamphlet and applied in widely differing circumstances is less likely to work. The officers who I talked to at this time seemed genuinely keen to know about ways of dealing with insurgents and were modest about their country's achievements in this field. Because the methods that we had developed differed from their general ideas about fighting, they had some difficulty in getting their people to accept them. Nonetheless, they had been successful at advising other countries how to deal with the problem, especially in South America, to a greater extent than they seemed to realise.

*   *   *

Our marriage was fixed for 21 August and took place in a village church in Devon. The ceremony over, Elizabeth and I walked through an arch of swords

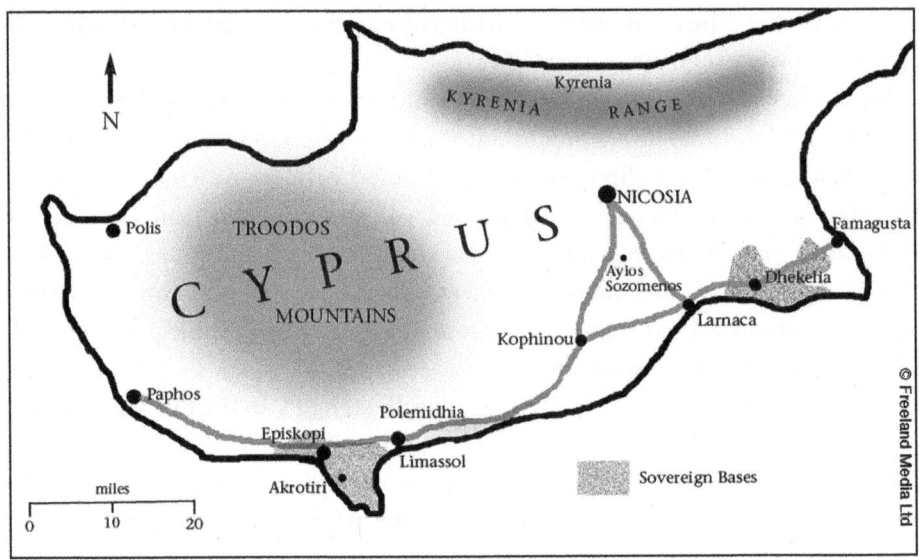

provided by warrant officers and sergeants of the Rifle Brigade and we then drove to the Spencer's house for the reception.

For our honeymoon we spent six wonderful weeks in Kenya. It was still then a colony but Jomo Kenyatta was now the Prime Minister and we saw him at a wedding to which we had been invited on our first day in the country. Thereafter we hired a car and drove around the countryside, meeting up with old friends and visiting various sites such as the game reserve at Meru, Amboseli, the Ngoro Ngoro crater and Lake Manyara. After our detour in Tanganyika we moved on through Tsavo to Malindi and on the way home we stopped at Tsavo East game-park where Dennis Kearney was the assistant warden. Our last appearance in Kenya was at the Royal Show outside Nairobi where we saw a lot of old friends and where we were able to thank Eric for the trouble he had taken arranging our trip.

Shortly after our return to England we flew to Cyprus to join 1 RB commanded by Hew Butler. The idea was that I should be his second-in-command, but on arrival it turned out that Tom Jackson, who was senior to me, was staying for longer than expected so I was given B Company to command until his departure in six months time. This was welcome news because commanding a company is always fun and I would have plenty of time to be second-in-command later on.

* * *

When Cyprus became independent in 1959 the United Kingdom retained two small blocks of land, each one being around 10 miles from east to west and 5 miles from north to south. They were known as the Sovereign Base areas. They were needed so that we could fulfil our international agreements to other countries in the Near and Middle East. 1 RB was stationed in the Dekhelia Sovereign Base area, which was on the south-east coast. The other area, also on the coast about 60 miles to the west, was called Episkopi. It incorporated the major RAF airfield of Akrotiri and Britain's Near East Headquarters. The Gloucestershire Regiment was the garrison battalion for this Sovereign Base area.

The Rifle Brigade was much as I had left it four and a half years earlier, although many of the people had gone or changed their jobs. In B Company Simon Dereham, one of Dick Worsley's platoon commanders in Malaya, was now my second-in-command. My three platoon commanders were Sam Shepherd, Peter Irby and Andrew Festing, third son of our colonel commandant, Field Marshal Festing. Jonathan Peel was Hew Butler's adjutant and Bagley, was now B Company's colour sergeant. There were many other old friends in the battalion such as George Blunden who was the quartermaster.

The primary task of the two battalions in Cyprus was to guard the Sovereign Base areas, but as far as we knew, no one wanted to attack them. We were not therefore overworked. For a full year after our arrival the battalion followed a peace-time routine in which training alternated with sporting activities.

In the spring, I took B Company to a training area just beyond Episkopi. On one of our exercises Andrew Festing's platoon was doing an advance to contact when it came under fire from a few men acting as enemy about 300 yards to their front. It so happened that Andrew was relieving himself in the bushes by the side of the road at the time, but his platoon signaller, the 18-year-old Acting Corporal Logdon, immediately gave out a complete set of orders for the attack to the section commanders. I was amazed at the speed and accuracy with which this was done. By the time Andrew had done up his buttons the attack was well on the way. Soon after we returned to Dekhelia the men were throwing grenades on the range and one of the riflemen was making a great hash of it. The target was three mortar carrying tubes placed in the vertical position about 25 yards away. Turning to Acting Corporal Logdon I told him to show the man how to do it and he immediately threw one that actually went into the top of one of the tubes, which was either a great demonstration of skill at arms or a fluke. Unfortunately Logdon lost his stripe after a brawl one evening but I kept an eye on him and a few years later persuaded him to try for a commission via Sandhurst, which he got. He finished his career as a lieutenant colonel with an MBE. In the army many warrant officers graduate to short service and then quartermasters' commissions but the Rifle Brigade had always made a practice of getting a few exceptional NCOs to go for commissions while they were still young. Oddly enough there was another exceptional NCO in B Company at the time who also pulled it off, finishing his career as Colonel George Smythe OBE.

*   *   *

In March it was confirmed that Elizabeth was with child and we took a few days off to visit the Holy Land. We went with a small group from Dekhelia and lodged at the Shepherd's Hotel in Jerusalem, which was then part of Jordan.

In June the whole battalion went to North Africa for a month's training in the Libyan desert and Hew Butler was able to revisit places he fought over during the war. Where we were, the ground was much harder than I expected and the nights far colder. Other aspects of desert life such as swapping army biscuits with the Arabs for eggs went as planned. On our return Tom Jackson left and I became second-in-command.

From the middle of the year until October Cyprus gets hot and steamy so that excessive effort becomes unpleasant. At such times keeping the men occupied without browning them off becomes difficult. Hew Butler was an exceptionally good commanding officer and his general policy decisions reflected his deep understanding of the men. It was my job to turn his policies into action. In doing so I received a certain amount of 'advice' from Hew, one bit of which has stuck in my mind. Hew was always aware that some activities, particularly in the realms of sport, were more suitable for officers and some more suitable for the riflemen. Throughout my service I tried to encourage men to go to church. On one occasion when discussing this, Hew piped up saying that church was an 'officer sport' and I should not badger the men about it.

Joyfully our baby, who we called Catherine, arrived in mid-October.

*   *   *

At this point it is necessary to digress for a moment in order to understand a bit about the Cyprus problem. In 1963 the population numbered just over half a million split between Greek and Turkish Cypriots in a ratio of about four to one. The Greeks were not for the most part related by blood to the Greeks in Greece. They are said to be descendants of the ancient Phoenicians whose Greekness derived from the fact that Cyprus was conquered by Alexander the Great and incorporated both politically and culturally into his empire. They retained an intense sense of belonging to the Greek community forever after, first as part of the Roman Empire, then the Byzantine Empire, then the Ottoman Empire and finally the British Empire. They were more Greek than the Greeks and longed to be united with mainland Greece, which was the main purpose of the EOKA insurgency, led by Grivas. For their part the Turkish Cypriots were mainly descended from 20,000 Turks who were forcibly settled in Cyprus after it became part of the Ottoman Empire in 1571. They were of the same blood as the Turks in Turkey and for this reason the Turkish government could not countenance the absorption of Cyprus into Greece.

When the British decided to leave Cyprus they had to do so in a way that acknowledged the Greek preponderance in terms of numbers but which safeguarded the Turks against future attempts by the Greeks to unite with Greece. The resulting constitution was inevitably a dog's breakfast, which hardly accorded with a purist's conception of democracy. But it was accepted with all its drawbacks by both of the main parties concerned and by Greece, Cyprus and the United Kingdom, all of whom guaranteed it. The constitution provided for an executive consisting of a Greek Cypriot President, a Turkish Cypriot Vice President and a cabinet of seven Greeks and three Turks. Cabinet decisions were taken by a simple majority vote, but were subject to veto by either the President or Vice President. There was a House of Representatives, 70 per cent Greek and 30 per cent Turkish, where most laws required a simple majority, although certain specific matters required the approval of a majority of the Greek members and a majority of the Turkish members separately. The civil service was to be manned on a ratio of 70 to 30 per cent and the Cyprus army on a ratio 60 to 40 per cent basis.

Clearly any constitution acceptable to Turkey whose airfields were 40 miles away and Greece whose airfields were 400 miles away could only be made to work by very delicate management. Undoubtedly the President, Archbishop Makarios, was capable of this, but the Greek members of his government were mainly former members of EOKA who were well practised in the use of violence and fully persuaded of its effectiveness. Furthermore, the Turkish Vice President was unyielding in his determination to preserve every scrap of influence given to his community by the constitution, underpinned as it was by Turkey's superior military strength in relation to Greece. During the first four and a half years of Cyprus' independence it became evident that certain changes to the constitution were needed for purely practical reasons. For example the Turkish Cypriots could not find enough people capable of filling the 30 per cent of civil service posts allotted to them. But when the President, pushed on by the EOKA members of his government, suggested amendments, the Vice President reacting to the hard-liners in the Turkish community, rejected them fearing that they would ultimately strengthen the Greeks in their desire to be united with Greece. By the autumn of 1963 it began to look as if matters were coming to a head.

When word of the dissension between the two communities reached us, there was little reason to suppose that we would be involved, although widespread disturbances might pose a problem to those of our families living outside the Sovereign Base areas in places like Larnaca. There were of course plans for protecting the families and other British nationals living outside the Sovereign Base areas, and these got dusted off and brought up to date where necessary. At the beginning of December Hew Butler went on leave to England. On 21 December Elizabeth and I took hounds down to Akrotiri in the other Sovereign Base area so that the members of the RAF saddle club could get some hunting. We were to stay with the station commander for the night and attend a dance given by the Commander-in-Chief Near East whose daughter Jeanie was 'walking out' with Jonathan Peel. During the evening there was a certain amount of coming and going of staff officers and it soon became known that fighting had broken out in Nicosia. On returning to Dekhelia next day we heard that there had been a bloody confrontation between Greeks and Turks in Nicosia but that it had died down. Nothing had happened in Larnaca or elsewhere in the island.

In the evening I went to Nicosia to meet Hew Butler on his return from leave so as to bring him up to date. On the way to the airport all was quiet, but as we entered the city I noticed a number of armed policemen lining the wall of a police station looking rather frightened. They were still there when I returned with Hew some time later and the sight made him laugh. He probably thought that my account of recent events was exaggerated and it was certainly difficult for him to imagine that the peaceful island that he had left three weeks earlier was about to become so turbulent. Later that night when back at our house in Larnaca, I heard two or three shots which sounded as though they had come from one of the two Turkish parts of the town. Throughout Cyprus, Greek and Turkish Cypriots seemed to co-exist happily. Communities tended to stick together, although in Nicosia particularly there were some mixed areas.

Next morning we heard that there had been further and more serious outbreaks of fighting in Nicosia and it seemed likely that Larnaca would follow suit. For this reason we cancelled the battalion carol service so that the married men could get back to their wives and we opened the operations room and got the vehicles ready should we have to activate our families protection plans. During the morning as the wives were doing their last-minute shopping, firing broke out in Larnaca. Elizabeth rang me up to say that she had been accosted by a gunman who threatened her with a pistol and told her to get back home at once if she did not want to be shot. We soon heard that similar situations had been experienced by many of the wives some of whom had to take shelter in various shops and houses if they could not get back to their own homes. We asked Headquarters Cyprus District at Episkopi for permission to move in to Larnaca to protect our families and those of the other units in Dekhelia Garrison.

Permission was refused because the Cyprus government maintained that they were still capable of looking after our families. In the afternoon Hew Butler sent me into Larnaca to see what was going on. From various vantage points overlooking the border between Greek and Turkish areas I could see defences being prepared and I heard a bit of shooting. It was clear that the families living near the border were having difficulty getting in and out of their houses but those living elsewhere were all right. Luckily our house was about equidistant from the two major Turkish enclaves. I called in on Elizabeth and found her none the worse for her experience earlier in the day, but I was worried at leaving her and the baby when I returned to Dekhelia as I had to do.

Fighting in Larnaca continued throughout the evening during which we discovered that one of our men had been killed. We also discovered where most of the families who had not managed to get home, were lying up. During the night we made a plan designed to rescue these people and also to evacuate all families in exposed areas and re-house them with other families in Dekhelia until safer hirings could be arranged. Next day, which was Christmas Eve, we were given permission to implement the plan and by nightfall most of the families living in dangerous areas had been moved. In the evening Elizabeth came to Dekhelia to spend the night with the Butlers and next morning we went to the garrison church together. Afterwards, as there was a lull in the fighting, she returned to our house in Larnaca to cook lunch. I followed later with two of the subalterns who we had invited as our guests. Just as we were finishing the meal there was a great commotion at the back of the house and we saw a large party of armed Greeks Cypriots passing down the road towards the Old Turkish quarter waving flags and blowing whistles. There was some wild firing and one or two bullets hit the house. Reluctantly leaving Elizabeth to look after the baby we followed the Greek advance and then took up a position to a flank while they attacked and captured a school on the edge of the Turkish quarter. Nothing much else happened in Larnaca that day, but we heard that the situation in Nicosia was extremely serious.

There fighting continued and after a few days both the Greek and Turkish Cypriots proposed that the two British battalions in the Sovereign Base areas should move in to separate the two sides. Major General Peter Young who commanded Cyprus District set up a headquarters in the outskirts of Nicosia and the Gloucesters from Episkopi moved into a concentration area nearby. The British would no longer be confined to looking after their families but would become part of a peacekeeping force responsible for restoring order throughout the whole of Cyprus, a formidable task. Because of the delicate situation in Larnaca one of our companies and the reconnaissance platoon was required to stay for family protection and another to guard the Dekhelia Sovereign Base until a battalion could arrive from England to take on these tasks. Initially therefore Hew Butler could only take the one remaining company to Nicosia. I was left behind to deal with Larnaca.

In order to do this I based myself on our house. By now the two Turkish quarters had barricaded themselves in but a certain amount of skirmishing took place along the borders between the two communities. For the next week I was kept busy rescuing individuals of either community who were lying wounded between the outposts or bringing help to the sick and aged. We had no authority to use force to stop organised attacks between the two communities. My aim was to prevent incidents building up into large scale engagements by persuading low level commanders to do nothing until they got proper orders from their own leaders. We could then help them to contact their leaders using our wireless sets, once we were happy that their leaders would give them the right instructions.

In Larnaca the leaders of both sides were friendly but the same could not always be said of the young fighters manning the barricades, especially on the Greek side where recollections of the EOKA campaign were still relatively fresh. On one occasion when Hew Butler was visiting me, we heard that one of our men had been shot and wounded. Soon afterwards the casualty appeared and Elizabeth looked after him administering hot sweet tea to fend off the effects of shock while waiting for the medical officer to arrive. It was soon clear that the shot had come from a Greek position about 70 yards from where our rifleman was standing so there was no possibility of it being a mistake. We immediately went to see the Greek district officer and police superintendent and Hew red in the face and loudly banging the table, protested vigorously. They both expressed regret and assured us that the culprit would be shot if discovered. We never heard whether this drastic remedy was put into effect, but no more of our men were attacked around Larnaca.

A few days later a battalion of the Sherwood Foresters arrived in Dekhelia and a detachment took over our responsibilities in Larnaca. The commander of it stationed himself in a tent outside our house and Elizabeth allowed him to come in for a bath until he absent-mindedly blew up the geyser, which provided the hot water. By this time I was with the battalion in Nicosia, but like many of our officers and men whose houses were in Larnaca I was worried at leaving my family in such circumstances.

On my arrival I found battalion headquarters established in a school just outside the walls in the north-east part of the city. Our company and platoon headquarters were tucked away in public building or houses, but the men in the posts established to keep the Greeks and Turks apart, sheltered on roofs or behind walls or sandbags. They built little fires to keep warm as it was unusually cold with ice on the puddles and even snow on the Troodos Mountains, visible in the distance from many of our observation posts. For most of the time life was boring for the men but occasionally an incident would threaten to flare up and then everything would depend on the actions of whichever rifleman or NCO happened to be nearby.

By this time further reinforcing battalions were arriving from England. Within the old city walls there were enough troops to keep the dividing line between the two communities permanently manned. In our sector, which was outside the walls where the two communities had been living together, bands of armed Greek fighters had attacked their Turkish neighbours over Christmas. Many houses had been ransacked and their occupants killed. Survivors of the local Turkish community had fled to their compatriots inside the old city or moved to a refugee camp which had been set up to the north of Nicosia. This camp was no more than 5 miles south of the Turkish held Kyrenia Mountain range, which gave the occupants a feeling of security. For the moment the fighting was over but our men kept turning up rotting bodies, often of women and children, in the wrecked houses.

The principal danger was that Turkey would launch an invasion of Cyprus to safeguard the Turkish Cypriots against their vastly stronger Greek neighbours. If this happened it might well lead to war between Greece and Turkey thereby destabilising the whole southern flank of the North Atlantic Treaty Organization. It was mainly for this reason that the British were trying to keep the two sides apart. As Turkey was stronger than Greece our intervention was to Greece's advantage. But in Cyprus, by stopping the stronger Greeks Cypriots from attacking the weaker Turkish Cypriots, we were helping the Turks, which turned the Greek Cypriots against us. They did not seem to understand that we were saving them from being invaded and it did not take long for their hostility to make itself felt in the form of an intensely hostile propaganda campaign. Although this did not worry us in our peacekeeping activities, it was a threat to the families who were living outside the Sovereign Base areas.

To start with General Young concentrated his limited forces on Nicosia because it was here that the situation could deteriorate sufficiently quickly to justify a Turkish invasion. The city was divided into sectors each of which became the responsibility of a battalion. During January, Roly Gibbs, now a brigadier, arrived with the Parachute Brigade Headquarters to take charge of the peacekeeping units in Nicosia and the immediately surrounding countryside which enabled General Young to look at the problem in the island as a whole.

Within our battalion sector the key to controlling events lay in establishing good relations with the local leaders of both communities, but the main difficulty facing the company commanders was to discover who these local leaders were. In fact finding out anything at all about the opposing sides was difficult. Both sides had built up their forces in secret and secrecy was a habit. No intelligence was available from the headquarters of the British Peacekeeping Force or from the British High Commission and any but the most discrete enquiries on our part tended to cause an immediate loss of goodwill.

The only way in which we could make headway was to build up a picture by collecting every scrap of information, which anyone happened to pick up as they went about their business. Initially we concentrated on collecting the names of all those who appeared to be taking an active part in the affairs of either of the two communities, even if it was only a Christian name or nickname. Using telephone directories or trade directories we discovered where some of them lived and where they worked. We then examined the background of people living nearby or working in the same business in the hope that a connection in ordinary civilian life would lead us to one or other of the fighting organisations.

Each company sent us the information as they collected it. We recorded every detail in files or card indexes so that we soon had a mass of names, addresses, telephone numbers and car numbers. Gradually by staring for hours at this conglomeration of facts and figures we began to discern the outlines of the opposing sides and the information started to snowball. We then sent back to the company commanders our ideas as to how things seemed to fit in and asked them to examine and test them. They could do this by putting soldiers into observation posts to watch the coming and goings of particular groups or individuals or by conversing with people. It sometimes happened that when a particular leader realised that we knew who he was and what his position was in the hierarchy, he would put us right about minor errors, especially if he thought that we had underestimated his importance. Company commanders also sent out patrols to follow new telephone cables, which might have been laid to connect one group of fighters with another and this could lead to more names and addresses. The whole business was an enjoyable game, which kept everyone usefully employed and greatly increased our potential as peacekeepers.

Journalists who had descended on Cyprus to report on the fighting, constituted another potential source of information. They mainly stayed in the Ledra Palace Hotel waiting eagerly for incidents to report. Having recently served with the United Nations Force in the Congo, Jonathan Peel knew a few of them so he and I would go to the hotel to meet them every now and then. His acquaintances sometimes produced useful bits of information and we were able to help them by affording them opportunities to take pictures and talk to our riflemen.

Across the road from battalion headquarters was a large Greek girls' school. When we first arrived the girls were friendly but as the propaganda campaign built up they became sullen. One day some journalists who had been told that there would be a spontaneous demonstration by the girls, turned up. When all was ready the girls assembled with banners saying 'Go Home British', whereupon the headmistress appeared telling them to control their righteous anger and remember that nothing could stand in the way of God's intention that Cyprus should be united with Greece. After this the girls spontaneously returned to their classrooms.

That evening I went on the roof as usual, to admire the sunset and the view towards the Kyrenia Range in the north and the Troodos Mountains to the west. If Turkish parachutists appeared they would come from the north and we still half expected this to happen because of the continuing tension that existed. Any further outbreak of fighting could serve as an excuse for Turkey to invade. As it got dark, the school across the road faded into the gloom but I noticed a light in one of the classrooms.

Some time later one of our patrols was shot at from the school. The patrol immediately broke in and found a nest of Greek fighters observing Turkish positions on the city walls a short distance away. The school was supposed to be out of bounds to both sides so the patrol brought the fighters back to our headquarters and Hew Butler rang up the Greek Chief of Police and told him to come and remove them. When Hew tried to find out why they shot at our men they all answered at once with wild gesticulations and great excitement. They claimed that it was an accidental discharge. When the police chief arrived the shouting and excitement continued. Soon afterwards a very tall man appeared who announced that he commanded all the Greek fighters in Nicosia. He soon disposed of the fighters and the police chief after which he settled down for a drink and chat with us. He was an imposing character called Petros who was helpful in confirming the positions of the Greek leaders that we had discovered. He also gave us bits of information that would help us do our job, but little that we did not need to know. He was a most likeable and entertaining person. Like most of the Greek Cypriot leaders he had been connected with EOKA and as I later discovered he had also made a considerable study of underground warfare. Although capable of becoming worked up over a particular incident, he was more level headed and objective than most of his countrymen and was totally uninfluenced by the Greek propaganda campaign.

* * *

The possibility of a Turkish invasion was of growing concern to the families, who might have to be evacuated to England should it occur. In anticipation, the Dekhelia Garrison Staff was circulating instructions to the wives telling them what they should do and what they should take if they had to leave. I wondered how Elizabeth viewed the prospect of being ready to move within an hour or so, taking nothing but the baby and a suitcase and flying out of one end of Cyprus as the Turks flew in at the other. It was not a cheerful prospect and must have seemed truly terrifying to some of the teenage wives of the riflemen. In order to reassure them, Hew Butler decreed that all married men should get one day off each week to visit their wives. My day could never come soon enough.

Because of this ruling Hew Butler was himself in Dekhelia when an interesting situation occurred. The battalion was allowed to patrol the area outside Nicosia for which it was responsible, but was not allowed to station troops there. On the day in question I heard that two Greeks had been ambushed and killed near a Turkish village about 12 miles south of Nicosia. Though not in our area, it was close to our border, which caused me to send the Reconnaissance Platoon to keep an eye on what was going on. Later we heard that Greek fighters were closing up to the village so I warned one of our companies to be ready to move at short notice. By this time the regiment in whose area the incident had taken place, had an officer on the ground but he was not finding it easy to get the Greeks to go away. At 12.40 pm we heard that shots had been fired and I was told by our brigadier, Roly Gibbs, to move in with a company and sort the situation out. Apparently the regiment responsible for that area could not spare a company at the time.

I first told the Reconnaissance Platoon to find a suitable place near the village for our company to assemble on its arrival and gave orders for the company to move as soon as possible. I then set off in my Land Rover with my batman, Rifleman Rogers. As we drove I wondered how best to deal with the situation bearing in mind that we were only supposed to shoot in self defence. We turned off the main Nicosia to Larnaca road and pushed on over a rough track for a few miles of flat country. After a while I could see Ayios Sozomenos, as the village was called, and behind it an almost vertical cliff face which stretched for several miles in each direction. Soon I met the officer from our neighbouring regiment who had been told to brief me on my arrival after which he left to take a badly wounded Greek fighter to hospital.

About 200 yards ahead of where I was standing I could see where the Greeks had established their front line and beyond the village there were men on the cliffs. Firing was coming from some dead ground on my left and it was clear that the village was surrounded. Leaving Rogers with the Land Rover, I ran forward down the track to try and find the Greek commander. On arriving in their forward position I found policemen in their familiar blue uniforms lying down in fire positions in the young corn. Two were dead. Walking down the line I found a police superintendent in a steel helmet who said that the men on the cordon were holding the ring while some fighters were preparing to assault the village from our left. Looking in that direction I could see smoke and some men darting up a line of trees toward the village. At that moment a helicopter started to descend near my Land Rover and guessing that it contained Brigadier Gibbs I ran back to tell him what I had discovered. He had sized up the position pretty accurately from the air and as soon as I had filled in the details we set off across the fields with one of his staff called Peter Morton, to contact the assault group. Passing through the cordon we crossed a particularly muddy field and eventually came up with the assaulting force. By now it had reached the edge of the village and set fire to a hedge, which was blazing furiously. Some men were moving under cover of the smoke to improve their positions whilst others fired at random at the houses.

We had great difficulty in discovering who was in command. The first man we asked said that it might be a police inspector who we could see some way away or it might be a sergeant who we could not see. The fact that an inspector is senior to a sergeant was irrelevant because the fighters had their own rank structure. We soon discovered that the sergeant had been wounded but it took time to persuade the inspector that he was now in charge. Roly Gibbs then suggested a ceasefire but the inspector said that his orders were to arrest the people who had killed the Greeks earlier in the day and that he could not stop firing while the Turkish population were obstructing him from doing his duty. Roly pointed out that the Turks probably felt that they were beating off an attack on their village rather than obstructing a policeman from doing his duty. He also pointed out that the Greeks would be unable to achieve their aim without capturing the village and that they would lose many men if they tried it without artillery support. He suggested that a better plan would be to let us enter the village to find out whether the Turks were harbouring the culprits and if so whether they would give them up. In this way the Greeks stood to lose nothing as they could stay on the cordon and resume their attack later if we were unsuccessful. I noticed that the inspector seemed glad of an excuse for not pressing on with the attack. Roly Gibbs decided to stay with the Greek commander to discourage further adventures. I was to return to our Reconnaissance Platoon and make my way into the village with two of the ferrets (small armoured reconnaissance vehicle). Once inside I was to keep one with me and send the other through to him. Thereafter we would be able to speak to each other over the vehicles' wireless sets.

I ran back through the muddy field and explained to the superintendent what was intended. I then returned to where our men were waiting, boarded one scout car and taking another with me headed off through the cordon towards the village. The Turks being as yet unacquainted with the idea of a ceasefire, were still shooting at the Greeks who were returning their fire. Bullets were cracking around, hitting rocks or buildings and whining away through the air so that I was glad to be in an armoured vehicle. Soon afterwards we stopped on a bit of grass in the middle of the village well screened by buildings from Greek bullets.

I soon found a number of men sheltering in doorways but none could speak English until someone sent for the schoolmaster. Whereas most of the men seemed friendly this individual was prickly and immediately started blaming the British for not preventing the Greek attack. He held us responsible for those killed already and said that unless we did something quickly they would all be massacred. I told him that stopping the massacre was the purpose of my visit and that he was to get the Turkish headman at once. When he arrived I explained our proposal for a ceasefire to which he agreed. By this time our second scout car with its wireless set had reached Roly Gibbs on the other side of the village and he passed the word to the Greeks to cease firing in accordance with the agreement. After a few minutes the shooting died down.

I then tried to talk to the headman about the two Greeks who had been murdered that morning with a view to working out how to satisfy the Greeks and get them to go away. Unfortunately our discussion was bedevilled by the schoolmaster, who kept inserting his own opinions into the conversation until I told him that he was there to translate and not to interfere. At this moment more firing took place and Roly Gibbs said on the wireless that it came from a Greek some way away from him who did not know about the ceasefire, but that a message had been sent to him. I passed this on to the Turkish headman but just as I said that the firing would stop, a number of bullets hit the houses near where we were talking, showering us with mud and plaster. I could not help laughing and most of the Turks joined in but the schoolmaster was beside himself with anger. I got on to Roly Gibbs to complain about the unmannerly behaviour of his Greeks only to be told that my Turks had just shot and killed a Greek lying immediately next to where he was standing. At this news the schoolmaster actually smiled for a change. This shot had come from a Turkish house on the edge of the village and, as I afterwards heard, Peter Morton at considerable risk to himself moved across the ground in front of the Greek position to tell the occupants to stop firing.

But ceasefire or not, the critical moment had arrived and the Greeks got ready to renew their attack. I asked the headman if he was prepared to surrender the men who had ambushed the Greeks in the morning, but he assured me that none of the villagers was responsible. I then asked him whether he would be prepared to come with me in the scout car to meet the Greek inspector. As the firing was getting heavier by the moment he agreed to do so. He was a brave and dignified man totally different from the repulsive young schoolmaster. (I have often thought that Shakespeare's character in Henry VI missed a trick when he suggested killing all lawyers. Schoolmasters and religious leaders are usually more of a menace.)

We drove through the village and met up with the inspector and brigadier. There was little chance of the headman reaching agreement with the Greeks but their discussion would at least take up a bit more time and it was already starting to get dark after which the attack would need to be put off until next day. In fact the affair ended suddenly when as a result of negotiations between General Young and the President, the Minister of the Interior called off the Greek fighters. Roly Gibbs gave a sigh of relief and headed back to Nicosia where the events of the day had heightened tension. I moved the company, which had been waiting patiently behind the Greek cordon, into the village to help clear up and attend to the casualties. Altogether five Greeks and six Turks had been killed and a lot more on both sides wounded. Perhaps the peacekeeping force had been at fault in allowing the battle to start but it had undoubtedly been responsible for preventing a massacre that might well have sparked off a Turkish invasion. I have often wondered whether the two Greeks, who it transpired had been inspecting an irrigation pipe, were murdered by Turks from outside the village for this very purpose. It was inevitable that the Greek would react as they did and the inhabitants of Ayios Sozomenos had no means of defending themselves against a determined assault.

I have described this incident in some detail because it highlights the problems that face peacekeepers who are working on behalf of both sides, but who can only use force in self defence. There were now plenty of troops in Nicosia, which meant that those desirous of furthering their aims by force, usually sparked off incidents in other parts of the island including Limassol in the south, Polis on the western side of the island and Kyrenia in the north. To counter these adventures, an increasing number of battalions were arriving from England, many of which came from the 3rd Division. In mid-February, the Divisional Commander, Major General Mike Carver, arrived with his headquarters to take over command of the British Peacekeeping Force. General Young returned to Episkopi to look after the Sovereign Base areas and provide logistic support for all British units in Cyprus.

Soon after his arrival, General Carver appeared at our school in Nicosia. He had got rid of his intelligence staff officer and having known me in Kenya and the War Office he decided to borrow me from the regiment until he could get a replacement. I therefore moved to a tent on the airfield at Nicosia where the headquarters was set up. Normally the job of the intelligence staff officer at a divisional headquarters is to put together and process information gathered by other people and feed it to the commander and to superior and subordinate formations. But circumstances were far from normal. There was little information of any kind and my first concern was to ensure that what little was known did at least reach us. Also in the Rifle Brigade we had discovered ways by which soldiers on the ground could collect useful information. There were by now the equivalent of eight infantry battalions and three squadrons of armoured cars in the British Peacekeeping Force. I therefore started by visiting units throughout the island to pass on the ideas that we had developed and to collect any information they might have picked up. In some unaccountable way Rogers managed to scrounge a Land Rover for me without which I should have been grounded.

The general wanted facts quick, regardless of how I presented them or of my views on them. This was sensible as he was better placed to work out what they meant than I was. Watching him as he went about his business was interesting. On the face of it he appeared to be doing little more than reacting to situations as they occurred. He spent most mornings going to meetings in Nicosia visiting such people as the British High Commissioner, President Makarios, Vice President Kutchuk, or high-powered visitors from outside the island. In the afternoon he visited units or trouble spots. He held a meeting of his own in the headquarters in the evening attended by the staff and officers called in to discuss the days' events. Later he might go out to dinner with someone with whom he wanted to have an informal talk or he might ask someone to the headquarters. I soon saw that he was spending as much time trying to prevent incidents from arising as he did sorting out trouble. Prevention involved identifying likely causes of trouble and taking action before it blew up. For example if one side looked as if it intended to occupy a building or a piece of high ground which would cause a reaction from the other side, he might order members of the peacekeeping force to pre-empt the move and occupy it themselves. If one side had already done so, he might try to negotiate a withdrawal possibly by negotiating a corresponding concession from the other side somewhere else. If tension was arising in a particular place for no particular reason he might speak to the leaders of the two communities locally in an attempt to persuade them against allowing the situation to deteriorate. It all came down to meeting the right people and talking to them and his daily round of visits and discussions was mainly conducted with this in mind.

To some extent General Carver was hampered in his desire to talk to influential people, by their desire not to talk to him. He could talk as much as he liked to the official spokesmen of the two communities but he also needed to be able to speak to the leaders of the fighters from time to time. On the Greek side the Minister of the Interior, an EOKA fighter called Georgadjis was a key figure, but to start with he tended to keep the general at arm's length. Eventually it was arranged that the two would meet for dinner in a restaurant after a reception

My parents with my brother Tom.

My portrait as a Rifle Brigade Lieutenant, 1946.

The House at Kamiti.

With the original team of Loyalists collected by Eric Holyoak.

Eric Holyoak. His local knowledge and language skills were invaluable to me throughout my time in Kenya.

Hooded Men. Jacky Miller extreme left taking notes.

A Pseudo-Gang. Kamau second from right.

Men of S Company leaving the jungle after six weeks.

Jonathan Peel (left) and John Starkey in their camp in the jungle.

Re-supply party with bicycles setting off through rubber trees on edge of jungle.

Our honeymoon. Elizabeth talking to Dennis Kearney and a young rhino.

Gremlin, responsible for my marriage and the existence of our children and grandchildren.

The Dekhelia Drag. I was Master and
Huntsman and Elizabeth the Whipper In.

Elizabeth talking to HRH The Duke of
Gloucester with Hew Butler listening in.

Elizabeth holding Kitty before her Christening
with my Mother (Lady Kitson, known as Boat)
and me.

General Carver (peaked cap and arms folded) and Brigadier Gibbs (beret and arms folded) sort out a problem in Nicosia with Greek spokesman, Mr Clerides.

reeks v Turks. Corporal Christian outside a UN Section Post.

Greeks v Turks. The Army outside our house in Larnaca.

Corporal Divine's Section Post after destruction by Greek mortars.

1 Royal Green Jackets Medal Parade. General Martola (saluting) flanked by Brigadier Harbottle (left) and our Colonel Commandant, General Mogg (right). Jack Dill standing to attention in front of his platoon.

Conferring with Roly Guy, Commanding Officer of 1RGJ in a Belfast street.

Aftermath of an explosion.

Mo, Chiggy and Kitty with Jomo and Brush.

The Troubles. A rampaging mob set fire to a bus.

An all too familiar scene of troops deployed on a riot-damaged street.

Troops manning a barricade.

General Sir Frank King, Commander-in-Chief BAOR, looks at me askance during a visit to my 2nd Armoured Division tactical HQ during a Rhine Army exercise.

The Queen's Silver Jubilee Review. Elizabeth being presented to HM. On Elizabeth's right is my old friend, David Alexander Sinclair.

300 Bandsmen playing the National Anthem.

General Sir Timothy Creasey, Commander-in-Chief UK Land Forces. A great soldier.

General Doktor Ferdinand von Senger und Etterlin (Deidi). A charismatic and intellectual German officer who had first-hand knowledge of fighting the Russians.

The Staff College Drag outside Staff College House; left to right: Elizabeth, myself, Susie Ross, Pat Sutto (Huntsman), the two Masters and Malcolm Ross.

The Kermit Roosevelt Lectures. Talking to the cadets at Westpoint.

Saying farewell to Kamau for the last time at Kahawa Kenya. He died nine months later.

Seeing them off to the Falklands. Talking to General Dwin Bramall and Sir John Knott, Secretary of State for Defence. Jamie Gordon, my ADC, looks on.

Seeing them back. The Colonel of the Parachute Regiment, Tony Farrar-Hockley talking to the Colonel-in-Chief, HRH the Prince of Wales. Admiral Fieldhouse is on the right.

Linda Kitson gets her Falklands Medal at HQ UK Land Forces. Major General Tillotson is between Elizabeth and me.

HRH The Duke of Edinburgh visiting HQ UK Land Forces.

Retreat Parade at Wilton House. Left to right: Sir Arthur Bryant, Elizabeth, Field Marshal Roly Gibbs, myself, Field Marshal Lord Harding.

A picture taken at the Regimental Depot in Winchester to mark the moment when the Royal Green Jackets had, in addition to their two Field Marshals, Gibbs and Bramall, and no less than ten serving general officers. The three Colonel Commandants, Guy, Kitson and Glover, are in the middle of the front rank.

Our three grown-up daughters. Left to right: Kitty, Chiggy, Mo.

My last parade. Mo's comment 'Crufts, Best in Breed, 1985'.

given by Makarios in Nicosia, to break the ice rather than have a discussion on any particular subject. I can not now remember whether I fixed it up through Petros or whether it was organised through the President's office but to underline the social aspect of the dinner it was agreed that I should accompany the general and bring Elizabeth as well. Accordingly we all met up at the reception, after which I went with Georgadjis in his car and Elizabeth followed with Mike Carver. I later heard that Elizabeth was concerned to see me disappear with this renowned terrorist and that Mike Carver patted her on the knee and assured that no harm would come to me. In fact we had a pleasant evening and thereafter Georgadjis was sometimes prepared to talk to the general, but at other times he would disappear for days on end, particularly at tricky moments when he was most needed. He was at best an elusive character whose second nature was to engage in plots of one sort or another. Some years later he was murdered when one of his devious schemes failed to work out.

* * *

The original idea that the British Peacekeeping Force would be able to stabilise the situation quickly, had long since been abandoned. The next idea was that it should be replaced by a NATO force but this was found to be impractical and a United Nations Force was considered instead. Once this became a possibility an Indian general called Gyani arrived to see what was going on and it soon became likely that he would become its commander.

Early in March the Security Council authorised the establishment of a United Nations Force for Cyprus. The first contingent would arrive at the end of March. When this happened General Carver became the Chief of Staff of the United Nations Force under General Gyani but continued to run things more or less as before, at any rate to begin with. The officers in the headquarters now changed into the blue berets of the United Nations Force. At this point I remained British and was transferred to work in the High Commission where I was joined by a high powered man from the Foreign Office called Dennis Speares. In the war Dennis Speares had been a fighter pilot and it was his delight to take over the controls of any aircraft in which we were travelling to remind himself of those heady days, long past. I seem to remember wishing that he would leave it to the pilot but, as good luck would have it, we always arrived in one piece.

* * *

I did not stay long in the High Commission. Hew Butler was due to hand over command of the battalion to Mark Bond at the end of April and it was considered unfair that Mark should take over in the absence of his second-in-command. By this time the battalion had got back to Dekhelia and settled down to its former peacetime existence. When I returned on Good Friday, people were paddling in the sea and boats from the yacht club were sailing through the waters of the bay. The reversion to a peacetime existence was abrupt. Outside the Sovereign Base areas men continued to live in schools, aircraft hangars or derelict buildings, working all hours just as we had been doing for the past three months. The contrast between this and the leisurely way of life in Dekhelia took a bit of getting used to.

I quickly settled down and found myself organising training courses, running the sports day or enjoying myself at the saddle club or on the beach with Elizabeth and Catherine. Also I was glad to be around as our child started to take an interest in her surroundings. In June I became what was then known as a brevet lieutenant colonel, which meant that I continued to do the same job and got no more pay. On the other hand when three years later I became a substantive lieutenant colonel, my seniority as such was backdated to June 1964. Up to ten brevet promotions were given in the army as a whole each year.

In Dekhelia Dennis Speares came to stay with us for a day or two now and then as a change from Nicosia. In this way I kept abreast of events in the country as a whole and learnt a lot about the inner workings of both sides to he dispute. It was particularly interesting to hear how the Greek Cypriots were divided amongst themselves. Grivas, a Cypriot who had been made a full general in the Greek army at the end of the EOKA campaign, had been sent out by the Greek government to take charge of the fighters. Grivas apparently remained devoted to the cause of union with Greece, an aspiration shared by most of the young fighters, but Makarios was now firmly in favour of an independent Cyprus, a course which also seemed to be attracting some of the older members of EOKA such as Georgadjis.

At the end of May a new security problem arose as a water pipeline within the Sovereign Base area was blown up and the battalion was told to guard it. As it stretched for some miles and was blown up on a number of occasions, guarding it was a difficult and time-consuming task, which continued until the end of July. In mid-August, I left Cyprus for England in charge of the battalion advance party.

I had been lucky to get such a good education in the business of peacekeeping in such a short time. Within a period of three and a half months I had been in command of a detachment in a small town, second-in-command of a battalion deployed in a capital city; and intelligence staff officer of the commander of the peacekeeping force. In this time I had been able to watch at close quarters two of the best operational commanders that the army produced during my service, i.e. Mike Carver and Roly Gibbs. In many ways they were very different, Carver being sharp and often critical whereas Gibbs was relaxed and usually laughing even when things were going wrong. But they were both courageous and decisive and a joy to work with. Peacekeeping is different from fighting insurgents because the peacekeeper is an outsider called in by both sides to help them settle a quarrel, whereas those acting against insurgents are operating as agents of their government, or possibly of an allied government. Nonetheless Peacekeeping has more in common with counter-insurgency than it has with other forms of military activity. In both cases units and sub-units are likely to be strung out over an extensive area and success depends as much on finding out, or working out, what the two sides are likely to do, as it does on using one's troops to stop them. Furthermore political factors, which tend to have a more direct bearing on fighting insurgents than they do in conventional operations, have an even greater impact on peacekeeping.

*   *   *

On our return from Cyprus we went to Monk's Hill for some leave in the course of which we visited Elizabeth's parents. At the end of my leave we moved into a small house in Felixstowe which is where the battalion was due to be accommodated in an ex-RAF seaplane base. The plan was that having settled the families, the battalion would go to Aden in March for a nine-month unaccompanied tour. It was a bit of a struggle making a seaplane base fit an infantry battalion and after a short time it was decided that 1 RB would go to Colchester instead. Then this idea was cancelled so it was back to the seaplane base. Soon afterwards we were told that instead of going to Aden in March the battalion would go to Hong Kong in January for three months and then proceed to Sarawak to take part in what was described as 'Confrontation' with Indonesia. I did my best to adapt to these rapidly changing instructions until in November Arscott Molesworth-St Aubyn turned up to take over from me as second-in-command of the battalion.

During the four years that had elapsed since the end of my sojourn in the War Office, the three service ministries had been huddled together into what was now described as the Ministry of Defence, in order to save overheads. In practice what had happened was that each of the old ministries had been co-located in one building and were now called the army, navy and air force departments. The old Minister for Defence was now called Secretary of State for Defence and the former secretaries of state for each service were downgraded to ministers of state. The organisation that had formerly operated at Storeys Gate, reinforced by a number of new defence services branches, was also crammed into the same building and was known as 'The Centre'. As no building was big enough to hold such a conglomeration of bureaucrats, the overflow was housed in various other buildings scattered around the West End. This whole edifice was presided over by Earl Mountbatten as Chief of the Defence Staff and a galaxy of senior Civil Servants known as Permanent Undersecretaries. Not many overheads had been saved.

My new job was in the Army Staff Duties Directorate (ASD), which was in effect the executive arm of the General Staff. The Director of Army Staff Duties was none other than Major General Carver who had two deputies and a number of branches each headed by a lieutenant colonel. Some of these branches dealt with the detailed allocation of posts and equipment to every unit and independent sub-unit in the army in packages called their establishment. There were three others branches. One known as ASD 5 and run by Hugh Beach dealt with the organisation and deployment of the Territorial Army. Another known as ASD 4 and run by Bill Scotter dealt with the allocation of manpower throughout the army. The third, ASD 2, dealing with the organisation and deployment of the regular army, was the branch that I was to run. It is remarkable that all three of us eventually became full generals; especially so in my case.

Most matters seemed to be dealt with by committees. In his position as Director of Army Staff Duties, Mike Carver chaired most of them at major general level while the lieutenant colonel running whichever ASD branch was relevant to the problem chaired the committees at the lower level. Horrified at the number of committees that I was expected to chair, I decided to get rid of as many as possible. I had a large team consisting of five grade two staff officers (majors), each with support at grade three level (captains) and I felt that my most important task was to know what was going on throughout the building in order to direct their efforts effectively. I would be of little use spending my time fiddling about with innumerable agendas and minutes all of which they would have had to process and prepare.

Deploying units of the regular army was a complicated business. First there was the routine movement of regiments and battalions together with their families between Germany, the United Kingdom and the various overseas garrisons such as Hong Kong. Superimposed on this was the requirement to send units, without their families, from their normal stations to carry out shorter operational tours. When I arrived in my new job we had to supply units for operational tours in Cyprus, Aden and Borneo. As a separate matter we had to work out the implications of sending units to other possible trouble spots should the need arise. These implications would include consideration of the training needed to enable them to carry out the new role, adjusting the tour lengths of other units to take account of their deployment, the provision of replacements should the commitment continue for longer than the unit sent could be spared and paying the costs of the extra commitment. There were also manning complications because the establishment of units varied according to the task they were given and it was sometimes impossible to send on an operational tour the unit whose turn it rightly was, if it could not muster enough men. All this was going on at a time when the strength of the army was being reduced as a result of the end of National Service.

It was our job in ASD 2 to work all this out time and time again, contacting the logistic, personnel and finance directorates to get the necessary information. Similar sorts of problems arose whenever organisational changes were being discussed to take account of policy reviews. Such complex studies often had to be completed within a very short time. In order to get the work done quickly, it was important to avoid examining matters that were in the process of becoming irrelevant. Mike Carver was good at knowing when this was happening and heading off unnecessary work, but it was obviously my job to discover as much as possible. It was a bit like Cyprus. From his contacts he knew more than I did, but I was still able to collect information that was useful to him and us.

In this context I quickly made it my job to identify useful sources of information. One particularly good person to know was Colin Mitchell, one of Mountbatten's briefers, who always seemed to have access to the draft minutes of cabinet meetings before the finished version was circulated and who had few inhibitions about passing on his knowledge. Letting me read them put me ahead of the game at a time when much of our work was connected with totally impractical ideas for ousting Ian Smith in Rhodesia. Such advanced knowledge saved much nugatory effort, to use a phrase frequently on the lips of the Civil Servants. The only problem was that I had to take care not to disclose my source as this would have got him into trouble. With the aid of Mitchell and a few others like him I soon got a reputation for being unusually well informed. In a Whitehall Ministry where secrecy for secrecy's sake was little short of a religion I became the object of suspicion amongst certain senior officers including the Director of Military Operations, a direct descendant of the Duke of Cambridge who was Commander-in-Chief throughout most of Queen Victoria's reign. Once when talking to one of his colonels I said something that this man passed on to his director. Thinking that it was tip-top secret his general sent for me to find out how I could possibly have got hold of it. After he had been haranguing me for some time about passing on information which, I should not have known anyway, he asked me how I had discovered it. In this case I was in the clear because, as I told him, I read it off the ticker tape in my club.

*   *   *

Perhaps the most serious long-term problem that arose during my time in the Ministry of Defence related to the government's decision to pull out of the Far East and Middle East and to concentrate on our commitments in Europe. Clearly this produced a lot of detailed work regarding the redeployment of units especially as the timing of withdrawals depended on the ending of the campaigns then in progress in Malaysia and Aden. But it was the long term implications that caused the most trouble as the government insisted that in future the size and shape of the army must be justified only by what was required to fulfil our obligations to NATO and the defence of the United Kingdom. Many of us said that this was dangerous because if the Russian threat subsided, we would be obliged to reduce the size of the army to such an extent that it would be unable to handle unexpected contingencies. Hitherto we had borrowed troops from Germany when necessary, as when the Greeks and Turks attacked each other in Cyprus and as we would have to do again when trouble broke out in Ireland at the end of the decade. In the event the Russian threat kept us in business for another quarter of a century, but since it receded the government has done its best to bleed the services dry in its determination to direct its resources towards projects popular with the electorate.

It would be tedious in the extreme to go into details of the work carried out by ASD 2 over the two and a half years during which I ran it. The main strength of my position derived from the fact that my grade two officers who did most of the work were men of exceptionally high quality. Apart from the senior one who was the co-ordinator and in effect my second-in-command, each covered a particular part of the world, i.e. NATO, Far East, Middle East and the UK. The UK desk had a particularly tiresome time because, in addition to its normal business it was often asked to deal with emergencies such as occurred when an oil tanker ran into Cornwall or when foot and mouth disease raged through the agricultural community in 1967. The Home Office, painfully aware of the political implications, always wanted the immediate attendance of a senior officer. Inevitably the general was too busy and I had no desire to get tied down with such time-consuming triviality, which meant that the unfortunate grade two officer had to go. Luckily this post was held by Peter Inge who was much better at keeping the Home Office calm and affording the necessary assistance than I would have been. He got much further in his military career as well, finishing up as a field marshal and a peer.

Whilst running ASD 2, I had fewer opportunities for overseas travel than when I was in MO 4. In view of my recent experience in Africa, the Persian Gulf and Cyprus it was not thought necessary for me to visit the headquarters in these areas, but apart from my year in Malaya I had no knowledge of the set up in the Far East. I was also a bit rusty so far as BAOR was concerned. It was therefore decided that I should pay a short visit to Germany in July and then undertake a protracted tour of the Far East in October 1965. After visiting Headquarters British Forces Hong Kong and being shown the frontier with Red China, I flew on to Labuan, which was the Headquarters British Forces Borneo. Here Major General Lea commanded thirteen infantry battalions together with artillery, naval and RAF support on operations designed to counter the infiltration by Indonesian troops. His force consisted mainly of British and Gurkha battalions but Australian and New Zealand units from the Commonwealth Brigade also took part. After being briefed, I was sent to visit two of the brigade headquarters. The first was 51st Brigade commanded by one of my predecessors in ASD 2, Harry Tuzo. This brigade operated in Brunei and in northern Sarawak. I then went on to the recently designated West Brigade at Kuching. The brigade commander was away and Mark Bond was commanding it in his absence. The troops were deployed into heavily fortified company bases designed to hold their own against attack by strong Indonesian regular army units. From them raids could be mounted against enemy forces identified by SAS style forward patrols or by wireless intercept. Next day I was flown by helicopter into one such base occupied by B Company, 1 RB commanded by David Ramsbotham. This was an altogether different sort of war to anything I had experienced previously and it was immensely interesting to hear how it worked. My tour ended with a visit to the Unified Headquarters Far East at Singapore after which I returned to England.

So far as rank was concerned, I had now progressed from being a brevet to a temporary lieutenant colonel, which meant that, though still not substantive, I was at least paid. This suited me all right but early in 1966 a proposal was made that a number of the best lieutenant colonel's jobs should be upgraded to full colonel and that brigade majors should become lieutenant colonels. Jobs to be upgraded to colonel included the two senior staff officers at the various divisional headquarters and my own job as head of ASD 2. I was asked to comment. My view was that the proposal was damaging because it took some of the most rewarding posts away from young and able officers in order to give them to older men who would get less satisfaction in doing them. Furthermore, so far as ASD 2 was concerned, it was difficult to argue that the responsibility for organising and deploying the regular army had increased, which was the ostensible reason for the proposal. On the contrary, as the army had been consistently shrinking since the end of the Second World War and was now no more than 180,000 strong, the responsibility for deploying and organising it had, if anything, decreased.

I submitted my views to the branch handling the proposal and also sent a personal minute to General Carver. In it I explained why I felt as I did, quoting a number of letters I had recently received from a friend in BAOR who was leaving the army because of the frustration he felt about the way matters were handled by the elderly officers above him. In reply I got three hand-written pages sympathising with my views and those of my BAOR friend but explaining the reasons which made it inevitable that some of the posts mentioned would have to be upgraded. My own job was one of them and I got paid as a full colonel until I left a year later.

There was a sequel to this almost two years later when I was commanding a battalion. On this occasion General John Mogg who was the Commander-in-Chief Strategic Command asked me to write a paper on the subject of officer promotion for him to submit for consideration at a Commanders-in-Chief meeting. In it I made a number of recommendations including the abolition of the rank of colonel which had no command responsibility. My suggestion was that all staff jobs between majors and brigadiers should be held by lieutenant colonels which is the rank held by the commanders of major operational and logistic units. It was a good paper, which naturally got nowhere.

Attempts to increase efficiency by cutting out unnecessary staff officers and providing satisfying jobs for those likely to go on, ran counter to the requirement to provide employment for all officers up to the age of 55 which is what the army guaranteed. This guarantee was thought to be necessary to ensure that schools continued to recommend the army as a career and as the recruiters pointed out, it was no good having a super efficient-army that could not get enough young officers to join it. The drawback was that surplus officers some of whom had come to the end of their useful lives, had to be found jobs commensurate with their age and seniority to the detriment of the overall efficiency of the army.

*   *   *

In addition to my work in the Ministry of Defence I continued to promote my views on handling insurgencies and on having the necessary specialised units available at short notice. In April 1966, I gave a talk to the officers course at the School of Infantry on the tactical handling of information by company and platoon commanders stressing the chain reaction system that I had used in Kenya and Malaya. In May, inspired by what I had seen in Borneo with particular reference to finding enough SAS to cover the frontier with Indonesia, I started a new hare in a talk I gave to 21 SAS. Pointing out the desirability of SAS being able to carry out a greater variety of tasks than pure deep patrolling and explaining how difficult it was to get the army to contemplate expanding it sufficiently, I suggested that the SAS should be closely associated with some other organisation. After discussing and dismissing various alternatives I suggested the Parachute Regiment, which also needed a new role as few supposed that they would be able to descend into battle on the end of a parachute in the face of modern anti-aircraft weapons and guidance systems. As expected my suggestion aroused a certain amount of opposition from both the Parachute Regiment and the SAS. I had sent a copy of my lecture notes to Peter de la Billiere, by now a major with the SAS at Hereford, which he discussed with his officers, but he felt that enlargement of the SAS or a widening of their role in the way I was suggesting would not be helpful.

Around this time I started writing about my experiences in Kenya, Malaya, Muscat and Cyprus. The result of my labours formed the basis of a book, which I only succeeded in finishing many years later and which I called *Bunch of Five*. In the midst of our busy life, Elizabeth found time to have another baby, our daughter Rosemary who arrived in February 1966.

* * *

When I started at the Ministry of Defence my next posting was uncertain. I would be in line for command of a battalion but timings would not fit so far as the Rifle Brigade was concerned as Peter Hudson, who had been selected to take over from Mark Bond, would still have over a year to do. General Lathbury as colonel commandant of the Parachute Regiment, therefore suggested that I should command one of his battalions which would become vacant at the right time, an offer that I gratefully accepted providing the Rifle Brigade did not need me. Soon afterwards it was suggested that I should take command of 22 SAS when Bob Wingate-Gray left, but this would have been at the expense of their current second-in-command who was hoping for the job. Indeed he rang me up a few days later to sound me out and I was able to reassure him that there was no danger as I had already accepted General Lathbury's offer. In the end these arrangements were turned upside down by the decision to combine the Oxford and Buckinghamshire Light Infantry, the 60th and the Rifle Brigade into a new regiment called the Royal Green Jackets as from January 1966. The commanding officer of the Ox and Bucks, which would become 1 RGJ, was due to hand over command in the summer of 1967 and I was appointed to take over from him. General Lathbury who had himself been in the Ox and Bucks, raised no objection. 1 RGJ was stationed at Tidworth and having arranged to let Horsley House in Surrey, we moved there on 5 October 1967.

A surprising post-script to my efforts in the Ministry of Defence came a few months later when I found that I had been awarded the OBE for my work. Despite my distaste for the place, I had evidently functioned to the satisfaction of Monkey Blacker who was no more enthusiastic about life in the Ministry of Defence than I was. Although I did not know it at the time, I would never again serve as a staff officer.

Chapter 7

Battalion Command: Royal Green Jackets 1967–1969

Alll the barracks in Tidworth are named after battles that the army has fought in India. When in Tidworth with 2 KRRC and again ten years later with 1 RB, I had been in Assaye barracks which was at the south western end of the camp, only Alliwal being closer to the open Plain. This time we were at the eastern end in Lucknow Barracks with Mooltan being the only one beyond, and that was empty at the time. It was odd that there was no Plassey Barracks.

Each barracks included a house for the commanding officer. Lucknow House and Mooltan House were joined together with a big wooden fence dividing the garden. Mooltan House was occupied by Lieutenant Colonel Tim Washington of the 12th Lancers, which was Colonel Spencer's old regiment.

At the end of October 1 RGJ flew out to Cyprus, each company carrying out a relief in the line of the company of the Duke of Wellington's Regiment from whom they were taking over. On 1 November 1967, I took over responsibility for the battalion's area known in UN parlance as Limassol zone, which covered the whole of the south-west part of the island, an area about 75 miles from east to west and 20 miles north to south. The zone was divided into four UN districts each presided over by one of our company commanders.

Battalion headquarters was at Polemidhia, camp which also contained Headquarters Company and C Company. C Company was responsible for Limassol District. Further west was B Company, which was responsible for Paphos District, its company headquarters being at Kitima. To its north was Support Company, responsible for Polis District. A Company looked after what was known as Kophinou District, which covered a relatively small area around the junction of the Limassol to Nicosia road with the Limassol to Larnaca road. In actual fact this was part of Larnaca District so far as the Cyprus government was concerned, but it was an area of key strategic importance and sensitivity so the UN had made it a district in its own right.

* * *

The United Nations Force consisted of six battalions drawn from Canada, Denmark, Finland, Ireland, Sweden and the United Kingdom, which also provided an armoured car squadron of the 5th Inniskilling Dragoon Guards. The force commander was General Martola of Finland, aged 71. He had fought in both wars and had retired as a corps commander in 1946. Since then he had been employed in many influential capacities and had at one time been the Secretary General's military advisor. Despite his age he was energetic and his knowledge of the United Nations combined with his considerable wartime experience as an operational military commander made him ideally suited to his task. His Chief of Staff was Brigadier Michael Harbottle who was also designated commander of the British contingent. He had formerly commanded the Ox and Bucks and could not have been more helpful to me on my arrival. He had taken over as Chief of Staff from Jim Wilson about eighteen months earlier.

My first task was to go round the districts meeting the spokesmen of the two communities as I did so. In the case of the Greek Cypriots, the official spokesmen were the district officers who had been brought up in the old British Colonial Service and who were friendly and helpful, although naturally obliged to carry out the policy laid down by Archbishop Makarios. In each district the Turks also had a person specified as the leader of the local Turkish community.

Based on what I had heard from Jim Wilson and Michael Harbottle and from what I could see with my own eyes, it was clear that the balance of power between the Greeks, Turks and the United Nations Force had shifted since 1964. On the Greek Cypriot side the various fighter groups had been incorporated into the National Guard, which was a properly uniformed and equipped force, officered by professionals from Greece. There were now also in Cyprus, illegally, Greek national army units including tanks and artillery amounting in all to at least 5,000 men. Grivas who had been made a general in the Greek army at the conclusion of the EOKA campaign, commanded all Greek and Greek Cypriot forces on the island. Turkish Cypriots fighters had been issued with uniforms and there were Turkish officers from the mainland in some places, but they had no artillery or tanks, nor were there any regular Turkish units illegally in the country. Turkish Cypriots still depended on Turkey to rescue them by invading Cyprus. Turkey would presumably have been happy to see the back of the Greek army units, but had the ability to overcome them should the need arise.

The UN battalions in Cyprus were spread around their areas in sections of six to eight men. Each section was responsible for manning an observation post in some prominent place, which consisted of a blue tin hut with the letters UN painted on the side and roof in white paint. The positioning of each post had been the result of painstaking negotiation over the years between the two sides and the United Nations Headquarters in Nicosia. No commander had the discretion to move a post or to alter the number of men manning it without getting the alteration accepted by both sides in Nicosia, which usually took many weeks. The purpose of the posts was to enable men to observe and thereby provide information which commanders at every level could use in negotiation. The men in them were not expected to manoeuvre or fight. None of the battalions had enough men to man all their posts and retain a reserve capable of intervening in any serious fighting. In order to get the best view the observation posts were often sited on rocky outcrops, greatly exposed to the weather. At some more spacious and sheltered spot within about 100 yards the section would have a tent or shed where the men could cook and sleep. Neither the observation post nor the living area was prepared for defence because this would imply distrust or hostility towards one or both of the sides to the dispute. The fact that the United Nations could not have afforded to fortify these positions throughout the island, though true, was not the point.

Another thing that struck me was that Grivas was interfering with the United Nations ability to observe events. He insisted that our helicopters should fly at certain heights and give notice of each flight half an hour before take off. Road movement in some areas was prohibited. It was natural that he should prepare to repel a Turkish invasion, and he would have been understandably nervous of United Nations forces leaking details of his defences to the Turks, either accidentally or on purpose. But he should not have been allowed to restrict our ability to forestall Greek Cypriot moves against Turkish Cypriot enclaves. In short the National Guard backed by Greek national units had now become more powerful than the United Nations force which had lost its ability to defend itself or to dictate to the two sides in an emergency, as the British Peacekeeping Force could have done in early 1964. This should not have mattered because peacekeepers are not supposed to achieve their aims by force, nor should they expect to be attacked by either of the contesting parties on whose behalf they are acting. But even if it was not significant, it was certainly noticeable.

Despite this weakness, there did not seem to be any feeling of imminent crisis. There had been no major incidents in Cyprus for some months, although there were one or two sensitive situations in my zone particularly in Kophinou District and around Kitima. At Kophinou, steep hills overlooked the village and the important road junction. Over the years the Turks had built up their ability to exploit this position and an undercover Turkish officer from the mainland was in charge of the local fighters. He was responsible for training them and his aggressive predecessor had brought about a series of confrontations with the United Nations Force as a result of which the Turkish leadership managed to impose restrictions on their movement around the area. He had been carrying out in a small way the sort of actions that Grivas was using over the whole island and for the same reason. He was trying to reduce the ability of the United Nations to see, publicise and therefore interfere with the preparations that he was making for preventing movement along the main roads at the junction. Another agreed restriction was that the United Nations would not communicate directly with the Turks at Kophinou. All contact had to be with the official Turkish spokesman in Larnaca 12 miles away, on the grounds that there was no Turkish leader in Kophinou, but merely a lot of simple farmers. We were told that they hated us because of previous confrontations. In fact the Turkish officer, whose very existence was officially denied, exercised such strict discipline that none of the local Turkish Cypriots were able to talk to us even if they had wanted to do so.

The official Turkish spokesman in Larnaca was a colourful character called Dr Orhan Muderisoglou who held a weekly meeting with the two UN commanders in Larnaca District, i.e. the British company commander in Kophinou and the Swedish battalion commander who covered the rest of Larnaca District. He could be charming but he roared with anger when he disagreed with what we were doing. When he was annoyed with the Swedes he was particularly nice to us and vice versa. He was a good actor. I went with Bob Pascoe who commanded A Company, to these weekly meetings and witnessed the performance at first hand. It was difficult to control Dr Orhan as he knew so much more of the background to past events than we did.

There was a Greek police station about one mile out of Kophinou on the main road to Limassol at Skarinou Bridge close to one of our observation posts. From here a small road ran south for about a mile and a half to a village called Ayios Theodoros which had a mixed population of Greek and Turkish Cypriots. A policeman had the right to travel down this road to the village, which he usually did about once a week, although his route lay between hills occupied and farmed by Turks. On arrival he had to pass through the Turkish part of the village before reaching the Greek part. About three months before we arrived, the policeman had temporarily desisted from travelling along the road because of Turkish unrest and when he attempted to restart his visits in September he found his way barred by Turkish villagers. This event immediately escalated to the highest level in Nicosia because free movement along the roads of the country was an important matter of principle. Soon the UN Secretary General was conducting negotiations in New York with the governments of Greece, Turkey and Cyprus. The Turks were in the wrong and both Makarios and Grivas wanted a settlement that would teach them a sharp lesson. But the Turks had genuine sources of grievance elsewhere in the island and wanted to get concessions in return for opening the road. When we arrived, negotiations had been going on for some time and in the usual way a settlement was expected that would involve small concessions from both sides. Indeed we were told that tension had recently eased because the Turks had agreed to open the road soon.

On 13 November, General Martola and the Secretary General's Special Representative in Cyprus, the Mexican Osoria-Tafall, were called to a meeting with Makarios, Grivas and Georgadjis because the road was still not open. Despite Osorio-Tafall's plea for more time, Makarios said that the Cyprus government could not be expected to wait any longer. An attack by Greek forces on the Turkish positions around Ayios Theodoros and Kophinou became a possibility. There was no question of the United Nations using physical force to stop such an attack because this would have meant fighting the Greeks in support of a Turkish line of action, which the United Nations had consistently condemned.

Next day I visited Kophinou and heard that a Turkish shepherd had disappeared. Bob Pascoe thought that the shepherd might have seen Greek forces moving into the area and been abducted to stop him spreading the news. Although we were not allowed to shadow the National Guard, we had every right to use the roads and Bob sent out two patrols, one towards Limassol and one towards Larnaca to see whether there were extra Greek forces around. As we discussed the situation, some RAF bombers from Akrotiri flew overhead. A bit later the National Guard Officer asked to see Bob at the Skarinou Bridge police station and I went with him. On arrival we were met by an efficient looking major of the Greek army who warned us that it was dangerous for the RAF to fly around the area. We pointed out that we were United Nations troops and had nothing to do with the RAF, but he merely repeated the warning. We returned to Kophinou wondering whether he thought that the RAF were spying on our behalf or whether he merely wanted to impress us that the situation was serious. On our return we heard that one of our road patrols had seen a group of Greek officers about 3 miles down the road towards Nicosia and that one of them looked like Grivas.

This was followed by another call for Bob to visit Skarinou Bridge. This time he was asked to escort a police patrol leaving for Ayios Theodoros in half an hour. If he declined, he was told that the National Guard would escort them. Clearly this request was designed to be refused, because it would be impossible to organise an escort in the time and because, as everyone knew, all requests had to be made through the Ministry of the Interior and not direct to United Nations commanders. I contacted our headquarters in Nicosia and was told that of course we should not offer the protection suggested. In passing this on to the National Guard, Bob urged them not to carry out the patrol because negotiations were still in progress. The police patrol, escorted by armoured cars and infantry, set off nonetheless. In Bob's operations room we listened to reports sent in from his observation posts overlooking the route and were surprised to find that the policeman and his escort got to Ayios Theodoros and back without any interference on the part of the Turks.

Breathing a sigh of relief Bob and I walked out into the compound beside the main road. At that moment three large staff cars drove past from the direction of Nicosia, one of which contained Grivas. As his car drew level, I saluted the bloody-minded old terrorist as he was officially a Greek general, but memories of his past activities with EOKA caused me to experience some mental reservations. All the same I admired his determination and had I foreseen the daring of his next move, I should have felt less inclined to grudge him a salute. At the time we assumed that he was going to congratulate his men at Skarinou Bridge but much to our amazement a moment or two later our observation posts reported that the three staff cars had turned left off the main road and were heading for Ayios Theodoros. On arrival Grivas got out and had himself photographed talking to the villagers. He then returned the way he had come and the Turks did nothing about it. The newspapers were full of the story. The Turks had been humiliated and had the Greeks left well alone, they would have gained an advantage that they could have used in future negotiations. But they intended to rub the Turks' noses in it and despite a warning from the Turkish leadership in Nicosia that further patrols would be met by force, another patrol went to Ayios Theodoros and back next morning.

At this time I was summoned to see General Martola at Nicosia who told me that if fighting broke out, our troops were not to become involved, but were to report events as they happened in order to provide accurate information on which negotiations could be based at his level. Osorio Tafall who was with General Martola at the time, said that he had again asked Makarios to stop further patrols as the point about freedom of movement had been well made and that further patrols could only end in disaster. After receiving my orders, Mike Harbottle came with me to my waiting helicopter and having checked that I was absolutely clear about what I had to do, warned me that the Turks really meant what they said. By way of emphasis he explained how he knew this to be the case which should have carried conviction with me in view of my past experiences in Cyprus. But after what I had seen the previous day I was not convinced. I headed off for Kophinou arriving around midday only to be told that yet another patrol was leaving Skarinou Bridge for Ayios Theodoros. At about this time a troop of armoured cars from the squadron of the 5th Inniskilling Dragoon Guards arrived at Kophinou to reinforce A Company.

Soon our observation post overlooking the route reported that there was an obstruction on the road some way outside the village and I decided to go out in my Land Rover towards Skarinou Bridge to see what sort of reaction there would be from the Greeks. The battalion signals officer, Nigel Mogg, came with me so that I could hear messages being passed between our posts and company headquarters. At 12.10 pm while still on the main road, one of our posts reported hearing three shots. The shots had been fired, almost certainly by a Turk, when the police patrol with its escort had tried to move the obstruction. Supposing that any fighting would be limited to the area in which this incident had taken place, we carried on in the hope of reaching a position from where we could see what was happening. We were still on the main road heading towards Skarinou Bridge when much to our surprise we saw a force of National Guard, led by armoured cars, appear over the crest to our right, at least 2 miles from the scene of the incident. We were even more surprised when they opened up with their machine guns over our heads onto the side of the hill beyond us. As the armoured cars pitched up and down over the rock-strewn scrub, the muzzles of their guns did likewise. The puffs of dust that the bullets kicked up, traced a crazy pattern over a large area of hillside. As if this was not enough, artillery and mortar fire began to land there as well. Heaven knows what they were shooting at, as there seemed to be no Turks in the vicinity.

From what we heard on the wireless it was apparent that the original confrontation on the road to Ayios Theodoros had provided an excuse for a well prepared assault on the whole of the Turkish enclave around Kophinou. I soon realised that only by returning to Bob's headquarters in the compound would I be able to work out what was happening and then pass back the information to General Martola's headquarters. As we arrived back we could see another assault going in on the high ground a few hundred yards away, which was occupied by Turkish fighters armed with recoilless weapons judging by the clouds of smoke and orange flame that accompanied their firing.

Inside the operations room it gradually became clear that Grivas had launched three simultaneous attacks immediately on hearing that the police patrol had been halted. One moving along high ground to the south-west of the road to Ayios Theodoros, was directed on the village itself. Another, which consisted of armoured cars and infantry was directed onto the high ground to the east of the road to Ayios Theodoros, presumably to destroy Turkish positions that might interfere with the other thrust and movement down the road itself. The third was designed to eliminate the Turkish position covering the village of Kophinou

Of immediate concern to us was the fact that each of these assaults was bound to run into our observation posts, as they were situated on places with the best view which meant that they were also places that the Greeks would need in order to dominate Turkish positions. Regardless of what the Greeks wanted, we had to stay put in order to keep sending reports to Nicosia, as the information would be of vital importance to those trying to bring about a ceasefire. I had not been back in the operations room for long before the first confrontation arose, when some National Guard approached a section observation post and ordered our men away. Here an experienced corporal called Savage confronted them and firmly refused to move. On this occasions the Greeks gave way. Continuing their advance towards Ayios Theodoros they passed close to another of our posts commanded by a subaltern which, though not directly molested, was caught in cross fire, one or two mortar bombs also falling close by.

The second attacking force which was the one that had been firing over my Land Rover, had as its objective a hilltop occupied by another of our posts. As they advanced towards it they sprinkled it with fire and when they arrived the Turks opened up on the area as well. To make matters worse the Greek company commander demanded that our men abandon the post and stop reporting events. At the same time his men looted their sleeping quarters. Fortunately a very robust young corporal called Bradford commanded this post. Although his section could not expel a whole Greek company, they set upon one of their officers who was trying to damage their wireless set and cut off his thumb. Soon afterwards two of the Greek platoons advanced to their next objective, leaving one platoon and the company headquarters around our observation post.

The behaviour of this Greek Company was inexcusable but those taking part in the third prong of the attack just to the north of the compound were worse. When the attack started this section 'stood to' in their slit trenches, one of which contained the section commander, Corporal Divine, and three men and the other, some way off, contained two more men. Before the Greeks reached them the fire of both sides passed close overhead. Several mortar bombs fired by the Greeks fell on the position, one of which scored a direct hit on the shed where the section did its cooking. Another landed within a couple of yards of the two-man trench, concussing the occupants. All this was being reported as it happened by field telephone until suddenly the line went dead. Bob sent two armoured cars to the area, which discovered that the line had been broken by small arms fire. They also discovered that when the Greeks arrived, they had forcibly disarmed the two men in the smaller trench and ordered the four men in the other trench to lay down their arms and leave the position. Despite the hammering that the post had received, Corporal Divine refused and the Greeks turned to looting the living quarters, stealing money, cigarettes and personal property. They also found the rifle of a man who had been sent off sick that morning which they stole. By the time the armoured cars arrived, the Greeks had moved on to their next objective.

While Bob Pascoe was keeping in touch with his observation posts and ensuring that they hung on to their positions, I was trying to make sense of the reports as they came in and send a coherent picture of events back to General Martola and Mike Harbottle. Had I not been present at Kophinou, Bob would

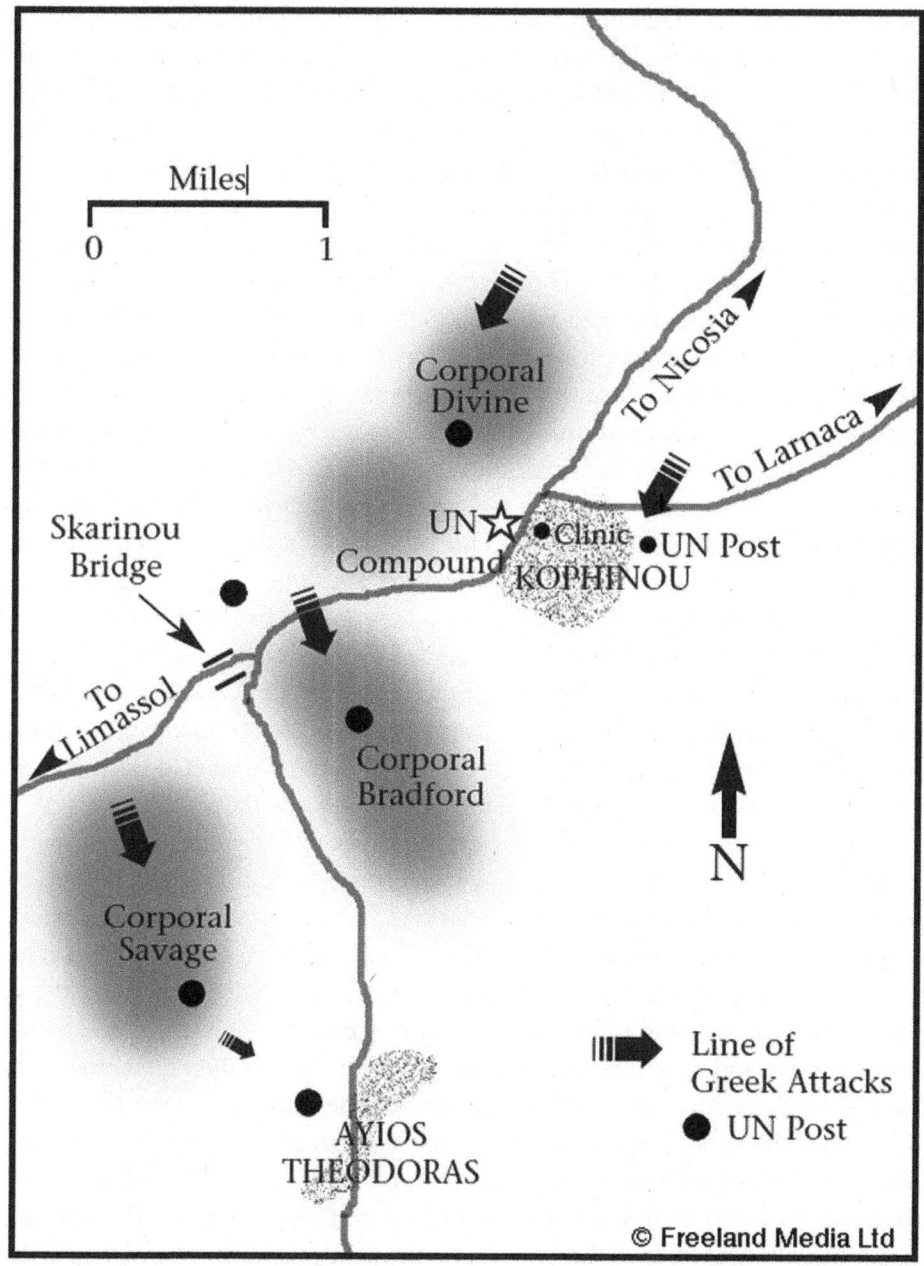

Miles

0   1

Corporal
Divine

To Nicosia

To Larnaca

Skarinou
Bridge

UN
Compound

Clinic   UN Post
KOPHINOU

To
Limassol

Corporal
Bradford

N

Corporal
Savage

Line of
Greek Attacks

UN Post

AYIOS
THEODORAS

© Freeland Media Ltd

have had to send the information to battalion headquarters at Polemidhia from where it would have been forwarded to Nicosia. Being at Kophinou with the signals officer I was well placed to work out what was going on and pass the information back immediately. I was also concerned about the possibility of trouble breaking out in Limassol and Paphos when the Turks there heard about the Greek attack on their compatriots. As I was in the wrong place to cope with repercussions of that sort, I telephoned Bill Chevis who was second-in-command of the battalion, and asked him to be ready to deal with them. I also asked him to put together two ad hoc platoons from headquarter company and send them together with the medical officer and some extra signallers towards Kophinou.

So far we had suffered no casualties because our men were reasonably protected from everything other than a direct hit in the slit trenches dug alongside the observation posts. All the same I greatly resented the Greek action which was massively out of proportion to the blocking of the road to Ayios Theodoros by the Turks and which represented a callous disregard for the safety of our men. To make matters worse the Greeks now started shelling and mortaring Kophinou village, which was immediately across the road from our compound. In the operations room we had lifted the window frames off their hinges to avoid the danger of flying glass, but shrapnel and muck thrown up by shells falling nearby was rattling against the walls. One of Bob's officers who had just taken a tour of the compound to see how the sentries and lookouts were getting on, reported one of the men saying that he was praying hard for the first time in his life. Hew Butler may have been right when describing church as an officer sport, but its not only the officers who need direct access to the Almighty 'when the guns begin to shoot,' (in this case a mixed battery of 25 pounders and 75 mm howitzers). The officer also said that the Charwallah's tent had been badly ripped and that one of our main wireless aerials was down.

Soon a lot of small arms fire was also cracking over our heads and a new Greek assault was directed on Kophinou village which also passed through another of our observation posts situated on a track near the Larnaca road. It was supported by fire from positions captured earlier. Bob had already sent two armoured cars to support this post which was reporting that fire was falling all round their position and ricocheting off the armoured cars. But this time the Greeks did not misbehave and once they had established themselves on their objective their company commander came back to enquire whether our men were safe.

At about this time Corporal Bradford reported that a Colonel of the National Guard had arrived and was insisting that he move his men from their observation post. Bob Pascoe therefore drove there in his Land Rover. He and the colonel asked each other to remove their men from the position. Both refused, and Bob insisted that his men should be left undisturbed to carry out their function of observation. In the end Corporal Bradford's section remained and the National Guard dug a defensive position around them. Bob returned to the compound just as it was getting dark.

Meanwhile the Greek forces having cleared the Turks from all their defensive positions started to move in to clear the village of Kophinou. They were already doing the same thing in Ayios Theodoros. In the course of clearing Kophinou a Greek armoured car sat itself down within 30 yards of the Turkish clinic which was immediately across the road from the compound and started shooting at it with a machine gun and its 2-pounder cannon. The racket was tremendous and once again stray bullets passed over or struck our buildings. The only occupants of the clinic were three nurses who managed to run across the road and take refuge with us.

From the start I decided to leave Bob free to command his company together with such reinforcements as might arrive, as he saw fit. I stayed in constant communication with Mike Harbottle in Nicosia who was sending reports to the Secretary General of the United Nations in New York. As a result the countries most closely concerned with preventing war between Greece and Turkey, were able to put forward a convincing case for a ceasefire, which they would have found difficulty in doing had they been relying on the contradictory reports provided by the contestants. Turkey insisted that all the places occupied by the National Guard during the fighting should be evacuated at once. If not, air attacks would start at first light next morning. As the evening wore on we heard that Greece had recommended Makarios to accept this demand. Then it appeared that Makarios was not prepared to give the necessary orders to Grivas, or it may have been that Grivas refused to accept them. Then we were told that the Prime Minister of Greece had given Grivas a direct order to withdraw the National Guard and that a ceasefire was to take effect from 10 pm. But when Bob tried to arrange with the National Guard Colonel for medical help to be sent into the two villages, he was told that he could only send it in when his men had finished clearing them of Turkish fighters. In the event firing continued in parts of Ayios Theodoros until well after midnight.

During the evening small arms fire and shelling round Kophinou died down. Soon afterwards a squadron of Canadian armoured cars and part of an Austrian field hospital arrived, as did the two platoons that I had sent for from Polemidhia. Space was limited and the compound was bursting at the seams with officers wondering where they should go and what they should do. I was worried that if by first light next morning the Turks were not satisfied that the National Guard had withdrawn, they would launch air attacks and some of our observation posts would once more be in the firing line. Corporal Bradford's post, smack in the middle of a National Guard company headquarters, would be in the gravest danger. Nothing could be more obvious, but one of the officers who had arrived with the reinforcements, supposing that I had not understood the danger, insisted on reminding me of it at regular intervals with the impractical suggestion that we should withdraw the section.

In the early hours of the morning Mike Harbottle paid us a visit, but not until 3 am did we hear that the Greek National Guard had been ordered to withdraw. We were to take over their positions and assume responsibility for all Turkish prisoners and the people who had been turned out of their houses. At 5 am the withdrawal started and was completed within the hour. As we took over the positions medical teams moved into the villages and our two ad hoc platoons started collecting the dead Turkish fighters, preparing them for burial and generally trying to relieve distress. Considering the damage done in the villages, casualties were light. Altogether twenty-five Turks were killed and about twelve wounded. The Greeks had one man killed and a few more wounded. None of our men became casualties: no thanks to the contestants.

*   *   *

Once I was sure that there would be no more fighting, my main concern was to see for myself the extent of the damage and then visit the other Turkish enclaves in my zone to prevent unnecessarily exaggerated rumours flying around that could lead to further disturbances. Accordingly, as soon as it got light, I set off in my Land Rover to take a look at the villages and to talk to our men who were in great spirits, rightly conscious of having fulfilled their task and survived the perils of the previous day. I greatly admired the way they had stood up to the National Guard and was particularly impressed by the courage of the section commanders who so robustly defied the heavily armed threats of the National Guard officers and their ill disciplined followers. The dead Turkish fighters in their lightweight uniforms looked very young with their wispy moustaches and staring eyes coated with grit blown around by the hot wind of the previous day. I later heard that survivors had sheltered in nearby hills and villages, returning some days later. This would have accounted for the comparatively few casualties sustained on the defensive positions. The dead found in the villages were middle aged men wearing civilian clothes who had obviously been killed, mainly by grenades thrown into houses to make sure that there was no resistance.

Having got a clear idea of the damage done, I drove to Larnaca to see Dr Orhan, expecting a flood of vituperation for our failure to avert the catastrophe that had overtaken his people. To my surprise he was very kind, enquiring after the safety of our men. He seemed certain that Turkey would invade Cyprus to ensure the security of he Turkish community throughout the island. From Larnaca I went to B Company in Ktima and tried to reassure the Turkish leader Mr Altay, after which I visited Limassol before returning to battalion headquarters. I was in need of a good wash and brush up after a busy, not to say alarming, twenty-four hours.

For the next few days much of my time was taken up talking to both sides throughout my zone in an attempt to ease tension. I also had to send accurate information back to our Rear Party in Tidworth so that the families could be given a true understanding of the position as accounts given on the wireless and in the newspapers must have caused them some concern. I realised only too well that Elizabeth would be worried and it was obvious that there would be many other wives feeling the same, not to mention anxious parents and girl friends. Over the coming weeks I also had to answer numerous enquiries from military sources in England and the Sovereign Base areas from people who had gained an erroneous impression of events.

Meanwhile Bob Pascoe's men occupied the Turkish defensive positions until they were taken over again by Turkish fighters, after which we established observation posts nearby. As a result of the support that our men gave to the injured and distressed folk in the two villages and thanks to the material assistance provided by the United Nations, relations with the Turkish community greatly improved. We were allowed to move freely throughout the area and football matches and social contacts took place. The Greek Cypriots apologised profusely for the looting and for stealing our weapons during the battle, returning the rifles and giving generous compensation for items stolen. We had been surprised when the National Guard violated our positions, tried to intimidate our men and took no regard for our safety when using their weapons, but this was probably done in a deliberate attempt to frighten us into not reporting their activities.

The overall situation in the eastern Mediterranean remained menacing with Turkey making overt preparations for an invasion of Cyprus. Sterling efforts were made by the United Nations and the United States to avert such a calamity with special envoys flying back and forth across the Atlantic, many of whom visited Cyprus, one at least getting as far as Kophinou. Escorted by General Martola, he was met by Bob Pascoe and myself for a tour of the battlefield. Late in November it looked as if all their efforts had failed and that the Turks were on their way. There was a meeting of zone commanders in Nicosia at which we received our orders. I can not remember exactly what we were expected to do but it would have involved exposing our men to a certain amount of risk. I was sitting next to the colonel commanding the Irish zone and at the end of the meeting he quietly told me that he was going to get his men to dig the deepest holes they had ever dug, and sit at the bottom until it was all over. I thought that this was sensible, but knew he would do nothing of the kind. The Irish were first class peacekeepers with experience in many different places. Because we sat in alphabetical order at General Martola's conferences, I was always next to this man who seldom asked questions and never complained.

In the end the Turks did not come but they exacted a stiff price for not doing so. All Greek, as opposed to Greek Cypriot, units had to leave Cyprus and this included their tanks and artillery. As the Turks had complete air superiority anyway, this meant that they would be able to invade whenever they pleased without much difficulty. The Greek government recalled Grivas three days after the battle and over the next three months Makarios progressively lifted many of the restrictions formerly imposed on the Turks. In fact the fighting around Kophinou constituted a turning point in the affairs of the island. Up to that time the Greek position was getting stronger by the day at the expense of the Turkish Cypriots and the United Nations. As a result of the bargaining that brought it to an end, the Greek position became rapidly weaker, the Turkish Cypriots became more secure and the United Nations more acceptable to both sides. After a few weeks life in Cyprus became more peaceful than it had been since the troubles began, although situations continued to arise which required careful negotiation in order to prevent them from escalating into open conflict.

But had diplomacy failed to prevent a Turkish invasion following the battle at Kophinou, there would have been considerably more bloodshed. Inevitably I wondered whether there was any way in which the United Nations could have prevented the battle at Kophinou from taking place. After only a fortnight in Cyprus we had little detailed knowledge of the way in which the dispute had built up over the months, or of the geography of the area, or of the personalities influencing events. The restrictions on movement, which the United Nations had been obliged to accept, meant that we knew nothing of the disposition of the National Guard units, nor did we know the strength and layout of the Turkish defences. We therefore had little idea how the situation would develop if the Greeks decided to force open the road to Ayios Theodoros.

Greater freedom of movement and better intelligence would have enabled us to give more accurate warning of how and in what strength the attack was likely to come, but it would only have been helpful in bringing pressure to bear on the Greek leadership to call off the attack. It would not have enabled the United Nations to oppose the attack by force, because there were insufficient uncommitted troops available and in any case the mandate governing the use of United Nations troops in Cyprus would not stretch to the use of force against either community. All the United Nations could do was to report what was happening so that diplomatic activity could proceed uninhibited by false reports put out by the contestants which is was what we had done anyway. General Martola's Chief of Staff later wrote:

'The information we were receiving (during the battle) was so good and accurate that Osorio-Tafall and Martola in their negotiations with the (Greek Cypriot) Government were able to give a detailed picture of events and to refute false reports and wild rumours from other sources. This running commentary which would have done credit to a football cup final at Wembley, also established the extent of preparedness of the National Guard for the battle and the excessiveness of the force used. At no time was a single UN post evacuated despite the great possibility of casualties. Had there been a withdrawal of UN, the claims and counter-claims of atrocities and damage would have seriously confused the issues in the settling up stage, but more important, the continued presence of UN acted as a deterrent to those bent on more extreme measures and probably did more than anything else to limit casualties and to influence the Greek Government to order the calling off of the attack and the withdrawal of the forces from the area.'

Although I could do nothing about the limitations which the United Nations were obliged to accept, I felt that it would be worth trying to get more information in order to strengthen our negotiating position during the build up of incidents. For this purpose I tried to make friends with those likely to have information of use to me, such as the military attachés of the various countries represented in Nicosia. I got on particularly well with the Russian from whom I tried, unsuccessfully, to obtain some Armenian brandy and I looked up old acquaintances like Petros. Using the dodges I had picked up over the years I eventually identified some of the people directing events in my area, who were not always the official spokesmen. Although continuing to pay my respects to the spokesmen, I did what I could to ensure that they received the sort of instructions that suited us as far as possible. This, together with constantly visiting our own outposts and attending frequent functions laid on by the other zone commanders, took up most of my time. It was not exhausting, but the vast amount of drinking involved did little to improve my liver.

*   *   *

Although the riflemen around Kophinou had experienced a certain amount of excitement in mid-November, life in the observation posts was usually dull and involved remaining alert in uncomfortable surroundings day after day. To provide some variety we moved each platoon to a new location every two weeks. Men were picked up by helicopters from near their observation posts, and flown to relieve a platoon in another part of the zone. As the district commanders who were also the Company Commanders, stayed in the same place to achieve continuity, they were often commanding platoons from a company other than their own. Movement was complicated by the fact that each district needed a different number of platoons i.e. Kophinou, five, Limassol and Paphos three each and Polis one. In Limassol District only one platoon was deployed in observation posts, the other two being in reserve which gave them a chance to train and take some exercise. Our experienced and hard working adjutant, Nigel Sale, arranged the rotation.

By visiting each section once in each place, I got to know the section commanders and riflemen quicker than I could have done in a peacetime station such as Tidworth. I also had an unrivalled opportunity for assessing the company commanders as I watched them sort out their day-to-day problems. The way in which Bob Pascoe handled the disturbance at Kophinou and its aftermath left no doubt in my mind that he was an exceptionally calm and competent commander. Paphos was the next most difficult district, which required much patience and quiet diplomacy to keep on an even keel. Here we were lucky to have Robin Eveleigh for the first two months followed by John Holroyd, both of whom developed a good rapport with the leaders on both sides so that none of the potential crises ever developed into a major outbreak of violence. Tim Hartley at Polis had an easier task as the two communities were obliged to work together in the sulphur mines in order to earn a livelihood. The local leaders, Inspector Ekonomidies and a Turkish schoolmaster called Salleh were both strong and sensible characters who seemed able to prevent the politicians in Nicosia from upsetting the apple cart, but they needed a lot of support from Tim and his men. Michael Massey-Beresford who commanded Limassol District suffered from being co-located with battalion headquarters at Polemidhia. Remembering my feelings when commanding S Company, 1 RB at Kuala Kubu Bahru in 1957, I realised that it was not what he would have liked, but he made the best of it and did a good job.

*   *   *

While all this was going on the process of turning the old Ox and Bucks into Royal Green Jackets continued. Within a month of arriving in Cyprus I had seen enough to know that the battalion was top class by anybody's standards. But the merger of the three old regiments had only taken place less than two years earlier and the great majority of the people in 1 RGJ had spent most of their service in the Ox and Bucks. There was plenty to be done to get everyone comfortable with the idea that we all belonged to one new regiment instead of one of the old ones by a new name. Taking a leaf out of Malcolm Douglas Pennant's book I decided that whenever an issue had to be resolved, it would be on the basis of common sense rather than precedent: there was little point in arguing about the relative merits of this or that old regiment. It must be said that the majority of the members of the battalion thought along these lines but there were naturally pockets of resistance particularly amongst the less intelligent officers and some of the long serving members of the sergeants' mess. With this situation in mind I prepared to meet our colonel commandant who was coming to spend five days with the battalion in March.

Lieutenant General Sir John Mogg, was Commander-in-Chief of Army Strategic Command based at Wilton near Salisbury. He was also father of our signals officer, Nigel Mogg. From Elizabeth's letters I knew that he and his wife had taken great interest in our rear party and dependants and that they had also been kind to her personally. I reckoned that through Nigel, or our wives, he would have a pretty good idea of what was going on in the battalion and this turned out to be the case. During his visit I took him round each of the companies and had ample opportunity to discuss matters with him. I soon realised how lucky I was to have such a splendid soldier and person as colonel commandant. Although formerly of the Ox and Bucks, he was totally committed to making the Royal Green Jackets work and approved of my way of doing business. He listened patiently to my opinion of the few officers I thought to be less than satisfactory and of my desire to be rid of them, merely suggesting that I should do nothing in a hurry. He did not say so, but technically 1 RGJ was his battalion, not mine. I commanded it on his behalf and was grateful for his advice. Naturally, in practice, if anything went wrong it would be me that was responsible and not him.

During the course of his visit we had our one and only ceremonial parade when General Martola came to Polemidhia to give out the United Nations Medal for service in Cyprus to as many men as we could spare. The rest would get them from me as I went round the companies later. Since arriving in Cyprus I had stopped all drill parades because I felt that the men had little enough time away from the observation posts and could be given better things to do than marching around the square. The regimental sergeant major had warned me that my ruling would lead to disaster when the medal parade came round and in view of the presence of the colonel commandant he begged me to relent and to allow him at least one rehearsal. But most of the men would have to be brought in from the companies by vehicles on the morning of the parade and returned immediately afterwards so that a rehearsal would mean doing it all twice. I therefore refused his request but suggested that he could put whitewash on the square where he wanted the men to stand and get them all in place before the parade started. He could then get the band to march up and down and in and out, doing as much complicated drill as he liked. All the men would have to do, was to come to attention and stand at ease a few times as General Martola walked along the ranks. They could then march past him in threes, which needed no rehearsal. On the day, it went like clockwork. So good was the band that it looked as though we had carried out a complicated series of manoeuvres and General Martola complemented the regimental sergeant major on an excellent parade.

During our six months in Cyprus many other officers visited us. Major General Deane-Drummond who commanded the division in which the battalion was serving when in England was one. As a result of our association in Muscat I greatly respected him as a commander and was more than pleased to see him again. Another visitor was Dwin Bramall who I had served with in 2 KRRC in 1951 but had not seen since. He was a high-class commander who had recently taken over the brigade at Tidworth and his visit enabled us to go over the programme for the rest of the year after our return to England in May.

*   *   *

It was now necessary for the battalion to cast off its peacekeeping role and to prepare for war as part of 5th Brigade in the Strategic Reserve. After a battalion study day and exercise, there was a brigade study day followed in August by Exercise Iron Duke run by Dwin Bramall on Salisbury Plain. It envisaged us as having deployed to Germany in support of a BAOR division that was being attacked by the Soviet Union. It was as realistic as such exercises can be and even now I remember having to think rather rapidly what I should do about the arrival of a couple of enemy tanks which suddenly appeared from totally the wrong direction while I was relieving myself behind a bush. The only other thing I can remember was slipping home for a quick visit to Elizabeth as we swept past Tidworth in pursuit of a fleeing enemy, or possibly as we retreated before a triumphant one.

After a period of leave the battalion moved to Sennybridge in Wales for six weeks of company training and field firing. Everything was perfect except for the weather: it rained almost the whole time. For a fortnight we were joined by 4 RGJ of the Territorial Army, commanded by Nick Eden, with whom we conducted two joint exercises. They were organised by my new second-in-command, Michael Koe, and their training major, Mike Carleton-Smith. Nick and I were the exercise directors, which meant that we controlled the umpires, up to a point. Exercising with Nick Eden was very pleasant as he moved around with a trailer attached to his Land Rover containing a lean-to, table, chairs and a seemingly inexhaustible supply of champagne with which he entertained the many distinguished visitors that arrived to cheer on the Territorial Army.

The next task for the battalion was to conduct trials into the new range of night fighting equipment in order to determine its affect on tactics and the scale at which it should be issued. Until Christmas Michael Massey-Beresford's C Company would be learning how to use the various devices on a training area in Norfolk. After that there would be a series of two-night exercises on Salisbury Plane in which C Company reinforced by elements of Support Company, an

Armoured Reconnaissance Troop and elements of a Light Artillery Regiment would be opposed by one of the other companies together with some gunners and armoured cars. Each of these exercises was designed to examine the value of the equipment in differing tactical settings and to answer specific questions posed by Brigade Headquarters. Michael Koe prepared the exercises and I directed them as chief umpire.

In fact, my main contribution to the trials came after they were completed. Michael Koe produced the detailed report by collecting the ideas of the many officers involved. He, more than anyone else, was responsible for the success of the trial. But it was my business to decide on the main tactical conclusions as well as the recommendations as to the usefulness of the various bits of kit. In the coming months I gave a number of talks about the trials in different places, the first of which was to the men of the battalion in which I explained how important had been their contribution throughout the past uncomfortable winter. My conclusions can best be summarised by saying that, although the new equipment would not turn night into day, it would turn one sort of night into a totally different sort of night. Furthermore any force without night-fighting equipment would have a thin time fighting an opponent possessing it.

At the end of April the battalion set off for five weeks training based at Camp Wainwright in Canada, accompanied by an artillery battery and logistic elements from our brigade. Each company spent time field firing at Wainwright but they also disappeared into the Rocky Mountains for a prolonged period of adventure training during which time I visited them and did a bit of fishing. Trips were also organised to Calgary by Princess Patricia's Canadian Light Infantry, a regiment affiliated to the Royal Green Jackets, which is based there. We concluded the training with a short but energetic battalion exercise on the Wainwright training area. The battalion thoroughly enjoyed Canada. We were back in Tidworth in early June and just before we returned Elizabeth gave birth to our third daughter, christened Marion but forever after known as Chiggy.

*   *   *

To say that I knew little about Ireland and its troubles over the past centuries would be an understatement. So far as I was concerned it was just a place one went to occasionally, to hunt or shoot and from where it was possible to recruit good soldiers. I knew that as a result of the settlement that had been reached after the disturbances that took place during and after the First World War, discontented persons sometimes left bombs at railway stations etc., but I had never taken it seriously. I now realised that there was a lot to discover pretty quickly. As a start, whilst still travelling in the aeroplane, I asked Alistair Stewart, who was acting as adjutant, how many Irishmen were in the battalion. It turned out that there were around forty of whom two thirds were Roman Catholics, mainly from the south, the rest being Ulster Protestants.

Our deployment resulted from rioting that had broken out in Londonderry, when Roman Catholics clashed with a march organised by the Apprentice Boys of Derry, a group of men who were closely connected with the Protestant Orange Order. The rioting spread to Belfast and troops of 39th Brigade normally stationed in Northern Ireland plus the spearhead battalion of the Strategic Reserve, were deployed onto the streets to keep the two sides apart. Headquarters 24th Brigade had also been sent from England to take over responsibility for Londonderry and the border with the Republic.

Our job as part of 24th Brigade was to deploy behind the border with Southern Ireland to ensure that no further trouble occurred in the counties of Tyrone, Fermanagh and Armagh. Battalion headquarters and Support Company moved in to share the barracks at Omagh with two resident squadrons of the 17/21 Lancers, most of that regiment being in North Africa and Cyprus. B Company, which was still commanded by John Holroyd, became responsible for Armagh and C Company, now commanded by Roger Preston, took over Enniskillen. Arish Turle's A Company was sent to Dungannon, a particularly sensitive town where some rioting and bombing had recently taken place. Arthur Douglas-Nugent, second-in-command of the 17/21 Lancers who could not have been more helpful to us in every way, became responsible for Tyrone, aided for the first month by Roger Kerr who commanded Support Company. A troop of armoured cars was attached to each of the deployed companies

My first task was to visit the senior police officer in each of the counties known as the County Inspector. In order to arrange proper co-ordination of our activities we set up County Security Committees consisting of the county inspector, company commander and the county commandant of the Ulster Special Constabulary, known as the B Specials. Thereafter I spent much of my time visiting these people and the men of our deployed companies. I also tried to make contact with the more influential members of the community to get their views on the causes of the trouble and the best ways in which we could help to defuse the situation. In this I was greatly helped by Arthur Douglas-Nugent whose family had lived in Ireland for centuries and who understood the background to The Troubles as only an Irishman could.

In Londonderry riots had broken out on several occasions over the past year as a result of Protestant reaction to demonstrations staged by the Northern Ireland Civil Rights Organisation backed by student hangers on of the People's Democracy Party. Both of these groups were trying to highlight grievances felt by the Roman Catholic section of the community because of unfairness in the electoral system and discrimination in such matters as jobs and housing. Many Protestants in Northern Ireland thought that such unfairness as existed was necessary to prevent the Roman Catholic community from becoming strong enough to undermine the union of Northern Ireland with the rest of the United Kingdom. In April the Prime Minister of Northern Ireland had been obliged to resign because of opposition by members of his own party to concessions he wanted to make to the Roman Catholics in order to defuse the issue. The new Prime Minister was my old friend from the Staff College, Jim Chichester-Clark, and he now found himself obliged to use British troops to maintain order while he got on with removing the unfairness that had sparked off the civil rights movement. In this work he was being pushed along by the British government who wanted peace and their soldiers off the street, whilst he was opposed by those Protestants who had unseated his predecessor for doing the very things that the British government now demanded. The Irish Republican Army (IRA), which had taken part in previous campaigns designed to drive Northern Ireland into the Republic, was being blamed, wrongly as it turned out, for various acts of sabotage that had taken place over the past few months. It remained almost entirely inactive during the rioting.

Against this background our task was to prevent outbreaks of rioting and to deal with any movement across the border with the Republic of people desirous of fomenting trouble or re-arming the IRA. To look after the border I had two Army Air Corps helicopters at Omagh and could call on troop-carrying helicopters from the RAF at Aldegrove. The Omagh helicopters kept roads from the Republic under observation and if any suspicious vehicles were seen, the RAF moved men to man roadblocks to intercept them. I spent a considerable amount of time flying along the border to get a good idea of the problem and of the lie of the land. In fact nothing much happened in the six weeks remaining before Roly Guy arrived to take over from me at the end of my two years in command, nearly half of which had been spent away from Tidworth.

I was very sorry to leave the battalion, which had turned up trumps in Cyprus and had responded magnificently to the business of getting itself quickly to Ireland when called on in the middle of a period of block leave. There is no doubt that the old Oxford and Buckinghamshire Light Infantry, which is pretty well what I took over, was a splendid battalion. By the time of my departure it was well on the way to being a battalion of the Royal Green Jackets and it was evident that this new regiment was going to be as good, or better, than its forebears.

Another source of regret was that my departure from the battalion marked the end of nearly twenty-five years service as a regimental officer. In future I would be a member of the General Staff rather than Royal Green Jackets, since that is the official designation of officers of the rank of full colonel and above. In practice I would still be part of the great Green Jacket family, but I could never again serve in a battalion of the regiment.

Chapter 8

Northern Ireland:
From Protest to Insurgency 1969–1971

At some time during the summer of 1969 General Mogg told me to volunteer for a Defence Fellowship which meant spending a year at a university studying a subject that would be laid down by the Ministry of Defence. At the end of the academic year one had to produce what was described as a thesis. If this satisfied the Ministry of Defence and the university one was entitled to put the letters 'd.f.' after ones name. He said that it would save me from having to go to the Royal College of Defence Studies at a later date, which was a pretty good waste of time. Defence Fellowships were the brainchild of Denis Healey who was the Secretary of State for Defence. Although no doubt he hoped that the studies might be of some use, the idea was also to widen the horizons of the selected officers by exposing them to contact with the higher reaches of the academic world. I duly volunteered and was accepted. Thanks again to General Mogg, the Master of University College Oxford agreed to take me in as a member of the Senior Common Room. I duly appeared in early October and was given a room in college, a gown and a mortar board type hat. Never having been to a university, except for my brief visit to Cambridge in 1944, I found my horizons being extended at record speed in a world that I had never even thought existed. My study was to be 'supervised' by Norman Gibbs, Chichele Professor of the History of War, who was based at All Souls College, a short distance away.

While I was coming to terms with my new surroundings, Elizabeth and the family moved back to our home, Horsley House, Surrey, where I joined them every weekend.

The terms of reference for my thesis, laid down by the Ministry of Defence, were to draw attention to the steps that should be taken in order to make the army ready to deal with subversion, insurrection and peacekeeping operations during the second half of the 1970s. Just about every book that had ever been written about subversion, insurrection or guerrilla war could be found somewhere within the university. Professor Gibbs read my script as I went along and at intervals of about six weeks told me what he thought about it. He did not regard himself as an expert on my subject but was good at ensuring that I only wrote what I could substantiate from a specific source that had to be quoted. He was hot on what he referred to as academic integrity, meaning that I was not allowed to quote that part of a man's views that supported my ideas and leave out the bits that did not. If I wanted to peddle my own ideas I was welcome to do so, but I had to show clearly that they were mine.

Over the coming months I made many contacts at Oxford with people who knew a great deal about the subject of my thesis. A particularly helpful man was a former officer of the US Marine Corps called Robert Asprey who was busy writing his monumental two volume work *War in the Shadows, The Guerilla in History*.

During the second half of the academic year I visited military establishments in England and America to see how the subject was being taught so as to be in a position to suggest changes where necessary. At Fort Bragg I had discussions with Lieutenant General Richard Stilwell who was Deputy Chief of Staff Operations, of the US Army. He was son of 'Vinegar' Joe Stilwell, famous in the Far East during the war, but the son was not in the least vinegary. Naturally I also had to write the thesis which, apart, from *Gangs and Counter Gangs*, was the longest document that I had ever written and easily the most difficult.

*   *   *

In June 1970, I was promoted to brigadier and told that at the end of the academic year I was to take over command of 39th Brigade in Belfast. As part of my work I had recently visited the security authorities in Northern Ireland to get their opinion of what would be going on there in the second half of the 1970s. The official line was that the situation was improving as the reforms needed to reassure the Roman Catholics were being implemented. This was encouraging, but what made me nervous was that there seemed to be no great effort to enlarge the intelligence organisation, which so greatly needed improving if the optimism regarding the implementation of reforms proved to be misplaced. Although the original rioting had developed out of a series of civil rights protests rather than IRA action designed to unify Ireland, it seemed unlikely that the IRA would forego the opportunity for turning protest into insurgency.

In July my thesis was finished and was passed as academically sound by Professor Gibbs. It also found favour in the Ministry of Defence. The next question was how to bring it to the attention of those who might find it useful. Realising that army officers seldom look at official publications, it was decided in the ministry that a commercial publisher should publish it. The government would of course hold the copyright as it had paid for my year at Oxford, including all the travelling, but agreed that I should have a share of the royalties. There was a member of All Souls College called Monteith who was the chairman of Faber & Faber and he undertook to publish it. He saw me briefly and handed me over to one of his editors called Mathew Evans who would look after its preparation. It was called *Low Intensity Operations* and General Carver agreed to write the foreword. With all this decided, I said goodbye to Oxford and prepared to move to Northern Ireland.

About ten days before I was due to take over the brigade I was told to attend a study day being held jointly by the General Officer Commanding in Northern Ireland, Lieutenant General Sir Ian Freeland, and the Chief Constable. On my arrival it was clear that matters had taken a turn for the worse since my earlier visit. Protestant riots were breaking out in Belfast and it was apparent that the Roman Catholics who had welcomed us so vigorously in 1969, were now less friendly. This was put down to the way in which soldiers had entered a Catholic area of Belfast in July searching for weapons, many of which were found.

The purpose of the study day was to discuss how the army would hand over to the police by the end of the year and retire to its peacetime locations. Most of the officers, thought that the idea was ridiculous: it seemed more likely that the army would need reinforcing than removing.

It was also apparent that the general and the Chief Constable were not seeing eye to eye. The Chief Constable was the highly distinguished Sir Arthur Young aged 63, who had amongst other senior positions, been Chief Constable of the Metropolitan Police and of the City of London Police. Harold Wilson had sent Young to Ireland when there was little if any insurgency, as part of the package designed to reassure the Roman Catholic population that their grievances were being put right. So far as the police was concerned, the package consisted of disarming them, disbanding their Special Constables, forming a police authority and redrawing boundaries so that there were now ten police divisions of which six were in Belfast. Although Young was well suited to turning an armed police force into an impartial police service, this method of policing would only work if the people of Northern Ireland were prepared to settle for the government's new concessions. It was now evident that neither community intended to accept them, which would give extremists on both sides of the religious divide the opportunity to derail the whole process. The lack of preparation for such a situation that I had noticed when visiting the Province in the spring, was likely to be serious.

*   *   *

In mid-September the family left Horsley House and moved into an army quarter in Lisburn within a protected compound that also contained Headquarters 39th Brigade and Headquarters Northern Ireland.

The general picture of what had happened up to the time of my arrival can be summarised as follows. The population of Northern Ireland was about 1.5 million of which 66 per cent were Protestants and 33 per cent Roman Catholics. Of the 615,000 who lived in Belfast, 60 per cent were Protestants and 40 per cent Catholics. In parts of the city Protestants and Catholics lived quietly together, but in other parts, mainly occupied by the poorer families, they lived in their own segregated areas in rows of small terraced houses. Behind each row of houses was a narrow passage which, along with the pattern of the streets themselves, constituted a veritable tangle of buildings and alley ways erratically lit by street lamps, when they were working. In Protestant areas the layout was much the same. It was here, in the segregated areas, that most of the trouble occurred, especially along the borders between the two communities.

Most Catholics looked forward to a time when the two parts of Ireland could be united peaceably but were meanwhile mainly concerned with making Northern Ireland fair for both Catholics and Protestants. They were known as Nationalists and were followers of the Social Democratic and Labour Party (SDLP). Those that favoured unification at once were known as republicans. The IRA was the armed wing of the republican movement. In August 1969 the IRA was ineffective having lost much of its support as a result of its failure in the previous campaign which foundered in 1962 and also because of its extreme left wing politics. After the August 1969 riots the IRA appealed to the Catholic community to support it on the grounds that it was the only true safeguard against further Protestant incursions, such as had recently occurred. IRA membership gradually built up and a split arose between those who wanted to use a little violence and a lot of left wing politics and those who wanted to stick to the old IRA methods of as much violence as was necessary to bring about a United Ireland. The former were known as the Goulding Group, or Official IRA and the latter the Brady Group or Provisional IRA. Because both groups were prepared to use violence to achieve their aims, they both intended to become involved in a campaign of insurgency. Insurgents are by definition criminals, but criminals who have the sympathy and sometimes the backing of a significant number of people both inside and outside the country. Stopping them is essential for many reasons, in particular to prevent them from intimidating those who oppose the use of violence. But it has to be done in a way that does not turn the population as a whole against the government. At the same time those risking their lives on behalf of the government, have to be protected and encouraged.

Plenty of Protestants objected to the concessions that had been made to the Catholic community for the same reasons that caused republicans to support them, that is to say they thought that the concessions weakened the position of those desirous of remaining part of the United Kingdom. Protestants were particularly enraged by the disarming of the Royal Ulster Constabulary and the disbanding of its reserve constables known as the B Specials who they regarded as their first line of defence against the IRA. For years the Protestant Orange Order had demonstrated their attachment to the union by marching along traditional routes, many of which skirted Catholic areas. The IRA, as it grew stronger, encouraged youngsters to hurl abuse and missiles at the marchers for the purpose of starting riots, which in turn would cause the Catholics to support the IRA as being the best defence against the enraged Protestants. For their part the Protestants organised riots of their own against the army to demonstrate their frustration at the failure of the government to stamp out Catholic dissent.

One of my earliest recollections of Belfast was looking on as a company of the King's Regiment tried to rescue the company commander, Major 'Kipper' Herring, from a bakery in a street off the Protestant Shankhill Road where he had taken refuge. Clouds of CS gas were swirling round the street lamps as the troops pushed down the road armed with shields and batons. Later that evening I found a platoon of the Coldstream Guards at the other end of the Shankhill drawn up in three ranks. They were being pelted with bricks and bottles by a crowd of youths intent on breaking the windows in the nearby Unity Flats, an isolated Catholic enclave. At least half a dozen members of the platoon had been damaged by these people.

The riots enabled me to learn quickly how the mechanics of moving troops around in Belfast worked. Each of the battalions in the brigade had its area, as did each company within a battalion. An elaborate system existed for reinforcing hard pressed companies from less hard pressed ones and for passing companies from one battalion to another. There was also a battalion in brigade reserve on the outskirts of the town, which could send companies to reinforce battalions on the street, or the reserve battalion could move as a unit and take over temporarily part of another battalion's area. All of this was very slick and worked well. The thing that the brigade commander had to do was to ensure that as soon as one reserve was used up, another was formed so that he always had something in hand should a new disturbance arise. I was full of admiration for my predecessor's arrangements and for the efficiency of the brigade staff in keeping the business working for four days. I was less impressed with the tactics of the battalions on the ground, which seemed to consist of standing firm while bricks and bottles were thrown at them, until dispersing the crowds with water cannons and large quantities of CS gas. This entered the homes of rioters and non-rioters alike, thereby annoying the population as a whole.

*   *   *

Before going further it is necessary to outline briefly the command structure of the security forces in Northern Ireland. General Freeland was not only the commander of all army units in the Province, but also Director of Operations. His Chief of Staff was Major General Tom Acton of the Rifle Brigade an officer I knew well. There was a Commander of Land Forces (CLF), Major General Tony Farrar-Hockley, who I also knew as he had been a Defence Fellow at Oxford when I was there and had only been promoted into his present job in August. During the early months of The Troubles, General Freeland had found difficulty handling the military demands of the confused security situation whilst at the same time keeping in touch with the politicians at Stormont and Westminster. As the Stormont government was responsible for the internal security of the Province at a time when the Ministry of Defence in London controlled the army, problems were unavoidable. Tony Farrar-Hockley had been inserted to take on the business of directing Freeland's subordinate commanders, that is to say the brigadiers, while Freeland handled the wider issues. The fact that Freeland's staff also looked after Farrar Hockley reduced the chances of crossed wires but for the system to work, Freeland had to forego any direct military contact with the brigadiers and deal with them exclusively through Tony Farrar-Hockley. Both Tom Acton and Tony Farrar-Hockley had considerable counter-insurgency experience.

Under Farrar-Hockley were two brigades; 8th Brigade in Londonderry which was responsible for that city and the whole of the border with the Republic of Ireland and 39th Brigade in Belfast. The six police divisions in Belfast came under the Assistant Chief Constable for Belfast, Sam Bradley, who was himself responsible to the Chief Constable. My task was to assist the police maintain law and order and I was lucky to have Sam Bradley as my partner. He was a wonderful person of great experience having joined the Royal Ulster Constabulary in 1937 as a band-boy and having served in it ever since. He was tall, immensely strong and totally unflappable: he had seen it all before several times over and was well respected by the main protagonists on both sides of the religious divide.

When I arrived there was no proper security forces plan for Belfast, although there was a lengthy booklet concerned with procedures for working with the police. The police and the army reacted to riots as they occurred and action between them was co-ordinated as and when necessary. The police had not only been disarmed as part of the reforms but had lost their riot kit and were not supposed to react to the disturbances that were taking place. All of this had severely affected their morale. There was no formal co-ordination between the police and the army in Belfast and no co-ordination of any sort between either of them and the civil authorities. This was disappointing considering that it had long been recognised that operational methods have to be closely meshed in with political, economic and psychological ones if violent civil unrest is to be brought under control.

In 1969 there had been no difference in kind between Protestant and Catholic riots. Both sides were rioting as an extension of the political process. There was an element of criminality to rioting, which concerned such things as affray, obstruction and imposing bodily harm, but these were common to both sides. As soon as the IRA started up, an additional element of criminality was introduced, as the IRA was trying to overthrow the government by force. This brought into their actions such crimes as sedition, seditious libel, deliberate murder and even treason, although the government was anxious not to use such uncompromising terms. There was always the possibility that Protestant extremism would develop along the same lines, but when Sam and I started to work out a long-term plan for dealing with the situation, there were no signs that this would be the case. Meanwhile we needed a plan to control the rioting and at the same time to identify and arrest those who were trying to use the disturbances to foster their seditious aims by violence.

We quickly got down to making a plan. Sam told me that all the previous outbreaks since the partition of Ireland had been brought to an end by the introduction of internment without trial on both sides of the border at the same time. This did not require additional legislation in Northern Ireland as the Civil Authorities Special Powers Act, which authorised the Chief Constable to implement it when necessary, was still on the statute book. Of course we both knew that he would not do so without the agreement of the government, but we both thought that it was bound to come sooner or later. Until that time it would be difficult to get rid of the men who were plotting sedition, since we would be hard pressed to get the sort of evidence against them that would stand up in a court of law.

The forces at our disposal consisted of around 1,200 police spread around Sam's six divisions and my six battalions soon reduced to five. Four of these were loaned to me on four months tours from their normal locations in England or Germany. The fifth was the 1st Battalion, Parachute Regiment known as 1 Para, commanded by Mike Gray, which was on a two year accompanied tour based at Holywood Barracks just to the east of Belfast. The four-month battalions, deployed in the city, were split up geographically with companies and platoons living in schools, shops, disused factories or police stations.

Our plan, which was endorsed by Headquarters Northern Ireland and by the Chief Constable, consisted of three distinct parts. First, to try and get the inhabitants of the core Protestant and Roman Catholic areas to support the government rather than the leaders of disaffected elements in the community.

This was to be done by a mixture of community-relations projects and the dissemination of information. Second, to prevent rioting by effective anti-riot tactics. I was not happy with the idea that the army should stand in lines being subjected to bricks, bottles and abuse until dispersing the rioters with gas and water-cannons. In order to work out better methods we set up a study to be run by Sam's deputy and Dick Gerrard-Wright, the commanding officer of 2nd Royal Anglian Regiment, based at Springfield Road Police Station. They were to report by the end of the year. Third, we would try to get enough evidence to convict in court at least some of those planning violence and stirring up trouble. For this to happen they needed to be caught red-handed with illegal weapons or carrying out some other subversive activity. We acknowledged the difficulty of getting sufficiently good evidence against those who took no active part in the disturbances themselves, but reckoned that sooner or later they would be likely to compromise themselves one way or another.

In order to put this plan into effect we set up action committees in each police division consisting of the Police Divisional Commander, the commanding officer of the battalion stationed in the division and a company commander of 1 Para, to provide continuity. 1 Para would also provide one or two senior NCOs to each Action Committee to provide continuity to community-relations projects. The Action Committees would co-ordinate all police and military work within the division designed to protect lawful activities within that division, although once rioting started our response would have to be directed by the normal chain of command through police and military operations rooms. This was necessary because the situation might then involve switching soldiers from one police division to another. On 22 October all the police divisional commanders and the battalion commanding officers met in Sam's office at Castlereagh Police Headquarters and I put our plan across to them.

Much depended on intelligence. There were no sources of intelligence directly available to us, as the Special Branch for the whole Province was centralised under an Assistant Chief Constable at Police Headquarters which was situated outside Belfast at Knock and a similar arrangement existed for the CID. The only contact Sam had with these organisations was through a Special Branch officer and a CID officer who worked in Belfast and who was supposed to keep him in touch with events. All intelligence gathered by Special Branch was passed directly to Police Headquarters to be collated. From there what was judged to be useful to the army was sent to HQ Northern Ireland and thence distributed to the brigades. Special Branch knew the names of some IRA members, largely related to the previous campaign and they also had some idea of which ones had stayed with the Official IRA and which has split off with the Provisional.

Anything produced by other intelligence agencies such as MI5 or MI6 would be passed to a Director of Security working at HQ Northern Ireland.

Soon after I arrived I attended a meeting of a non-governmental co-ordinating body for the defence of the Catholic community in Belfast called the Central Citizens Defence Committee (CCDC). A respected member of the business community was chairman and there were one or two priests including Canon Murphy who had been active as a go-between during the 1969 riots and who, I had been told, would help me to understand the viewpoint of the Catholic community.

I sat next to the secretary, a working class man from Falls Road, who smoked non-stop and who was clearly suffering from asthma. We seemed to be getting on pretty well and at one point I lent him my inhaler to relieve his breathing. I got the impression that the chairman was rather nervous and reluctant to agree anything unless re-assured by the secretary that it was OK. I later discovered that the secretary was the chief staff officer for the Official IRA in Belfast and that amongst the delegates were members of both IRA groups. As time went by I attended meetings of many of the branches of the CDC and made the acquaintance of a number of individuals.

Fierce riots instigated by both communities continued for the first two months of my time in Belfast. Sometimes they lasted for several days, building up in the late afternoon, raging in the evening and early part of the night until dying down about 2.30 am and restarting the next afternoon. Buses were hijacked and burned or used as barriers across the streets to hinder the movement of troops. Missiles such as bricks, bottles and petrol bombs were hurled with great enthusiasm. From November onwards, an increasing number of nail bombs consisting of a stick of blasting dynamite with long nails stuck round it, added to the excitement of the conflict. We suffered plenty of casualties from cracked skulls to abrasions and bruises but no fatalities. Battalions on the ground, assisted by 1 Para when necessary, controlled the riots easily enough. In November and December the tension eased to some extent.

*   *   *

I spent my days getting to know the battalions and the police in Belfast. The soldiers had a hard time. Their living conditions were basic and they had to work long hours in order to keep abreast of the situation. Some time before the arrival of a new battalion, the commanding officer and other key players such as the company commanders spent a few days in Belfast where they received a thorough briefing on the situation from the brigade staff. Shortly after its arrival I tried to give a talk to the men of each company separately, to explain what we were trying to do and why, in order to give some meaning to their endeavours. I went on doing this throughout my time in Belfast as the battalions came and went.

I also tried to gain an understanding of the varying influences at work in the city. For this purpose I spent much time visiting prominent members of the community for a chat.

Whilst this was going on some of the commanding officers developed useful contacts and Dick Gerrard-Wright got well acquainted with an IRA man who warned him that the armed neutrality between them and the army would turn to open hostility as soon as the IRA were ready to 'declare war'. By armed neutrality he evidently meant organising riots as opposed to shooting at us.

If riots broke out in the evening, I usually sat in the operations room at Lisburn listening to the brigade command net to get some idea of the way in which the situation was likely to develop. If it became clear that several battalions would become involved I would often go to the headquarters of the one most at risk. There I could discuss the situation with the colonel and decide when to bring more troops into his area if needed. If the colonel was with his men on the street, I would join him there. Sometimes Sam Bradley would appear and we would chat away until the situation eased off. At other times I might do the rounds of several of the battalion headquarters, especially if there was trouble in different parts of the city.

Occasionally, if things were going wrong, I might get personally involved in the fighting. On one occasion there was a riot on the Crumlin Road. Protestants and Catholics were confronting each other across the street and a company of Royal Marines from the Tennant Street Police Station were holding the two sides apart. I went to the Commando Headquarters to talk to the colonel, Pat Griffiths, only to hear that the company commander had been hurt and that Pat Griffiths had taken charge. As I went out of the building to find him, I passed a casualty being brought in. A nail bomb had gone off behind him and there were about a dozen nails sticking into his legs and back. I hurried on but as I approached the scene of the riot I saw Pat being carried off unconscious having been stuck by a brick which cracked his skull. For a short time I was the only officer present and found myself having to move a platoon to head off some Protestants wanting to throw bricks at the Catholics opposite. Soon other officers arrived and I managed to extricate myself. It is no part of the brigade commander's job to lead from the front in such circumstances, as it prevents him from fulfilling his proper function.

But it should not be supposed that there were riots every evening. Sometimes all that happened was the occasional explosion set off by the IRA for the purpose of encouraging their supporters during the time when they were building up their strength for active operations against the army.

Even so, when tucked up in bed, the telephone frequently rang. Usually it was the duty watch-keeper letting me know that something diabolical had occurred, but sometimes it was the local Bishop or Member of Parliament complaining that my soldiers were doing dire things to their flock, or constituents, and what was I going to do about it? It was during this period that I became aware that certain republicans seemed to be changing their names. For example the IRA Chief of Staff in Dublin who people had formerly known as John Stevenson, an ex-RAF Londoner, became Sean Mac Stiofain and a Belfast man called Frank Card became Proinsias Mac Airt.

* * *

One of the first things to strike me during these early months was the lack of civilian representation on our action committees, or with Sam and me at city level. This was particularly important in the Roman Catholic areas. After every riot there was damage to lights and pavements to say nothing of clearing up the mess. Under normal circumstances representatives of the local community, aldermen and councillors, would approach the civil authorities in the City Hall, but now they regarded this source as being strongly Protestant and unwilling or incapable of paying for and putting right the damage caused by their own people. If we had a civilian representative with access to the necessary resources they would probably come to us, but the absence of such a link provided a vacancy into which militant republicans could step. I was convinced that, if we wanted to dissuade the uncommitted members of the Catholic community from supporting the IRA, we needed to provide the civilian back up that they lacked. There were other important tasks that a civilian representative could carry out. For example civil development plans in the city could involve the provision of new housing estates, or they might result in evictions caused by the demolition of slums. In either case members of one community might find themselves moving into areas formerly dominated by the other community which in turn might land us with additional protection commitments. I felt strongly that the planning authorities should take account of our requirements in this respect which meant that we had to be represented at their meetings by a civilian who understood their ways of doing business as well as our needs. At a lower level there were many other circumstances such as sorting out rent arrears or mending power cables that required us to have proper civilian representatives within our action committees.

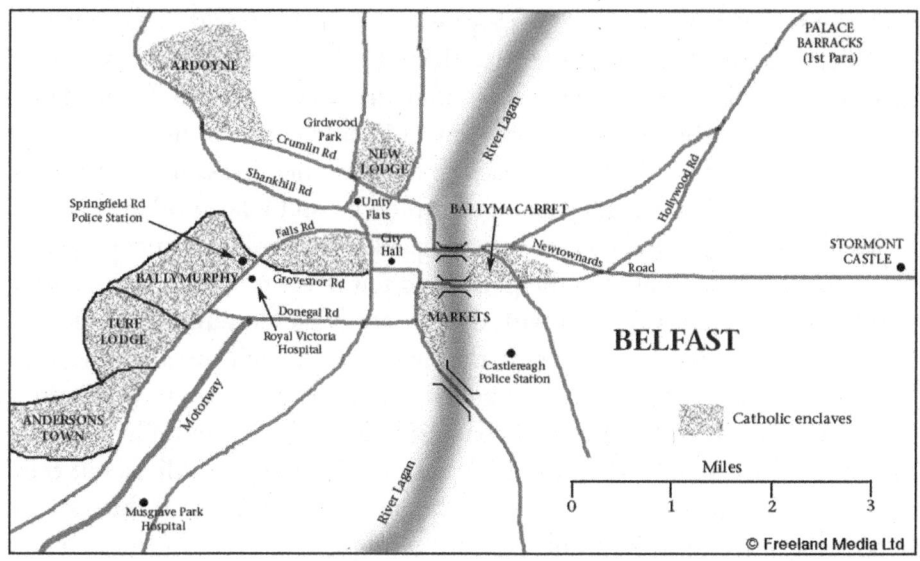

I first raised this matter with HQ Northern Ireland in early November 1970 and continued to exchange letters with them thereafter. All sorts of difficulties and red herrings raised their heads such as whether we should have Northern Ireland Civil Servants and if so from which ministry should they be drawn, or UK Civil Servants. I spent many hours discussing the matter with both Northern Ireland and UK civil representatives over the coming months. One stumbling block was that Stormont ministers were reluctant to let the army become involved in what they naturally regarded as their business. Virtually no one seemed to understand the absolute necessity of preventing the IRA from filling the local government function left open by the inability of the City Hall to operate in Catholic areas. After about a year we got our first civil representatives but by then much damage had been done.

Early in January Sam Bradley and I took another look at the tactics of handling riots in the light of the enquiry and experiments carried out by our deputies. The more we had seen the more sure we were that it was wrong to allow people to hurl abuse and missiles at soldiers or policemen and then for us to chase them away unpunished by releasing clouds of gas which seriously affected numerous uninvolved bystanders. Operating in this way amounted to condoning a serious offence and it engendered a lack of respect for the forces of law and order. Another consideration was that it naturally infuriated the troops so that they were tempted to get their own back when dealing with the civilian population during searches for weapons or at vehicle checkpoints. We agreed that it was essential that every time there was a riot some of the rioters should be arrested, put in front of a court and punished.

The system that we decided to adopt was that there should be a front line of soldiers sited to hold the rioters, so that snatch squads could be sent into them from the flank or rear, very soon after the trouble started. Each snatch squad would be lightly equipped and armed mainly with batons so that they could snatch a rioter and get him back to a place where he could be put and held in a vehicle. The snatch squad could then go and take another prisoner. In this way each of a number of snatch squads could collect a few prisoners who would be handed over to the police and put in front of a magistrate next morning. When experimenting with this system Dick Gerrard-Wright found that most riots broke up as soon as the first lot of snatch squads moved in. Anyone resisting would be swiftly subdued, using the minimum force required for making the arrest. No one would be hurt unless they resisted. These tactics had to be adjusted later when the IRA took to shooting at soldiers, but they eventually developed into a doctrine that became standard practice throughout the Province. We introduced one further reform, which was to prohibit the use of gas in Belfast in order to avoid hurting those not involved in violence. Small patrols continued to carry gas canisters but only for use if surrounded by a hostile crowd. Long after we had stopped using gas, it continued to be used in Londonderry, so that in Belfast we called it 'Londonderry Air'.

During January 1971 the pace quickened and there were some vicious riots in the middle of the month in Ballymurphy, which included the use of large numbers of petrol bombs. As the days went by riots broke out in other parts of the city, some of which included the use of firearms. To give some idea of the pace of events it is worth looking at what happened during the first week of February. During the morning of 3 February some houses were searched near Falls Road. As a result a crowd of protesters assembled, hurling abuse and the odd missile at the soldiers, who soon dispersed them using a few baton rounds. In the afternoon a small crowd erected several barricades in a nearby street using hijacked vehicles which they set alight. Later, more crowds gathered and troops were greeted with bricks, bottles and petrol bombs. Eventually these people were dispersed by a combination of baton guns and snatch squads but by now disturbances were developing in other parts of the Belfast such as Ballymurphy. In two places automatic fire was directed at our posts without much damage being done.

Later in the evening some Protestants set off from the Shankill towards the Catholic area and further troops were needed to contain them. At this point 1 Para was moved onto their usual concentration area at the city end of the Shankill Road outside the Catholic Unity Flats. At the same time our armoured car squadron moved in to guard the bridges across the Lagan, which we could not risk having blocked because we needed them to move our reserves and heavy engineer equipment. Shortly afterwards a soldier received a nasty wound from a nail bomb and there was an exchange of missiles between Catholics and Protestants across Springfield Road that runs north-west from Falls Road. There was also minor trouble in Andersonstown. Just before midnight a soldier was seriously wounded by gunfire in a street just to the south of Falls Road and early next morning another was wounded by a bomb nearby. Next, trouble broke out in the small Catholic enclave either side of New Lodge Road, some way to the north and a bit east of the Falls where several soldiers were injured by bombs and another shot and seriously wounded. Here it was necessary to use 1 Para to restore order. Thereafter the whole city settled down so that peace reigned by about 3 am. It had been a busy day but fairly typical except that there was rather more shooting than usual.

Events followed a similar pattern next day, which was 4 February, with rioting around Falls Road following a morning search for weapons. A soldier was seriously wounded by a nail bomb in the afternoon and a normal scale of rioting got going in the evening and continued with some shooting but no further casualties until about midnight. There was also minor rioting in Ballymurphy. The New Lodge area also played up into the early hours. The Ardoyne which was the other most active Catholic area caused some trouble including the erection of barricades, some use of explosives and a bit of shooting, but all was quiet there by the early hours of 5 February.

During the afternoon of 5 February there was a further spate of hijacking and burning vehicles. On this occasion the worst incidents occurred in the Ardoyne which necessitated the deployment of 1 Para for the second night running. Late in the evening one of their snatch squads breaking up a riot, was fired on and their vehicle set on fire. As the crew baled out one of the soldiers was shot and wounded. In the subsequent fire-fight several of the assailants were thought to have been hit and later, after an army post was shot at, a gunman was definitely killed. At about this time further trouble erupted in the New Lodge area and troops advancing down New Lodge Road came under fire, one man being seriously wounded and another killed. He was the first fatal army casualty since the army was deployed in August 1969. Over the next few days things gradually eased off. It usually happened that periods of intense activity only lasted for three or four days at the most, after which there would be a period of comparative quiet.

During a busy period such as we had just experienced the men on the street got very tired. In the Brigade Headquarters Operations Room in Lisburn the brigade major, Peter Graham, assisted by the GSO 3, Ralph Cowdy and a raft of watch-keepers would be constantly following events in order to keep me fully informed. It was my business to ensure that reserves were despatched to the right place, which included the provision of the heavy engineer equipment needed to remove barricades made of burning buses and cars. If I was temporarily unavailable the brigade major would take the necessary action. The vital thing was to ensure that there was always at least a company capable of moving at short notice to prevent a disaster and also that the route along which it had to go was not blocked. From the point of view of the team in the operations room it was like playing a complicated game of chess for hours on end.

Meanwhile I would probably be moving from one battalion to the next as the situation developed, sometimes in their headquarters and sometimes on the street. Over the coming months I seemed to spend quite a lot of time with companies of 1 Para on the waste ground outside Unity Flats where they would be waiting to be launched in the required direction. On these occasions I was well provided with cups of tea and the usual banter by the driver/operators of their respective commanders many of whom I got to know pretty well.

At this time soldiers were still allowed to visit hotels and pubs in civilian clothes away from the troubled areas when off duty. Early in March an ex-serviceman approached three men of the Royal Highland Fusiliers in a bar and offered to take them off to have a drink with some of his friends. Soon afterwards, glasses in hand, they were relieving themselves outside a pub when they were all shot in the back of the head. They were 20, 18 and 17 years old, two being brothers. There was a great outcry from Protestants and Catholics alike. Both wings of the IRA claimed to have had nothing to do with the killing, although there is little doubt that it was the work of some Provisionals from the Ardoyne, possibly unauthorised by their senior officers.

*   *   *

By now Jim Chichester-Clark, the Prime Minister, was being severely harassed by his supporters, who were fed up with the concessions being given to the Catholics and what they regarded as the feebleness of the Westminster government's approach to the business of wiping out the IRA. Jim, therefore, demanded massive military reinforcement and a change of approach, which the British Prime Minister Heath either could not or would not provide. Jim resigned, probably with a sigh of relief, his place being taken by the experienced politician, Brian Faulkner. Although he had not been in the army and was therefore looked upon with some suspicion by a certain section of the community. My own feeling was that at this particular moment political expertise was more use than a good regimental background.

By March I was beginning to see that our plans for persuading Catholics not to support the IRA, whilst trying to weaken it by such direct action as could be carried out within the law, were not progressing too well. There were probably many reasons for this but two were more obvious than the rest. The first was that we were constantly alienating the Catholic community by searching for weapons on the strength of Special Branch information sent down to us via Headquarters Northern Ireland with direct orders that we should use it. On many occasions the commanding officer in whose area the search was to take place, complained that the fuss it would cause was not worth the damage done to the IRA, even if we did find the odd rifle or pistol, but I was given no discretion in the matter. I was told by the Commander Land Forces (CLF), Tony Farrar-Hockley, that informers would have risked their lives to get the information and if we did not act on it they would no longer work for Special Branch.

It seemed to me more likely that Special Branch was feeding us the information to help the Stormont government, in the knowledge that the ensuing search would cause a disturbance that we would then have to put down. This would enable Stormont ministers to say to their supporters that we were 'ruthlessly pursuing' the IRA. What I wanted was for Special Branch to give our battalion commanders the information, copy to me, so that we could use it to harass the IRA when it would not harm our relations with the population as a whole and not use it when it would. General Freeland, the Chief Constable and Tony Farrar-Hockley had endorsed our plan, which was now known as 'De-escalation and Attrition' and commanding officers, together with the police divisional commanders, were the best people to work out how to balance the two prongs of our approach. But of course in all sorts of war, long term plans are often subject to dislocation when confronted by immediate political pressures. I did not expect to be immune from this, but I should have liked to know exactly what was going on so that I could explain it to the people responsible for implementing the plan.

In February, Ian Freeland came to the end of his time as GOC and was replaced by Lieutenant General Erskine-Crum who died almost immediately of a heart attack. Erskine-Crum was then replaced by Lieutenant General Sir Harry Tuzo. Tony Farrar-Hockley, had therefore been obliged to get on terms with two new GOCs within as many months. This would have restricted his opportunities for getting the GOC to persuade Special Branch to operate in a more sensible way, had he wanted to do so. But I did not even know whether he did want to. Sometimes he accepted my objection to doing a search and sometimes not. Because he was loyal to a fault he would never say I agree with your objection but my orders are to do this or that. Except for matters relating to the deployment of forces to cover processions or periods of widespread unrest, I wanted to decentralise most decisions to the battalion and company commanders, not just the decision to do this or that search. I saw my job as being to teach them in general terms how to do their business and then to put them in to bat in the best possible circumstances. My view was that the acquisition and exploitation of information, meant absorbing so much detail that the work needed to be done by someone on the spot. By contrast Farrar-Hockley felt that we should get involved in the day-to-day conduct of local operations, presumably so as to meet he political needs of the GOC.

And from the GOC's point of view the political position was difficult in the extreme. The nub of the problem was that he was serving two masters whose needs and aspirations were diametrically opposed to each other. As GOC Northern Ireland he was responsible through the Chief of the General Staff, to the Westminster government whose policy was based on removing the unfairness between the two communities in Northern Ireland in order to defuse the trouble. As the Director of Operations he was responsible for assisting the Northern Ireland government to fulfil its responsibility for maintaining law and order. But the Northern Ireland government's electoral support came from the Protestant community which was determined to hang onto many of the measures that the Westminster government wanted to remove because it saw them as existing to prevent the unification of Ireland.

The only sensible way in which the problem could be resolved was for the Westminster government to take direct control of the Province, as later happened. But at the time the Westminster government wanted to avoid this, probably because it needed the support of the Northern Irish Unionist MPs at Westminster to get important parts of its legislative measures through Parliament and because removing it might result in a Protestant backlash. As a result the GOC was sometimes obliged to do things to keep the Stormont government in power, that ran counter to the Westminster government's requirements and at other times he had to go against the wishes of the Northern Ireland government to satisfy Westminster. Furthermore both governments tended to live from day-to-day which meant that the GOC sometimes found himself pressed to do something or other, merely to save one or other of the governments from a public relations embarrassment. Tony Farrar-Hockley's preferred way of doing business provided the necessary flexibility, but made the long-term plan agreed between Sam Bradley and myself and approved by him and the GOC, less likely to work. The difference of approach between us made life a bit difficult at times.

*   *   *

By the middle of March it was very clear that, quite apart from the matter of searches, the getting of intelligence and the handling of it, was not working. As in Malaya, battalion and company commanders not only needed any contact information that Special Branch might discover, but they also needed direct access to Special Branch officers so as to benefit from their detailed background knowledge. Without it they would not be well placed to exploit the information gathered by their patrols and from men in observation posts. At the end of the month I wrote a long paper about intelligence which I sent to the Director of Security at Headquarters Northern Ireland. In it I spelt out in great detail exactly what was needed. I even included a fictitious example showing the many steps that a company commander might have to go through in order to find and capture an IRA man taking a weapon from an arms dump. This was just the sort of attrition that we could inflict within the law as it stood, because the evidence would support a conviction in court. I also explained how important such close contact would be to Special Branch if at some future date, it was decided to bring in detention without trial.

Anticipating opposition from Special Branch, I pointed out that no great organisational changes were required. They already had men on the ground some of whom were actually based in police stations that were co-located with our own battalion or company headquarters. Furthermore the Special Branch superintendent covering Belfast worked from Sam Bradley's headquarters where I maintained a small operations room. All that was necessary was to accept that these people should work directly with us and not just pass everything up to Special Branch Headquarters. I also pointed out that such a change would assist the splendid Special Branch men themselves, as they would pick up useful information from us. As a result of our constant presence on the streets we might even be able to put them in touch with potential informers. I knew all this to be true because we had already been working unofficially with some of the Special Branch men to our mutual benefit. In any case we had just such a link with the Criminal Investigation Branch despite the fact that they officially operated in the same way as the Special Branch.

By the end of March 1971 I was convinced that we were suffering from one other serious handicap which was that the four-month tour for our deployed battalions was too short. It took the first month for them to get a full understanding of the situation and to sort through such information as their predecessor's had left them. After that there were only three months when they were fully effective and even then, in the last week or two, they were thinking about their next move and briefing the advance party of the battalion that would be taking over from them. I wanted tour lengths increased to six or nine months.

At this time I wrote down on a sheet of paper the things we most needed, if we were to achieve our aim and pinned it to the wall of my office where it stayed until I left the Province over a year later. These were: CIVIL REPRESENTATION. BATTALION TOURS EXTENDED TO AT LEAST SIX MONTHS.

DIRECT ACCESS TO SPECIAL BRANCH, WITH INTELLIGENCE
PASSED DOWN TO COMPANY COMMANDERS. THE CO-
LOCATION OF MILITARY AND POLICE AS FAR AS POSSIBLE.

By Easter there was an easing off of direct IRA action, probably because their
recent activity had alienated some members of their own community who either
thought that they were going too far or who disliked having their immediate
surroundings turned into a battle ground. Also in March the feuding between
the Official and Provisional IRA came to a head. We did not know the details
at the time but realised that something was going on. Apparently my asthmatic
friend from the Central Citizens Defence Committee having been shot at in
a pub by Provisionals, later captured a number of them including Frank Card
otherwise known as Proinsias Mac Airt. The captives were on the point of being
murdered when the feuding was brought to an end by negotiations brokered by
the local priests. It would have saved us a lot of trouble had the rival factions
been allowed to get on with it, but one can hardly blame priests for trying to
save the lives of their flock.

I was never quite able to decide how the Roman Catholic Church viewed the
fighting. We, perhaps naively, supposed that their priests must be on the side of
law and order and deplore the violence of the IRA. Probably most did deplore
it, but there were some who were republican sympathisers and others who
possibly thought that the security forces brought the violence on themselves. I
had constant contact with them, particularly the ones based at St Peter and St
Paul's twin-towered church just down the hill from Divis Flats. Their leader,
Canon Murphy, was courted by politicians and other influential visitors. I
did not find him particularly easy, though always polite, but his number two,
Father Taggart became a good friend. If I ever mentioned the name of an IRA
man he would usually describe him as a foolish old man who meant no great
harm, even if he was one of the leaders. Priests as a whole seemed to dislike the
Officials more than the Provisionals because of their Marxist background. I
well remember Father Taggart saying one day after an Official had been killed
'Far be it from me to wish anyone dead, but if anyone had to go, he was one
that we could all afford to lose.' On another occasion he asked me who we were
referring to on the command net, when we mentioned 'uplift' or 'downdraft.'
He said he knew all the terms normally used in the appointment code such as
'Sunray' for the commander or 'Seagull' for the chief staff officer, but he had
never heard of theses two. I explained that they were names we had invented
for the padre and the pioneer sergeant as they were not included on the official
list. I asked him in return why he was listening to our wireless net and he said
that he had to keep in touch with events so as to know when to nip out and
give someone the last rites.

The easing off of direct IRA action was offset by the advent of the Protestant marching season. From Easter until the middle of August innumerable Protestant processions wound their way along sensitive interfaces between the two communities, goading the Catholics and increasing the IRA's ability to foment trouble. Protestant marching also helped to turn uncommitted Catholics against us for not stopping the nuisance.

Only those who have witnessed Protestant marches, can have any idea of what it was like. If the procession was sponsored by an Orange Lodge, it was headed by a uniformed band followed by the officers of the Lodge, wearing neatly pressed suits, bowler hats and carrying drawn swords, escorting the banner of the Lodge. Behind them marched the rank and file. If it was only one Lodge on the march, the procession was soon over and the marchers usually well behaved. In this case the provocation lay mainly in the route taken and in the sound of the band playing the well-known Protestant tunes. But sometimes when passing the ends of Catholic streets, unruly members of the rank and file raised two fingers and shouted uncomplimentary things about the Pope, in which case equally unfortunate suggestions regarding the Queen might wing their way back. Such banter often developed into an exchange of missiles and a full-scale riot if not stopped. This meant that whenever a march was passing a sensitive area, there had to be an adequate police or military presence.

* * *

One advantage of the marching season was that as the marches were planned well ahead, it was possible to predict likely moments of tension and make our arrangements accordingly. Most of this planning was being done by the brigade staff, who were working with great efficiency under the direction of Major Peter Graham and on the administrative side, under Major Tony Hare. Peter was brilliant at keeping any number of balls in the air at the same time and had a wonderfully soothing effect on the priests, Stormont MPs and visitors who wanted to discover what was happening or burden me with their troubles. Without him acting as a filter, I would have had no time to get anything done. Tony Hare had a formidable task trying to improve the lot of the soldiers dotted around in the city in all sorts of odd places on whose behalf he worked day and night. His tireless efforts greatly improved their conditions. I also had an efficient deputy, called Colonel Nick Carter, who was perfectly capable of commanding the many battalions and companies that had to be deployed for even the most complicated marching programme.

But despite all this high-powered help I was still busy even in quiet periods. By now I was commanding my seven battalions plus two battalions of the Ulster

Defence Regiment, plus an engineer regiment and an armoured reconnaissance squadron. I also had administrative command of 3 Queen's, the Province Reserve Battalion commanded by Ken Dodson, that lived at Ballykinler and which came under my operational command when not required elsewhere in Northern Ireland. The Ulster Defence Regiment had been formed when the Police Reserve was disbanded in order to retain its military potential, but under the control of the army and therefore the Westminster government as opposed to Stormomt. My two UDR battalions were not supposed to be used in large numbers in Belfast for good political reasons, but they did an immensely useful job providing static guards, escorts and vehicle checkpoints around the edge of the city. Without them the tasks they carried out would have fallen to the regular battalions and therefore would have eaten into the number of regular soldiers that we had available. Like the police, they lived in their own houses and came on and went off duty as required. They and their families had little protection when off duty and many were murdered in the course of The Troubles. The United Kingdom owes them a tremendous debt of gratitude.

In early May Sam Bradley and I ran a study day for all police divisional commanders and battalion commanding officers, company commanders and intelligence officers, to take stock of our de-escalation and attrition plan. Introducing it, I said that the most important factor governing our activity was the legal situation, which obliged us to deal with subversive elements of the population in accordance with the ordinary law of the land as there were no emergency regulations giving us additional powers. We then covered four different aspects of the plan, each introduced by a police or army officer, namely community relations, other methods of communicating with the population, developing projects designed to get at extremists, and riot tactics.

I took the period on developing a project, during which I explained how a chain reaction of information, leading to action to get more information, leading to further action might be applied. Starting with a bit of background information to the effect that there was an IRA company in one area of Belfast which was part of a battalion whose headquarters was somewhere else, I produced a series of possible events to show how the idea might work. For example many bits of information obtained by patrols and by overt and covert observation posts, could be put together and possible links between suspect persons and places, worked out. Vehicle checkpoints could then be sited specifically to test the validity of these theories. And so on through several stages leading, possibly, to the arrest of an IRA member or supporter. In the course of carrying out this procedure it should be possible to get enough evidence to get the person convicted in court for some offence that would at least get him sent away for a short period. My purpose was not to say exactly how it should be done, but to stimulate interest in the process, thereby giving our people the feeling that there was at least something that they could do within the existing law to harm terrorists. It was similar to the example I used in my letter to the Director of Security in March.

A worrying aspect of the situation that we did not touch on during our study day, was the extent to which public opinion in both north and south of Ireland, as well as in the UK and even abroad seem to be manipulated to our disadvantage by republican sympathisers. It was of course natural that the IRA should attempt to get their line across in the media and to discredit the government and its forces by accusing them of all sorts of abuses. That is a normal facet of any campaign of this sort. But it is essential that the government should monitor such activity, refute the accusations, prosecute those advocating criminal activity when expedient and put across its own line, hard and continuously. I often discussed the matter with Tony Farrar-Hockley who eventually managed to establish an information policy cell in Headquarters Northern Ireland which did great work. But the army can only assist the government in getting the right information across to the public. It can advise and help but there is such a strong political aspect to the business that it can not set up and do the job itself. Nonetheless the situation was depressing. On several occasions Sam Bradley made the point that we were not having our hands tied by the law so much as by not being allowed to use the law fully. He felt that we could do considerable damage if permitted to charge people for conspiracy and seditious libel, but prosecutions in these categories were not being permitted.

Apart from the marching, April had been a quiet month. Early in May I was glad to welcome Roly Guy and 1 RGJ to Belfast. They were to look after the Catholic heartland of Lower Falls and the area around Divis Flats and also the markets. Soon after their arrival they had a corporal killed in an ambush but on the whole Belfast was again reasonably quiet in May except for an increase in the number of explosions. In one of these an IRA supporter left a parcel in the charge office of Springfield Road Police Station when it was full of women and children. Had it not been for the supreme bravery of a sergeant of the Parachute Regiment who hurled himself across the bomb, there would have been a lot of casualties. In the event he was killed but the others escaped. That police station was also the headquarters of a police division and of 3 Para, which looked after a stretch of Belfast that included several of the worst Catholic areas including Ballymurphy and the western end of Lower Falls.

With the marching season at its peak, June 1971 miraculously passed without any serious confrontation, although in July things warmed up considerably. Now the number and size of explosions increased and there were four in the city centre on the day before the culmination of the marching season when all the lodges combined to commemorate King William III's victory at the Battle of the Boyne in 1691. That battle must have been a noisy affair but probably no more so than that the racket made in Belfast on 12 July 1971. Fortunately nothing worse than noise happened on that day but on each of the six days following the 12th there were a series of large explosions which caused much damage and a number of civilian casualties. They included the destruction of the *Daily Mirror*'s offices and the telephone exchange.

The IRA also opened fire on some of our bases, which resulted in the loss of another soldier killed and a number of others wounded.

Up to this point we had relied on our men in observation posts to give us warning of gathering crowds or the erection of barricades but they could not see a terrorist surreptitiously depositing a bomb. It was in response to this threat that the idea arose of having what amounted to mobile observation posts in the form of soldiers in plain clothes patrolling in unmarked civilian cars, on the look out for bombers. They could drive around or sit in car parks or other suitable spots and call up foot patrols to investigate suspicious movement. They could even tackle a bomber themselves if necessary. Who originally thought up this idea I can not now remember, but like all original ideas it probably came from a couple of people chatting together and then someone picking it up and putting flesh and bones on it. Certainly I backed it and Tony Farrar-Hockley was enthusiastic. As a result HQ Northern Ireland provided us with a captain to head the team and a number of NCOs to man it. In its early days it was called the Bomb Squad but we soon changed it to the Mobile Reconnaissance Force or MRF. As time went on we enlarged it and provided it with a lot of sophisticated night-fighting equipment and weapons.

*   *   *

Tony Farrar-Hockley was due to hand over his job in August and it was thought desirable that I should get some leave before he departed. For the last ten months I had been pretty busy in Belfast and with the children's school holidays coming up I too thought it would be a good idea. Just before I left Tony told me that there was a plan to arrest some of the IRA leaders whose names we knew, even though it would probably be impossible to convict them of an offence. I said that it would be total madness, as it would put them on their guard and make it much more difficult to catch them if internment was ever brought in. He said that the increased level of violence which was affecting Londonderry and other parts of the Province as much as Belfast, had made it politically necessary to do something and no one could think of anything better to do under the circumstances. As usual I did not know whether he agreed with the idea or not. All I could get him to say was that nothing would be done until I returned from leave. With that I went.

Chapter 9

Northern Ireland:
Insurgency and Internment 1971–1972

W e had arranged to spend part of my leave at Monk's Hill and part in Devon. On 24 July I read in the newspaper with intense annoyance, that a number of IRA members had been arrested in Northern Ireland; presumably as a result of the operation that Tony Farrar-Hockley had said would not happen until after I returned from leave. General Carver who was now Chief of the General Staff, had asked us to go to his house for a drink after church the next day and on arrival I asked him what on earth was going on in Northern Ireland. He said he thought I was going to tell him, implying that he knew nothing about it. I told him what I knew, adding that I was strongly opposed to that particular line of action as it would prejudice the success of any subsequent arrest operation that might take place if internment was introduced. I also said that I had been assured that nothing of the sort would happen while I was away. He changed the subject and we stopped talking about Ireland.

I returned to Ireland early on the morning of 3 August to discover that Tony Farrar-Hockley had already left. My first task was to discover what had been going on in my absence and to prepare a briefing for the new Commander Land Forces, Major General Robert Ford. Although he had little direct knowledge of counter-insurgency operations, he had other sorts of combat experience. He also knew a lot about the workings of the higher reaches of the Ministry of Defence, having worked there for the Chief of the Defence Staff when I was in ASD 2. As I soon discovered, he was a commander who understood exactly how to delegate responsibility to his subordinates whilst keeping a close watch on the success of their efforts.

That Saturday shots were fired at Springfield Road Police Station, which now housed 2 Para as well as the police divisional headquarters. There were several Protestant marches to protect and some trouble at a football match. In the evening there was rioting in Springfield Road and barricades were erected in Falls Road which we had to remove. There was also shooting and rioting in the Ardoyne. It was noticeable that incidents persisted later than usual and even at 4 am on Sunday morning the streets had not cleared. Not wanting to start the operation on Monday morning while disturbances were still in progress, we decided to delay it until 4.30pm.

On the Saturday evening a police superintendent arrived at 39th Brigade Headquarters with a letter from the Chief Constable requiring me to assist the police in carrying out the arrest of members of the public, as listed. Although the decision to implement internment had been taken by the government and I had been ordered by my military superiors to make the arrests in conjunction with the police, I still had to be asked by the Chief Constable to do so before it could be justifiable in law. Furthermore, once asked, I was obliged by law to provide the necessary assistance. When we looked at the list we were amazed. There were 280 names on it most of which had never been given to us by Special Branch before. It looked to us as if Special Branch had added anyone they thought to be subversive to their known list of insurgents in order to boost the numbers. The superintendent who brought the list was obviously hugely upset if not totally distracted, so Peter sent an officer in a Land Rover to follow him home in case he ran into the ditch. We rapidly broke down the list, sending the relevant names and addresses to battalions.

Sunday turned out to be even worse than Saturday with riots and hijacking going on in several areas. There were no less than thirteen major shooting incidents and another soldier was killed. On the Sunday night I visited the units in Belfast most heavily involved with the fighting, as usual. Our efforts that night were directed at getting the disturbances over as quickly as possible by being very firm and in this we were successful as the streets were clear by 3.30 am on Monday morning. By 4.30 all our arrest teams were ready and in they went. They either found their man or drew blank, thereafter getting back before the IRA could come into action.

The prisoners were all taken to the Territorial Army Centre at Girdwood Park where Special Branch screening teams set to work sorting out the take. We succeeded in picking up about half the men on the list, which was considered to be a success.

During this period I remained in Belfast to get a first hand impression of the IRA's reaction which was much as expected. Busses and lorries were hijacked and burnt at the entrance to all the main Catholic areas, whilst houses, factories and other buildings were set on fire. By now it was broad daylight and moving between the battalions I saw the clouds of smoke that hung across parts of the city. After visiting Girdwood Park, I returned to brigade headquarters to get a good overall assessment of the situation in the city. Naturally the media were actively enjoying themselves especially when a senior IRA man held a news conference in Ballymurphy in an attempt to demonstrate the impotence of the security forces.

In order to make up the number of arrest teams required, I had attached companies of 1 Para to the most exposed deployed battalions. I left the companies with these battalions during Monday to help with handling the backlash, with particular reference to preventing any confrontations between Catholics and Protestants along the interfaces. That evening we received two extra battalions to cover us for the immediate future and I speedily withdrew the companies of 1 Para so as to have them concentrated and ready for the next job. By the early hours of Tuesday the streets were clear of rioters but every Catholic area was totally barricaded and access was impossible for our men.

I had anticipated that this would be the case and was quite determined that there would be nowhere in Belfast where our troops could not go, which was in any case the general's policy. In all insurgencies a most important objective for the enemy is to have an area where they alone hold sway and where they can take people from all around the world and say this is our territory where only our flag flies. I also knew that unless we got on with the job of establishing our position, there would be a number of people offering to negotiate the barricades down over a period of weeks or months, in return for various concessions that would inevitably provoke the Protestants. We therefore issued orders for a series of operations to take place to remove the barricades over the next few days.

At first light next morning, Tuesday, 10 August, I was sitting in the command vehicle of the battalion that was starting to dismantle barricades round the Ardoyne. Actually I was lying rather than sitting, as I thought that while they were busy I might as well take a nap to prepare me for the next day, nonetheless remaining available should anything go wrong. All went well, resistance was light and after a vast amount of rubble was moved from the road we could come and go in the Ardoyne from then onwards as we wished.

On Wednesday we cleared out the markets area, Ballymurphy and Turf Lodge and on Thursday we cleared the remaining barricades in Falls Road and Springfield Road. All these operations involved a certain amount of shooting so that our men experienced what amounted to a low level of street fighting rather than normal counter-insurgency. Early on Friday, 12 August a few isolated pockets were tidied up and by midday the whole city was opened up and quiet.

Overall resistance would have been worse had not many members of the regular IRA, both Provisional and Official, disappeared to the Republic leaving defence of the barricades largely to the auxiliaries and the youth movement. But, as in the Ardoyne, the security forces never again in my time had any difficulty in going wherever they pleased in Belfast. The past week had been tiring for all of us and we had sustained about thirty casualties. It is difficult to know how many casualties were inflicted on the IRA and their auxiliaries because, in accordance with their normal procedure, the IRA tried to spirit their wounded away and get them over the border to be treated where they could not be arrested.

It was a great stroke of luck that at this testing time we had such splendid battalions in the most difficult places. As always, 1 Para, which Derek Wilford had taken over from Mike Gray in June, had done wonders, helping out in one trouble spot to the next.

From a purely military point of view the operation had been successful to the extent that we had picked up a reasonable number of the people on the Chief Constable's list and quickly overcome the subsequent disturbances. But I was annoyed for a number of reasons. First, because the July arrests had alerted the major IRA players to the danger so that few of them were arrested. Second, because of the 140 arrested in Belfast, only nine were to be interrogated: the facilities for interrogating more of them did not exist so anything they might have known would be wasted. Third, because the government information services were not ready to monitor republican propaganda and put over the government line effectively while the republican press was pouring out its version of events at record speed with scant concern for the truth. Fourth, because internment had been introduced in such a way as to ensure the maximum amount of opposition from the Catholic community which received no apparent advantage except for the banning of all marches for six months.

Although this would at least mean the cancellation of a Protestant march in Londonderry on 12 August, it did not amount to much. Sam Bradley and I had on one or two occasions discussed the way in which internment should be introduced. His idea was that it should be restricted to an initial lift of around twenty people of whom two or three should be Protestants who, though not actually involved in terrorism at the moment, had been in the past and would certainly be so again if the opportunity arose. My idea was that there should be no great operation, but when someone was arrested who we wanted but could not get to court, we should detain him and say that he was being held under the Civil Authorities Special Powers Act. There would doubtless be an outcry in the press, which would have to be followed by an official announcement from the government that it reserved the right to use the Act as and when necessary. It appears from other peoples' recollections that at a conference held by the Robert Ford soon after the internment operation, I described it as being 'the right measure introduced in the wrong way, at the wrong time, for the wrong reason.' I certainly do not remember saying it, but it perfectly reflected my views at the time.

Of course, in a wider context, we were now in a stronger position to the extent that our powers of attrition were hugely improved. Because it was no longer necessary to get a person convicted in court, we could get rid of the IRA leaders who we had never been able to touch before, providing that we could identify and find them. All we needed was the intelligence and we could start weakening the hold that the IRA had on the Catholic population. And as that happened it was vitally important that we should be able to fill the gap with our own civil representatives. On the Sunday after internment was introduced, I fired off another brief letter to HQ Northern Ireland saying that this was our last chance and that unless we got our civil representative and direct access to the intelligence organisation immediately, we would not succeed. Looking back on it I am slightly surprised that this letter, taken together with my remarks at Robert Ford's conference, did not result in my removal.

Luckily I was not removed and the reforms that I had asked for started to be implemented, bit by bit. Within a fortnight a Northern Ireland Civil Servant was appointed to work with Sam and me and it was agreed that additional Civil Servants would be appointed to the Divisional Action Committees providing that the first man confirmed that they were necessary. This he did and additional men arrived over the next few months.

*   *   *

In order to ensure that wanted men should at least be interviewed in future, Sam Bradley decided to set up a police holding centre in Belfast, which he would man with uniformed police. I agreed that the army would build it. Miraculously Special Branch Headquarters agreed to lend Sam a few men under an inspector to carry out the interviews and authorised that they should be held for up to 48 hours before being passed on into the detention centre. Now at least anyone arrested in Belfast under the Special Powers Act would be sensibly processed. The scheme proved so successful that Belfast was soon being asked to take men captured in other parts of the Province. Eventually police holding centres were set up in other places to handle this commitment.

The next advance came about because the Special Branch men charged with the responsibility for talking to the prisoners found that they could not do so unless they knew a bit about the person being interrogated. When Special Branch HQ was asked for the records they were found to be out of date or non-existent. By contrast our records based on what Special Branch had told us over the years together with what our patrols and observation posts had discovered, were properly collated and available. In order to overcome the delay of requests going to and from our intelligence staff at Lisburn, we moved a small records section with a duplicate set of records to the police holding centre. Initially these people merely provided information from the records to the interrogators as required, but soon they were also able to insert information gained by the interrogators into the records thus adding to our overall knowledge. Also, although the members of the army records section were not permitted to take part or attend the interrogations, commanding officers or their intelligence officers could ask the interrogators to see whether they could discover things that they particularly wanted to know. But like the members of the records section they were not permitted to be present at the interrogations.

Apart from a swift and impressive addition to the amount of intelligence gained, the closeness of the relationship between the army records section and the interrogators forged a bond between the two sides which turned out to be as strong as the links between the interrogators and their superiors at Special Branch HQ. Soon official recognition was given to what had happened and we were allowed to supply a second records section to work with the Special Branch cell at Belfast City Police HQ. Finally in December 1971 it was agreed that direct links could be established between Special Branch and the army and police at police divisional level, which is exactly what I had been asking for since October 1970, at which time it was already a year too late.

But the army and the police could now get on with arresting and interning members of the IRA without having to get the sort of evidence necessary for obtaining a conviction in court, which meant that there was a clear purpose to our operations that all could understand. Before internment, the message coming down from HQ Northern Ireland was blurred and subject to endless adjustments designed to fit the confused political position. We never quite knew where we were. Now Robert Ford was able to tell us exactly what was expected of us and he was very good at doing it. But I am getting ahead of events because a certain amount happened between August and December 1971.

The rest of August and the first three weeks of September were relatively quiet so far as rioting was concerned but there was a steady series of explosions and a number of sniping incidents. There was also a degree of Protestant discontent at what they saw as the failure of internment to deal with the IRA, which could have resulted in incursions into Catholic areas had we not deployed a considerable amount of troops to prevent it. It was at this time that a number of small local Protestant groups coalesced into the Ulster Defence Association (UDA) designed to defend their community against attacks by the IRA. Hitherto the only Protestant paramilitary force of any consequence had been the Ulster Volunteer Force (UVF) which liked to trace its ancestry back to 1914 but which had in fact been put together in 1966 to dispose of active republicans. After a short time during which it committed a few very unpleasant murders, the Northern Ireland government banned it.

*   *   *

By the autumn of 1971 the most urgent thing was to dismantle the IRA's organisation so that a political settlement could be reached with a Catholic community no longer living in fear of their own people. At the time of internment the Provisional IRA had a brigade headquarters and three battalions each of about six companies, each of which consisted of about twenty-five men. It was backed by companies of auxiliaries, less well armed than the regulars, a number of youth companies and a woman's section. The officials also had a brigade headquarters and three battalions though with fewer companies, also backed by auxiliaries, a youth movement and a woman's section.

Some of our people thought that both organisations were much bigger than necessary for waging war on the government, but they failed to understand that their main purpose was to maintain a grip over the Catholic population for which they needed a large number of adherents. It was our job to break up these organisations to the extent where the Roman Catholic community ceased having to support them and could engage in a realistic relationship with the government. In any case, from our point of view, the size of their organisations gave good opportunities for penetration and the collection of information.

By the end of September we had nine regular battalions in Belfast, some of which were in fact armoured or artillery regiments operating in the infantry role. We also retained our armoured reconnaissance squadron, our squadron of engineers and our two battalions of the Ulster Defence Regiment.

In practice our efforts had to be split between defensive operations such as controlling riots and defending people and installations on the one hand, and offensive operations designed to root out the IRA on the other. It was imperative to get the balance right. If we put too much of our resources into offensive operations at the expense of security, the death and destruction caused by the ensuing riots and explosions, would pressurise the government into coming to an agreement with the republicans that would cause a serious reaction from the Protestants. If we put too much of our effort into defensive operations, we would not be able to free the Catholic population from IRA intimidation to the extent needed for a sensible settlement to be reached. Inevitably for political reasons, I was obliged to expend much of our effort on defensive tasks. It was therefore important to make the very best use of what was left for rooting out the IRA. That meant getting the battalion and company commanders to build up projects as described earlier, making maximum use of the vastly increased flow of information now available and the fact that it was no longer necessary to have the sort of evidence need for a conviction in court.

The publicity evoked by the internment operation resulted in the arrival of a record number of visitors who had to be briefed and taken round Belfast 'to see the situation for themselves.' Newspaper editors and opposition politicians arrived in droves, many of whom were taken round the city by my long suffering deputy, Nick Carter. But obviously I had to brief and conduct most of the senior officers and members of the government, which took time.

The first to arrive, just two weeks after the operation, was the Parliamentary Undersecretary for Defence, Geoffrey Johnson Smith, who was also one of the most clear minded and understanding of our political visitors. He appeared at the very moment when a great uproar was going on in the press about the way the few people that had been interrogated after the operation, had been handled. These people had been taken to an installation specially set up for the purpose outside Belfast. Here they had been subjected to various procedures, allegedly based on those used by the Chinese in Korea, but adapted to teach our own special forces and aircraft pilots how to resist questioning if captured. I had never encountered this before and knew little about it. My concern about the interrogations that had taken place after the internment operation was that it had been conducted centrally by police who might not know what we wanted and that most of those captured had not been interrogated at all. I was therefore annoyed by a press article that said that the army had carried out the interrogations at Palace Barracks, in Belfast which was where 1 Para was stationed. This would further alienate the Catholic community from the army. I asked that there should be an official statement to the effect that the interrogations had not been carried out by the army or in Palace Barracks, but I was told that this would put pressure on the police whose morale had been much affected by recent events. I later raised the subject with Robert Ford who said that it was necessary for the army to shelter the police in this matter, especially as the methods used must have been suggested by the army. I had no option but to agree, but it was the start of many subsequent accusations that the army in general and me in particular, were responsible for ill treating prisoners. These accusations were made despite the fact that the army was never responsible for interrogating or even holding prisoners as far as I know.

When briefing senior officers and politicians there is always the temptation to give them the impression that one is broad-minded and understanding of their difficulties, even if it results in presenting the situation in a more favourable way than is justified by events. In practice this does nothing to help them and undermines their true interests. I therefore made a conscious decision to tell them as precisely as possible what the security situation was in Belfast, which was not always appreciated in the spirit that I would have wished. But I have always felt that if we do not tell our politicians where we stand, it is unlikely that we will get what we want.

When the Chief of the General Staff, General Carver, paid one of his regular visits in early September, I briefed him at Cloona House in the presence of

General Tuzo. This time I was able to say that at last we had got the first of our civil representatives and that access to Special Branch was beginning to improve but that we still seemed to be stuck with the four month tour for deployed battalions. After the briefing I took him on a tour of Belfast. There had been a lot in the papers about continual fighting and mayhem and I wanted to show him that it was all open and quiet. We travelled in a Land Rover complete with flag and his four-star plates, straight through some of the worst areas such as Andersonstown, the Ardoyne and Girdwood Park. I drove, he sat next to me and there was not a sign of hostility anywhere. We finished up visiting one of my two Ulster Defence Regiment battalions. Of course, I made it clear that things often got troublesome in the evening and that snipers and bombers were still busy, but these were isolated incidents and that the long hours of rioting and street disorders seemed to be over for the moment.

*   *   *

As mentioned earlier Harry Tuzo, as General Officer Commanding, had to deal with the brigadiers through the Commander Land Forces, if the system was to work. As a result he seldom spoke to me directly about the situation, although I often met him and his wife Monica socially and found them easy to get on with and extremely generous hosts. From contacts with him in the past I knew him to be intelligent, flexible and calm under pressure. What I did not know was how well he understood insurgency and how clever he was at handling politicians. When I was briefing Mike Carver, Harry Tuzo sat in the room but said nothing, so that I did not know whether he agreed with my views or not. A few weeks later Lord Carrington, the Secretary of State for Defence, visited Northern Ireland and much the same thing happened. That evening the Tuzos invited him and us to dinner and afterwards, the ladies having withdrawn, there was a more general conversation during which Harry Tuzo listened to what was being said without putting his own views forward to any great extent. Doubtless his major difficulty lay in having to reconcile what he knew to be necessary from a military point of view with the diverse political requirements of the Stormont and Westminster governments, as described in the last chapter.

The flow of visitors continued for some time culminating in visits from the Home Secretary in mid-December and the Prime Minister two days before Christmas, who not only wanted to be briefed but also to visit battalions in the most seriously affected parts of the city. I spent most of the day with him but although he smiled a lot he said very little. I think that he was partly jet lagged, as he arrived in Northern Ireland on his way back from discussions with the US President in Bermuda. He was also probably feeling the cold as he was wearing a very lightweight suit more appropriate to southern climes than to the streets of Northern Ireland.

Between mid-August and Christmas there were fewer large scale riots of the sort that burst out in several different parts of the city at the same time, lasted for several days and required co-ordinating from brigade headquarters. But there was a seemingly endless series of local rioting, stoning and abuse, which meant that the men in the deployed battalions got few breaks and little rest. Sometimes these disturbances came about as a result of searches being made by battalions for wanted men or weapons and at other times they were brought about to entice the army into a confrontation. The verbal abuse to which the soldiers were subjected to on these occasions, not to mention the spitting and the throwing of bricks, bottles and filth off the streets, almost defies description. Although our men knew that it was done to provoke them into carrying out some illegal action, it was still difficult to stomach. And while this was going on the crowd might suddenly melt away and a gunman open up on the soldiers. There would then be a follow-up designed to catch the gunman. In addition to all of this it was still frequently necessary to control crowds gathering at interfaces and soldiers had to be employed to ensure that Protestants and Catholics did not come to blows.

On one such evening I found myself on Crumlin Road with a crowd of Protestants on one side jeering at the Catholics on the other side who had been returning the compliment with interest, to say nothing of a few bricks and petrol bombs. I well remember that the bodyguard provided for me by the brigade headquarters and Signals Squadron was not one of the ones who usually came with me. Thinking that he was an Englishman I turned to him and said 'I bet you're glad that you don't come from an area like this.' 'In fact I do', he replied. 'My parents live in one of the houses in that street.' He pointed to an area of the Ardoyne directly in front of us. Just then there was a burst of fire from a Tommy gun in the area he had indicated and I wondered whether it came from one of his school friends. After a while I decided to have a closer look and went into the Ardoyne where I found Ronnie Eccles standing on the pavement with one of his officers and a few soldiers. He pointed out the house from where the rounds had been fired and tried to hustle me out of the way. He seemed concerned for my safety but he was probably worried that some terrorist, seeing my red hat, would take a pot shot at me and hit him or one of his men. Anyhow as his men were already moving in on the target, I felt that there was no likelihood of any further shooting on their part. The gunman would be withdrawing hurriedly in one direction while his weapon was being whisked away by a woman or child. Such was the usual routine followed by the IRA.

With the increase of shooting and the many explosions that continued to take place, life was becoming more dangerous for the soldiers. During the seven months before internment, units of the brigade had about ninety casualties of whom seven were killed. In the four and a half months between internment and the end of the year we had 130 casualties of whom seventeen were killed. Naturally much more attention was paid in the press and elsewhere to those killed than to those wounded, but it is important to remember that some of those wounded were crippled for life or blinded and some died later of their wounds. In short the casualty figures were quite high and caused us all a certain amount of sadness and concern.

As usual bare statistics only tell a small part of the story. To get the matter into perspective, each of the 130 casualties suffered in the period after internment, needs to be viewed against the way in which the soldiers in Belfast were living at the time. These men, mostly housed in company sized bases, were almost always dog-tired. They were constantly patrolling the streets, sometimes ignored by the population but at other times jostled, reviled or pelted with muck. On returning to their base they might get time off to rest, but as often as not that would be interrupted by the need to turn out suddenly and deal with a riot or unexpected incident. At other times they might be searching houses for arms, or manning a vehicle checkpoint. Another unpopular task was manning an observation post, probably on the roof one of their own bases but sometimes on a nearby block of flats. We were constantly trying to make our observation posts safer by fitting the most up-to-date protection, because the people manning them naturally felt like Aunt Sally. I knew how they felt because when moving round Belfast, I sometimes went into one to work out how useful it was in the context of existing operations.

Whilst doing any of these jobs a soldier might become a casualty. If shot while occupying an observation post he would, dead or alive, have to be extracted and carried down through the building, whilst another soldier was detailed off to man it in his place. If hit on the street, his mates with whom he had been living at close quarters for weeks or months, would have to administer first aid, call for assistance and get him off to hospital wondering whether they would ever see him again. Many of our casualties were the result of nearby explosions in which case they would be engulfed in falling masonry and flying glass with nothing but clouds of stinking dust to breathe. There were dozens of explosions in Belfast alone, between the start of internment and the end of the year. They not only killed or maimed our men but also brought death or desperate injuries to members of the civilian population, most of whom needed help from us or the police.

It was interesting to see the way that the different commanding officers reacted to the injuries inflicted on their men. Most just accepted them as the inevitable result of doing the job properly, but some seemed to feel each attack as a personal insult. These people suffered a lot more wear and tear than the rest. By contrast Derek Wilford became ever more determined that the men of 1 Para would be so well trained that they would have the best possible chance of surviving a surprise attack. He took immense trouble to keep them up to the mark and they benefited accordingly. Naturally they could not avoid casualties altogether, as they were constantly being committed into the worst situations, but they came out of it remarkably well.

Perhaps the people most exposed to danger were the Ammunition Technical Officers, known as ATOs, whose job it was to defuse the bombs that the IRA so liberally scattered around the city. There were not too many of these highly skilled and immensely brave people available and they were constantly employed. I have no record of the number of bombs that they dismantled but there is a record of the number of explosions that took place during 1971. From the start of the year until the end of July there were very roughly thirty-five explosions of varying sizes, excluding the nail bombs. Thereafter the numbers rose steeply. In August there were about the same number as had taken place in the whole year up to that time. In September there were more than seventy-five after which a steady decline set in. There were about sixty in October and then about fifty in each of November and December and thirty in January. This gradual reduction came about because of the erosion of the supply of explosive and because a number of the bomb makers were being arrested or blown up by their own bombs. Even so explosions caused much damage and many casualties, particularly to non-combatants.

When a soldier was severely wounded his first stop was likely to be the Royal Victoria Hospital close to the Springfield Road Police Station where the surgeons were superb and the care of a similar standard. Further outside the city was the Musgrave Park Hospital where there was a military wing manned by the equally skilled and devoted members of the Royal Army Medical Corps (RAMC) and Queen Alexandra's Royal Army Nursing Corps (QARANC). This is where most of the wounded were taken and also where men went if they were ill. I tried to visit this hospital at regular intervals.

One day, having talked to some of our soldiers I thought it would be a good idea to look in at the ward where wounded IRA men were treated. Accompanied by the ward sister I walked round asking the inmates if they were being well looked after. There were five there, four of whom were countrymen from outside the city. They were friendly and grateful for the care they were receiving. The fifth man called Mulvenna, was from Belfast. He was young, defiant and anything but friendly. Although he grudgingly said that he was being looked after all right, his only desire was to get back to his unit. Regardless of sister's orders that he should stay lying down, he insisted on getting out of bed and lifting his pyjama top. There was a long red scar running up his tummy held together by stitches. A Royal Marine had bayoneted him a few days earlier as he was trying to plant a bomb. I could not imagine how he could bear to move let alone stand up. Two days later I was in the Operations Room when one of the watch keepers said that an IRA man called Mulvenna had escaped from the Musgrave Park Hospital by climbing down a drainpipe. Despite being followed by tracker dogs, he had got clean away. It was a magnificent effort by a brave and determined man. When I visited Northern Ireland about ten years later I enquired after him and was told that he had been killed.

*   *   *

Despite the damage and casualties inflicted by the IRA, they themselves were suffering even greater losses. As the information flowed in and projects developed by the battalions bore fruit, we started to find men on the wanted list. In September we picked up sixty-five and in October another sixty. Thereafter we improved our performance considerably getting 140 in November, 170 in December and 120 in January. We also collected an ever increasing quantity of arms, ammunition and explosives. We found rifles, pistols, carbines, sub-machine guns, shotguns and even an anti-tank gun on one occasion. We also found grenades, detonators, fuses and explosives of various different types. The Scots Guards who took over from 2 Para at Springfield Road were particularly successful, but all played their part.

One of the reasons for our rapid success was that in November we worked out a new and effective way of getting further information. As the IRA started to weaken we discovered a few of their number who were prepared to help us out. We collected some of these people and housed them outside the city. Then we lent them to battalions operating in the areas in which they had been active. The battalion concerned would take one of the men around with them, carefully concealed in a vehicle from where they could point out IRA men who could then be arrested. Armed with the detailed knowledge provided by our guests, the police could often get hot information out of the prisoners, with particular reference to where weapons were hidden and sometimes where other IRA men could be found. This worked so well that in the first month that the system was in use, we recovered more weapons and ammunition in this way than was collected by all the battalions combined using normal methods. When these men ceased to be of use because their information became out of date, the police arranged for them to be moved to a safe place, usually outside Ireland, where they could live in peace. We referred to them as 'Freds'.

Like so many ideas, this one came about as a result of a casual conversation based on what might work in the situation prevailing in Belfast at the time. Inevitably some journalists jumped to the conclusion that I was trying to re-run the pseudo-gangs that had worked so well in Kenya, but there was no similarity between the two systems. At no time did we try and produce a phoney IRA gang to infiltrate the real ones. There was perhaps a faint resemblance to the use we made of hooded men in Kenya, in so far as in both cases we got certain members of the opposition, carefully hidden from their former friends, to identify them. It was apparently necessary to get ministerial agreement to the use of former IRA men in this way, which I only discovered when reading Lord Carver's autobiography, *Out of Step*, some eighteen years later in 1989. The system remained effective during the rest of my time in Belfast. Great credit is due to those of our own people involved in running it.

*   *   *

The result of our activities was gradually becoming apparent. First indications came from intelligence sources reporting that IRA companies were being obliged to amalgamate or close down and that the leadership was expressing grave concern. As IRA members were moved from the streets to the detention camp, the population became more friendly and responsive to the approaches of our officers and civil representatives. Soldiers started to be invited into peoples' houses for tea and meals in a way that had not been seen for many months. The Catholics never dreamt that interned IRA men would be allowed back until The Troubles were well and truly over.

By the end of the year it seemed that the situation had improved to the extent where a further political initiative would have a chance of moving things on, to a significant extent. So far as I was concerned there was never any chance of military action alone ending The Troubles. Insurgency consists of a mixture of political, psychological and economic methods used in conjunction with force, so the response to it must also consist of a similar combination of measures combined with the action of the security forces. What we had been trying to do was to weaken the insurgents to the extent where action in other fields had a chance of success. Quite what form a political initiative might take was difficult to imagine. The thing that would impress most of the Catholics would be the abolition of Stormont, but it was difficult to see what could be offered to the Protestants in compensation, since they had already got what they most wanted which was the introduction of internment. Perhaps they could be bought off by an undertaking that internment would be used more vigorously, but this would be likely to undermine the effect of the abolition of Stormont on many of the Catholics. The politicians were in an awkward position.

Another problem was that our successes, such as they were, were coming too late. The republican propaganda campaign was eroding support for government action both within the United Kingdom and overseas, especially in the United States. Our complete inability to come to grips with republican propaganda in time, must rank with our lack of preparation in terms of intelligence gathering, as the two main reasons why the campaign lasted for so long. As usual much of the British media, gave priority to exposing our shortcomings rather than attacking the enemy, which did not help. Anyway that is not strictly speaking part of my story.

What is part of my story is that in the weeks following internment the republican propaganda machine got it into its head that I was a suitable person on whom to concentrate their attacks. One reason was that they no longer had Tony Farrar-Hockley to blame for their woes and another was that I was known to have been a danger to insurgents in past campaigns such as Kenya. Be that as it may, I was soon being described as the architect of internment and the person responsible for the interrogation techniques that were being called into question. When in November my Oxford thesis was published under the title of *Low Intensity Operations* they had access to material that they could misquote to back their accusations. They also maintained that many of the operations undertaken by the security forces were the result of soldiers and police commanders following the ideas expressed in my book. The fact that few of our people would have had the time to buy and read it, even had they wanted to do so, was completely ignored. Surprisingly perhaps, the book did eventually have some influence on the way in which the army thought about counter-insurgency, but it would take years rather than weeks, for this to happen. Nonetheless the republican propaganda machine did succeed in making most of the Catholic population of Belfast think that I was a wicked fellow.

This adversely affected the security of my family, as a result of which the children were removed from their school and both Elizabeth and myself were obliged to have a bodyguard even when I was not on duty. Roly Guy provided a young lance corporal from 1 RGJ called Barry Byng to fill this post and he became a great friend of the family. Elizabeth was also taught to handle an automatic pistol, which she was supposed to keep on her person when outside the house. Despite the fact that she became proficient at handling it, worry regarding the security of the family added greatly to the stress of her existence. The fact that she never allowed it to rub off on me, or the children, did not alter the wear and tear that she suffered herself.

*   *   *

During the last three months of 1971 I was worried that the Royal Ulster Constabulary, which had suffered considerably from the way in which events had developed, was becoming discouraged. The radical re-organisation and disarmament of the police implemented by Sir Arthur Young had left them totally vulnerable and dependent on the army even for the defence of their own police stations. And despite being disarmed they were still required to be present at marches and other gatherings such as the movement of football fans through sensitive areas and they had to help in keeping the two sides apart. The police were the target of much republican propaganda and they sustained a number of casualties; some fatal. To cap it all the police were constantly being accused of using excessive force against rioters and for taking part in arresting and mistreating prisoners.

In every police division there was an appreciable number of Roman Catholic policemen as well as Protestants and when they went off duty they had to walk home and live in the community like everyone else. Although the proportion of Catholics to Protestants was low, it included many of the key players. For example the senior superintendent in charge of the division based at Springfield Road was a Catholic, as was the superintendent in charge of the Special Branch officers working in Belfast and one of the senior CID officers. The republicans campaigned to get all Catholics to leave the police force so that they could say that the police was part and parcel of the Protestant campaign to suppress the Catholic population.

On three mornings each week I held a conference of commanding officers in order to discover who needed what and to co-ordinate activities for the next few days. We held each meeting in one of the battalion headquarters, as I did not want to waste the commanding officers' time by getting them to trail out to Lisburn. Afterwards I usually went round to see Sam Bradley and thereafter to one or other of the police division headquarters to have a chat to the senior policeman in charge. Throughout my time in Belfast I tried to make the police think of us as equal partners with them in the business of making Belfast safe for all law abiding citizens. I wanted them to feel that I was as much concerned for them as I was for our own people. My links with Sam Bradley remained close.

One innovation that I introduced at this time was to produce a mobile headquarters for us both to use in the event of large-scale disturbances. It consisted of a pig, i.e. an armoured personnel carrier, in which were wireless sets on both the brigade forward and rear links. We also had the necessary gear to enable us to stop under any telephone pole so that we could connect a telephone to the main Belfast exchange. In this way Sam could be in touch with all his police stations. This meant that we could drive to anywhere in the city to see what was going on and remain in touch with events. Finally we had the ability to maintain direct contact with any helicopter that was observing from above and if desirable could call it down on a nearby open space so that I could go and have a look myself.

Towards the end of 1971 the Northern Irish Civil Rights Association (NICRA) was resurrected to act as a focus for demonstrations against internment. At this time in Belfast, it was largely under the influence of the Official IRA. In the third week of December it announced that it intended to hold a march through Belfast on Christmas Day despite the fact that marching was still banned. Robert Ford reminded me that we should be very firm with any sign of violence and when I asked Sam whether he had been given any guidance by the Chief Constable he said that the 'wee man' as he called him, would like us to break it up. On enquiring whether he thought we should be firmer than usual, he said 'Not at all. Would you want to have our photos splashed round the worlds' newspapers as the men responsible for attacking a collection of poor daft creatures on Christmas Day?' We discovered that the marchers were to assemble somewhere in Andersonstown and move down Falls Road to Donegall Road, which would take them to the edge of a Protestant area. We decided that we would secure the area where they intended to assemble, warn them that the march was illegal and that anyone taking part stood a chance of being prosecuted. We then erected a barricade at the point where Donegall Road joins the motorway so that when the head of the procession reached that point the only place they could go was onto the motorway heading for Lisburn. They then had a nice long stretch of road before finding a second barricade strategically sited by Dick Vincent who commanded 12th Light Air Defence Regiment, at a point where the motorway on a steep embankment runs over a stream. Shortly before reaching the barricade, there was a convenient road leading back into Andersonstown. When the head of the procession reached the barricade Sam told the commander of the police division to go and wish them all a happy Christmas and tell them to get along back to their 'bairns' and their dinners. A few keen young protesters ran down the embankment into the field at the bottom where they found the stream with some of Dick Vincent's men on the far bank but not much to throw at them. Everyone else took the advice of the police and went home. Sam said that maybe a few people would be prosecuted after Christmas, based on photographs taken at the time. He then advised me to be 'away home' and departed.

In the New Year there was another demonstration against internment. As before we secured the start point and put a barricade to prevent the protestors getting into the Protestant area but before they got there they turned into a park to listen to a number of impassioned speeches. Sam and I watched from our mobile command post and a helicopter overhead estimated the crowd as being about 2,500 strong as opposed to the 20,000 that the organisers subsequently claimed to have been present. A breakaway group of about seventy youths tried to damage the local bus station, but were quickly dispersed by the army, a number being arrested. Otherwise the event passed off peacefully.

These semi-political events tended to be easy to control for a number of reasons. First, because the officials who were running them did not want trouble, which would weaken the impact of the speeches on the attending press, and the Provisionals who would benefit equally from the press reports, did not want to disrupt the proceedings. Second, because we had plenty of troops covering the whole area through which the people were moving so that any violence could be quickly contained. Third, because the attendance of so many outside activists such as university left wingers, enabled us to insert plain clothes men into the crowd without fear of them being singled out by the locals and these men could slip away and keep us informed of any signs of impending violence.

*   *   *

At this juncture it is worth trying to summarise the position of the various sections of the Catholic population active in Belfast. Probably the majority still supported the SDLP in its attempt to achieve social reform by non-violent means. But in order to attract votes the SDLP felt it necessary to include in its programme the abolition of internment, some of the extreme socialism of the Official IRA and the unification of Ireland, which was the one and only aim of the Provisional IRA. The Official IRA also included the unification of Ireland and the ending of internment as part of its programme, which was mainly concerned with left wing politics. The strength of the Provisional IRA's position was that its aim of unifying Ireland was its only aim. But its aim was so emotionally attractive that the SDLP and the Official IRA both had to adopt it, despite the fact that the SDLP disliked the Provisionals for their use of force and the Official IRA regarded them as a danger to their very existence. Thus the people who had most to gain from the way in which internment was weakening the Provisional IRA, found themselves opposing internment. They also felt obliged to support the unification of Ireland, which was not particularly important to them. Even the Roman Catholic Church which had by this time wrested control of the Citizens Defence Committees (CDCs) from the Official IRA, felt that it had to oppose internment and back the idea of the unification of Ireland in order to retain and increase its influence with its flock. The effect of all this was to make it appear that there was strong backing for the Provisional IRA throughout the Catholic population, when in fact many sections of it merely feared it and would have been happy to see the last of it.

By the start of 1972 the Catholic enclave in east Belfast was almost entirely clear of IRA and in most other places except for Andersonstown and the Ardoyne, their influence was waning. There were some disturbing signs such as the use by the IRA of a few more modern weapons, but on the whole the city seemed reasonably quiet. We continued to arrest wanted terrorists and recover weapons and explosives as we waited for the long heralded political initiative.

By now two of my main requirements had been met, that is to say civilian representatives had been appointed to most of the police divisions and there was a good working relationship between Special Branch and the battalions on the ground. I had made no progress on my third major requirement, which was longer tours for the deployed battalions and I was beginning to feel that this was a lost cause. The reason why I was so keen on it, was to avoid losing the battalion and company commanders just as they were absorbing the information that would enable them to damage the IRA. Their ability to do so depended largely on the intelligence records, which each battalion built up during its tour and which got lost when the battalion moved away. If we could not keep the commanders for longer than four months, I thought that we should at least keep the records intact by appointing an officer or NCO on a one-year tour to look after them. In this way the records would in effect be tied to the area rather than to the battalion, so that the relieving battalion would then take them over complete, together with the person charged with keeping them up to date. Thereby commanding officers of replacement battalions could get themselves into the picture quickly. To strengthen the links with Special Branch I felt that this continuity officer or NCO should be attached to Special Branch in the same way as a military intelligence officer is attached to it. Although he would live and work as an officer or NCO of the battalion, he would in theory belong to the police Special Branch.

I also decided to make the most tremendous fuss if the army tried to replace a commanding officer during his four months tour. This happened twice in my time, and on both occasions, despite lobbying hard, I never succeeded in getting it stopped, even though the men in question were merely going to staff appointments in non-operational places. This clearly indicated a failure to understand the basic need for continuity in counter-insurgency operations, prevalent in the army at this time.

Early in the New Year I heard that I was to take over as commandant of the School of Infantry in the third week of May. I was also told that not having had any leave for the last six months and as my deputy was due to change in early February, I should take a short break at the end of January. Shortly before departing, Robert Ford asked whether I thought it would be safe for him to remove 1 Para from Belfast for about 24 hours at the end of the month, to reinforce 8th Brigade in Londonderry during a NICRA internment protest. I said that provided Belfast continued to remain quiet, it should be all right.

A day or two before we were due to return to Belfast we either heard on the wireless or read in the newspaper that there had been a serious disturbance in Londonderry. On my return I asked Derek Wilford about his trip to Londonderry and he told me that when launched at a crowd of youths hurling stones at a barricade, his men had been shot at and that in the ensuing action a number of presumed gunmen had been killed. Apparently the press were saying that some of them were not gunmen at all, but innocent bystanders and I was concerned that 1 Para would become less effective for a time because of the number of men that would have to go and give evidence to the military police investigating the incident. I was also told that there had been some reaction in Belfast in the form of an increased level of rioting, but that it was settling down.

February and March were relatively quiet so far as attacks on the army were concerned, although the IRA were making further advances on the propaganda front resulting from the Londonderry incident, by now the subject of an enquiry presided over by the Lord Chief Justice of England. A new development was a massive increase in robberies of banks, shops and Post Offices. Although apparently designed to boost IRA funds, it is likely that some at least of the proceeds found their way into the robbers pockets. Clearly a culture of criminality was getting a hold of the IRA. There was also an increase in the number of punishment shootings inflicted on the Catholic population by the IRA, either in the form of kneecapping or by gunmen shooting their victims from cars.

During the early months of 1972 it was becoming apparent that the Ulster Defence Association was increasing in size and becoming more visible. This reflected the fact that the Protestant population was becoming nervous about the long expected political initiative. At this juncture they were in no way hostile to us, but they were clearly a threat. They were demonstrating as strongly as they could that they would not remain inactive if the Westminster government tried to force unacceptable measures on Stormont. They were showing that the much-vaunted Protestant backlash was ready to be released and should not be disregarded.

Meanwhile although we continued to pick up wanted men at an increased rate, there was by March, a slight increase in the number of explosions that were taking place, despite the fact that many bombs were being discovered and defused. One bomb went off while being taken to the target area by four IRA all of whom were killed and their weapons left in the debris. But despite the occasional own goal, the IRA was succeeding in setting off two or three explosions most days with a proportional increase in the number of civilian casualties. The worst explosion resulted in six civilians being killed and about

150 injured, and there was another in which two were killed and 160 injured, mostly cuts and bruises, but some horribly maimed. Furthermore as bombs went off at random throughout the city, both Protestants and Catholics suffered alike. Going home in the afternoon after witnessing the aftermath of one of these incidents gave one a strange feeling. One minute all was rubble, broken glass and bloodstains. A few minutes later there were our children playing in the garden with the dog and probably some friends. I imagine that members of the emergency services, sorting out a multiple car crash or the blazing remains of an aircraft, get something of the same feeling.

* * *

The 24th of March 1972 was the day of the long awaited political initiative when the government's decision to suspend Stormont and impose direct rule from Westminster was announced. Apparently the British government had only wanted to take over responsibility for law and order from Stormont, but Faulkner had said that as this was fundamental to the existence of Northern Ireland, there was no point in Stormont continuing without it. Almost immediately there was an improved atmosphere in the Catholic areas so far as the army was concerned, with IRA slogans being painted over in a few places. On the other hand there were immediate signs of Protestant indignation as shipyard workers marched on the city hall. The next few days saw some large scale rallies staged by the Ulster Defence Association complete with speeches by their political leaders.

At the end of March there was a massive assembly at Stormont Castle when a crowd of at least 20,000, was addressed by Faulkner and others. Emotions were running high and there was a good chance of trouble as those making their way to Stormont moved past the Catholic enclave bordering Newtownards Road which was lined by army and police. Sam and I were standing in the line at one point when a small cheeky looking man passing by, knocked my hat off into the road. As he did so Sam's long arm stretched forth and caught him by the collar lifting him bodily off the ground. 'Pick it up', said Sam and the man did. 'Dust it off', said Sam and he did. 'Now behave yourself', said Sam. 'Sorry Mr Bradley', he said as he scuttled off as fast as he could go. Everyone in Belfast knew and respected Sam Bradley.

Ten days later General Carver again visited Belfast and I briefed him as usual. This was not an easy moment because coming so soon after the suspension of Stormont, it was difficult to know how things would turn out. Briefly my line was that whatever happened we would need to go on with our defensive tasks. We still had to disperse rioters, secure the Catholic areas from possible Protestant incursions and guard vital points including police stations. We also had to look after specific individuals such as judges, try to prevent explosions and help clear up the mess when they occurred. The main difference lay in the methods we should use when trying to root out the IRA. Although accepting that we might be able to operate against them in the way that we had developed since the introduction of internment, I felt that we should first try to avoid giving opportunities to republican backers both at home and abroad, by not attacking the IRA too openly. My recommendation was that whilst using uniformed soldiers for all defensive tasks, we should base our offensive operations on a special forces/plain-clothes capability, organised to get information and then act on it discretely. For this purpose I suggested combining the Mobile Reconnaissance Force, the Freds and Special Branch. So long as internment remained, such a force should be able to find and quietly capture wanted men and weapons, without getting involved in the massive search operations that so alienated the Catholic population. Should internment be abolished as the situation improved, it would be necessary to add a CID and legal element to the force in order to carry out successful court prosecutions. My final point was that as the police would not be able to find enough suitable people to provide their share of the force from within their own ranks they should be reinforced as necessary by the army or police forces in England.

Regardless of these considerations, I was in no doubt that however discreet we became, we would certainly have to continue our efforts to root out the IRA. Until the IRA was rendered incapable of terrorising the Nationalist population, members of it would be unable to support any government initiative that the IRA did not like. It is an unfortunate fact, demonstrated throughout the ages, that people are forced to support those they most fear, rather than those whose policies best suit their interests.

I had of course floated most of these ideas with Robert Ford when we had been looking forward to the great political initiative that was going to break the deadlock and he may have mentioned them to Harry Tuzo. Unfortunately Mr Whitelaw, the new Secretary of State for Northern Ireland, who took over the political direction of the Province from the government at Stormont, started by undermining the progress we had already made in weakening the IRA, by releasing selected IRA men from internment. The first batch of sixty-eight was let out on the very day that I was briefing General Carver. His aim presumably was to persuade the Catholics to support him, but the result was the opposite of what he intended. In the event the returning terrorists set about regaining control of the people in the areas that were beginning to turn in our direction, with a spate of kneecapping, tarring and feathering and murdering of backsliders. Worse still was the fact that never again could moderate Catholics be sure that the IRA men that we were capturing, would be held until they were no longer a threat to them. Nonetheless all was not lost. We still retained the information we had collected and our links with Special Branch were intact.

Another unfortunate decision soon followed which was that we should no longer make a point of keeping all roads open. For the time being we were told to keep the main roads open, but not to press the matter if clearing barricades from lesser roads was likely to cause trouble. The end result was that within a few months a major set-piece operation became necessary to regain control of Belfast as well as Londonderry where some obstructions had been tolerated since the previous August.

It was a depressing period and one that would soon become worse as hardcore Protestant paramilitaries who were just as brutal as the IRA, started targeting prominent republicans. I was glad that my time in Northern Ireland was coming to an end. I have two vivid memories of those final days. One was walking round the square outside the City Hall with James Templer, the battery commander of 3 RHA responsible for the security of the area. It was a favourite place for car bombs and he was looking through the windows trying to spot bits of wire and packages that might be a bomb. I felt very unsafe but he wandered round as though making sure that no one had left a dog inside without adequate ventilation. The threat of cars exploding was not at all remote as car bombs were becoming increasingly popular with the IRA. When considering the fuss that arises when the occasional bomb explodes in England, one begins to understand what the long-suffering people of Northern Ireland endured for years on end.

The other memory is of my last outing with Sam Bradley in our mobile headquarters a few days before I left Belfast. On this occasion we had parked our vehicle at a spot from where we could watch some gathering or other. Suddenly we noticed that we were being shot at from a builder's yard some considerable distance away. I therefore asked Sam whether he would prefer to move to another place where we could see what was going on without being shot at. 'Och the foolish creatures' he said 'let them shoot away.' Thinking that 'the foolish creatures' might include an ex-soldier, I popped my head out of the turret and gave the butt marker's signal for an 'outer', i.e. a bad shot, thereby registering my disapproval of his standard of marksmanship. I also took the precaution of telling the commander of the armoured reconnaissance squadron to send a couple of cars to the scrapyard.

*   *   *

Despite the fact of having had enough of Northern Ireland for the time being, it was painful to say good bye to the people in my headquarters with whom I had been working. Every one of the officers of 39th Brigade Headquarters and the members of its splendid Signals Squadron, had worked themselves to the bone. In this connection it is worth remembering that in addition to Peter Graham and Tony Hare, many of them were constantly moving around between the battalions in Belfast and not just sitting at their desks in Lisburn. This was particularly the case with Captains Thompson and Roberts who dealt with intelligence and its distribution to the regiments. For most of these people their hours of work were as unsettled as my own and their wives in the quarters at Lisburn would, like Elizabeth, be standing by at all hours of the day and night to keep them fed and rested. It would be difficult to think of a better lot. I was particularly sorry to part from Peter Graham without whose help I would so often have been in a great muddle.

At Headquarters Northern Ireland, Robert Ford had been wonderfully helpful and much better at explaining what was going on in the world beyond Belfast than his predecessor. Sam Bradley had been a constant support and a great friend. Harry Tuzo was always encouraging, friendly and evidently appreciative of my efforts since a few weeks earlier my name had appeared in a supplementary honours list as the recipient of the CBE for Gallantry. Plenty of OBEs and MBEs had been given for gallantry, but I was told that never before had a CBE been awarded in this way to a British officer, although a Canadian brigadier had previously received one for his work in the Congo.

I was particularly sorry to say goodbye to 1 Para. Throughout my time in Belfast they had been continuously employed in all the roughest places and had pulled my chestnuts out of the fire on more than one occasion. Nothing was ever impossible for them: nothing too dangerous or too much trouble. Sometimes complaints had been made that they were over-rough when handling crowds but those complaining failed to realise that by preventing Protestants getting into Catholic areas or republican inspired hooligans from attacking Protestants, they were heading off major confrontations that could have cost lives.

I was also very conscious of the debt that we all owed to the thirty eight regiments that had passed through Belfast since my arrival just twenty months earlier; some of them twice. The pressure of work and the lack of sleep experienced by these soldiers had been enormous. They had done great work rooting out the IRA and at the same time defending the two communities despite the endless harassment they had received from the very people they were trying to save. Their own forbearance and the strict discipline to which they were subjected, ensured that few unfortunate incidents occurred. Inevitably there were some lapses, which were eagerly tossed around by the press, but overall their behaviour was a magnificent example of sustained restraint.

*   *   *

In the afternoon of 30 April we put the children and their belongings into the car and set off for the ferry. We had a calm crossing with only one slight upset. We were, for security reasons, travelling under an assumed name. Just before going to sleep Catherine went to the lavatory and got lost trying to find our cabin. Eventually she was taken to the ship's purser where we found her with tears running down her poor little face. The purser kept asking her what her name was and she kept saying that she could not remember, which sounded odd from an 8 year old girl. The trouble was that she knew she must not say that she was called Kitson and she could not remember that she was supposed to be Catherine Crabtree.

*   *   *

Before leaving Ireland behind for good, it is perhaps worth mentioning two points, which may not be clear from the foregoing narrative. The first concerns the Protestants who have mainly been mentioned in the context of the threat that they might pose to the Catholics and therefore as a reason for Catholics to support the IRA.

But although it was that aspect of Protestant activity that affected our operations against the IRA, the Protestant community had many other things on their mind such as the prosperity of the Province and all the many aspects of government that bear on it. Their various interests impinged on mine in lots of different ways. I was particularly involved with matters such as urban development leading to population movement, community relations, the maintenance and guarding of essential services not to mention military links with ex-servicemen often in relation to remembrance. Accordingly during my time in Belfast I met many Unionist MPs, leaders of Orange Lodges, the Lord Mayor and his staff in the City Hall, trade union leaders and clergymen from all three of the main Protestant religions, i.e. Church of Ireland, Presbyterians and Methodists. In terms of hard work, decent living and the care they took of their homes and families, the Protestant community in Northern Ireland compares favourably with anything that can be found elsewhere in the United Kingdom.

My second point concerns timing. We were always doing things too late. In retrospect it is easy to see that when the British government decided to defuse the civil rights movement in 1969 by offering long overdue concessions to the Catholics, it should also have foreseen the likelihood of a further insurgency and prepared for it. The fact that this was not done in time, meant that the Westminster government was pushed into a corner in the first half of 1971 and had to implement internment hurriedly when unprepared to do it properly. Despite the advantages gained by internment, the inability of the British government to sell this ill thought out operation both at home and abroad, meant that pressure from outside Northern Ireland forced them to change their approach before enough members of the IRA had been removed from the Catholic population. Their method of doing this was to suspend Stormont and release many of those who had been interned specifically to get them off the back of the Catholic community. By suspending Stormont at a time when it had nothing to offer the Protestants in return, the government infuriated the Protestants. By releasing some detainees much of the ground that had been gained by internment, was lost so that the IRA soon became stronger than ever. It may be that political pressures on the government from within and without the country had already made it impossible to continue with the policy of destroying the IRA, in which case there was no course open other than the long haul. But it led to twenty-five bloody years spent proving to the IRA that their aim could not be met by violence. In the end the IRA politicised itself and brought the Catholic community to a peaceful outcome based on the sort of reforms that the civil rights movement and the SDLP were seeking in 1969. And these could perfectly well have been achieved within a year or two had the right action been taken from the start.

Although not difficult to see what went wrong, it is less easy to work out why. In the early stages, either the military did not understand the situation sufficiently well to make clear to the politicians what was needed, or the politicians were unwilling to do what the military suggested. There were probably faults on both sides. One of the troubles was that the army could only be given the influence it needed in the affairs of the police and civil authorities, at the expense of the civilians concerned. Furthermore change usually involves financial cost. The result was that decisions were delayed in the hope that things would improve to the extent that they would not be needed.

Another problem was the political and constitutional difficulties involved. As mentioned in the last chapter, after the general election of 1970 the Westminster government sometimes needed the support of the Northern Ireland Unionists to get its legislation through Parliament. An example of the way in which this might have affected us, concerns the bill authorising British entry into the European Economic Community. This was due to reach Parliament in October 1971 and could have been closely contested. Clearly getting the votes of the Northern Ireland Unionists to help the bill through Parliament, would have to be given priority over introducing internment at the ideal moment. I have never heard that this was a reason for implementing internment in August 1971 and it may well not have been, especially as governments seldom look that far ahead. But it shows how outside events could affect affairs within the Province.

Naturally consideration and decisions on all these matters were going on well above my head, but they are worth mentioning because of their relevance to one of the points I had been trying to get across from the time I left Kenya in December 1956. Insurgents are highly vulnerable when first they become active and should be disposed of at once. It is up to the government to ensure that the security forces are ready in advance to deal with all likely external and internal threats and also to take the necessary political decisions that will enable any threat to be confronted as soon as it is discerned.

* * *

An incident occurred more than twenty years after I left Northern Ireland, which may be of interest as a postscript to the time I spent there. On this occasion I was in Hatchards Bookshop in Piccadilly when I bumped into Mike Carver, by now a Field Marshal and a Peer, long since retired from active service. While we were talking Edward Heath walked past us and turning to me he said, 'You know I wanted to put you in charge in Northern Ireland, but the generals would not let me.' He walked on without waiting for either of us to say anything and Mike Carver continued talking about whatever it was we had been discussing before he appeared.

Chapter 10

The School of Infantry and RCDS 1972–1975

T he School of Infantry came as quite a relief after 39th Brigade, both for me and for the family. Whereas the parts of Belfast that mainly occupied my attention were noisy, grubby and dangerous we were now stationed in an exceptionally beautiful part of Salisbury Plain, surrounded by hundreds of acres of unspoilt, open countryside, within a few miles of the Wylye Valley. The only thing to remind us of Northern Ireland was Battlesbury House in which we would be living for the next two and a half years, as it had been built at the same time as the house in Ireland to exactly the same design. The only slight snag was that I had to take over the job at once without getting the prolonged leave that we were expecting, because my predecessor was urgently needed in Oman to command the Sultan's army.

The School of Infantry was not exactly a school: more a federation of training establishments spread over a wide area backed by various units and sub-units for which I was responsible. The headquarters together with the Officers' Wing, the Small Arms Wing, the Signals' Wing and the Administrative Wing were co-located at Warminster. The Support Weapons Wing was at Netheravon, the NCOs Tactics Wing was at Brecon in Wales and the Jungle Warfare Wing was at Kota Tinngi at the Southern extremity of Malaya. Each wing was commanded by a colonel or lieutenant colonel. In addition there was a demonstration battalion and an armoured squadron under my command stationed at Warminster and a battery of artillery at Larkhill, which was in support. I was also the commandant of the Small Arms School Corps (SASC) which had its regimental depot at Warminster.

The task of the School of Infantry, as laid down, was to train individuals so that they could return to their battalions and instruct. We were not responsible for training units, which was the business of the normal chain of command. The School had a subsidiary task, which was to provide a centre of thought on infantry matters. For those interested in statistics, a total of 110 separate courses were run each year, attended by over 4,300 officers and men. In addition there was a never ending stream of visitors to the school ranging from a senior dignitary accompanied by his entourage, to large collections of people from other army schools and colleges such as the Staff College, and army cadets.

It looked at first sight as if I should have an interesting time balancing the army's ever-changing need for instructors, with the resources available within the various wings. I did not suppose that I would have to concern myself overmuch with the running of the component parts of the school because each wing was commanded by a highly experienced senior officer. On the other hand it would be necessary to spend time travelling to the various wings and visiting the infantry schools of some of our allies. Altogether I reckoned that there would be plenty of time left for catching up with old friends and I looked forward to enjoying a more leisurely lifestyle than had been possible in Ireland. But events of a different kind were soon to force themselves upon us.

The first of these was an article, which appeared in *The Sunday Times* two weeks after our arrival at Warminster. There had been a number of reviews of *Low Intensity Operations* since its appearance in the previous November, but they had been basically uncontroversial, concentrating on discussing its usefulness to those concerned in dealing with the type of operations described. *The Sunday Times* article, written by two competent and well respected journalists was in most respects favourable so far as I was concerned, but it drew attention to parts of the book which they considered to have political implications far beyond anything intended by me.

Soon afterwards a *Times* reporter visited Headquarters United Kingdom Land Forces (UKLF) at Wilton and spoke with a number of senior staff officers who led him to believe that there was widespread concern amongst army officers regarding the state of the country. His article included a number of unfortunate remarks made at the dinner table. He expressed the opinion that many officers felt disdain for politicians.

Although I was not involved and scarcely knew any of the officers mentioned, certain Labour politicians, confusing me with the people met by the reporter at UKLF, tabled a string of parliamentary questions. In some of these my name was coupled with the officers at UKLF whose statements had nothing to do with me. On the other hand Mr Hattersley who had been Minister of State at the Ministry of Defence when I was doing my Defence Fellowship at Oxford and who was now in opposition, asked specifically whether my book was the basis for part of the syllabus at the School of Infantry. He also went on to say that certain parts of the book dealing with industrial disputes within Great Britain, were abhorrent to the Opposition and asked that the government should disown and dissociate themselves from these contentious paragraphs. It soon became clear that one of the abhorrent bits related to part of a paragraph in Chapter 1 in which I tried to forecast the sort of tasks that might be allotted to the army between 1975 and 1980. Writing at the end of 1969, a few months after the army had been committed in Northern Ireland, I mentioned the possibility of trouble arising elsewhere in the United Kingdom, pointing out that the army might be called on to help if political extremists resorted to so much violence that the police required assistance. The other abhorrent bit was a reference I made in the last chapter of the book to the fact that the army had recently, for reasons of economy, lost the specialised units it formerly contained, capable of running ports, railways, power stations, sewage works etc. I said that if the army was required to take part in peacekeeping or counter-insurgency operations outside the UK, it might need them and that even within the UK the army might sometimes be asked to provide men for this purpose. This was hardly a revolutionary suggestion considering that governments had from time to time used the army to handle essential goods in the docks, clear rubbish from the streets, or put out fires when the firemen were on strike.

The minister answering the parliamentary questions merely said that *Low Intensity Operations* reflected my views, not the government's views and left it at that. Thinking that Hattersley, as the opposition spokesman on defence, needed to know what was going on at Warminster, I arranged for him to visit the school and see for himself. I explained that *Low Intensity Operations* was the result of a Defence Fellowship and was not an official army document and therefore not the basis for any syllabus. I also made it plain that my proposals were only designed to make the army capable of doing what the government might require it to do. He seemed reasonably happy. I therefore asked him to make it clear to his friends in the Labour Party that they had no cause for concern so far as I was concerned. On his return he issued a helpful statement about what was going on at the School of Infantry but continued to profess little bits of abhorrence about parts of the book. He seemed a decent and friendly person.

But regardless of his efforts, the piece in *The Sunday Times* together with the questions in Parliament, sparked off a series of articles in other publications and interest in the matter continued for several years, not only within the United Kingdom, but also overseas. As time went by, some of the articles became ever more ridiculous, suggestions being made that certain military officers, including myself, might try to stage a coup or push the army into breaking strikes or suppressing civil rights. As they appeared at a time when a certain amount of industrial unrest was taking place, it made the allegations seem vaguely possible to some people who would not otherwise have given them credence. This unwelcome publicity resulted in my being invited to address all sorts of unlikely clubs and associations. In addition I received letters from many strange people, which had to be answered. This took up time.

The next excitement occurred in June when Peter Graham rang up from Belfast to say that both wings of the IRA had been telling journalists that the ceasefire, then being negotiated in Ireland, would certainly not apply to me.

The IRA were said to be unhappy at the damage I had done to them, blamed me for the interrogation methods used after the internment operation and considered that by my very existence I was a danger to the working class of the world! Peter wondered whether the threat to our security was being taken sufficiently seriously, as he believed that we were to be attacked in the near future. On moving to Warminster I had assumed that there was no threat to us, as I was no longer involved in the Northern Ireland problem. Enquiries by the staff at Warminster indicated that Headquarters UK Land Forces and the Ministry of Defence shared my views. However a few hours later, all changed. Roadblocks were erected at both ends of the road passing our house. A guard was mounted on the house found by the demonstration battalion. I was to be accompanied by a military policeman when on army land and by a Police Special Branch officer whenever I left it. Both Elizabeth and I were to carry an automatic within and outside the School of Infantry. This all took a bit of getting used to. Like the newspaper articles, security precautions were to dog us for many years to come.

*   *   *

At some stage in early June I was approached by a member of the Parachute Regiment who said that a number of officers at the Ministry of Defence were making critical statements about the way in which the Parachute Regiment had behaved in Ireland. Apart from one reference in the report made by the Lord Chief Justice investigating the disturbance in Londonderry, to the effect that some of the firing by members of 1 Para bordered on the reckless, there was no excuse for anyone denigrating the immense contribution made by this regiment. I therefore asked for an interview with the Chief of the General Staff in order to discover whether there was any official disapproval of their performance and if not whether anything could be done to prevent insinuations being made unofficially.

On my arrival I was ushered in to see General Carver who said that he had heard nothing of that sort and would not put up with it if he did. He then took me in to see Lord Carrington, the Secretary of State. On returning to his office, General Carver told me that he wanted me to go to the Australian CGS's annual conference as one of his representatives and give a talk on the British Army's activities in Northern Ireland. I was to clear what I intended to say at the conference with him and then use it as a base for any other talks I might have to give in Australia. My departure for Australia was timed for early August.

*   *   *

Sir Alan Taylor, General Officer Commanding South East District, was CGS's principal representative at the Australian CGS's conference and we travelled out together. On Monday I gave the first of my talks to members of the British High Commission. The conference itself which started next day, was not only attended by all the senior officers of the Australian Army, but also by senior representatives from America, Canada and various other friendly nations. It is not surprising that General Carver took some trouble to ensure that I said more or less the right thing. The first part, lasting for an hour, dealt with the general situation in Northern Ireland. The second, after a break, was for a further hour during, which I was supposed to explain in detail how our tactics in Belfast developed. The audience were generous in their appreciation of my efforts.

At the end of the conference I set off to carry out a number of visits to Australian Army Headquarters and units, making my way from Canberra to Sydney and then north as far as Cairns where the British were carrying out tests at an Ordnance Storage Depot to discover the problems of maintaining equipment in a hot, humid conditions. On the way I gave a shortened version of my Northern Ireland talk at the Australian Army's Jungle Warfare Centre at Canungra.

I got back to Warminster by the beginning of September. The family had experienced some excitement when I was away, following a telephone call in the middle of the night saying that there was a bomb in the house which was due to explode within a few minutes. Elizabeth woke the children one by one to take them outside, but as soon as she moved to the next room the first child returned to bed and went back to sleep. Eventually she got them all out together with Brush and the cat, Jomo, only to find that it was pouring with rain. They took refuge with Clive Brennan, the commanding officer of the demonstration battalion, who lived nearby. Our house was searched by the bomb disposal team and found to be clear, so they returned after a few hours. On another occasion the alarm went off, also in the night. The indicator showed an intruder in the drawing room so Elizabeth went down with her pistol and flung the door open. There was a rustling noise by the sofa, but just as she was about to fire there was a miaow. It was Jomo! In retrospect it seems hilarious, but at the time with only the children in the house, it must have been jolly frightening.

It might appear that my thoughts since arriving at Warminster had been centred on Ireland and the political fall out from *Low Intensity Operations*, but that is far from being the case. Getting to know the problems of the School of Infantry and the officers working there had been far more important. I was particularly lucky in having Tod Sweeny, a Green Jacket officer, as the deputy commandant who, though many years senior to me, was wonderfully supportive. Admittedly on one occasion he left me with egg on my face when a French

General was dining in the officers' mess. As we took our places behind our chairs I called on the padre to say grace, only to find that he was not present. Turning to Tod I asked, under my breath, if he knew a French grace and he told me to say '*un, deux, trois allez*'. Not knowing what it meant, I did, and the whole mess started to laugh.

The colonel commanding the Officers' Wing was another Green Jacket, David Mostyn, who lived next door to us. After a few months he went off to command the brigade in Londonderry and was replaced by an old friend from the Rifle Brigade, David Stileman.

* * *

In November, I paid a short visit to the British Army of the Rhine calling in at the Infantry Training Centre at Sennelager, the Corps Headquarters and one or two regiments to see whether our courses were delivering what they wanted. Tony Farrar-Hockley was now the General Officer Commanding 4th Division at Herford.

My next trip abroad came at the end of January when the Chief of the General Staff told me to give my talk on Ireland in America; first at the Army War College, then at the Army Staff College at Leavenworth and then at Fort Bragg. The Army War College was at Carlisle, Pennsylvania.

After three weeks back at Warminster I was off again, this time to the Jungle Warfare Wing. The purpose of the wing was to train officers and NCOs as instructors in jungle warfare, mainly for units about to be stationed in Singapore, or about to visit Malaysia for training. The army at that time was required to have a brigade group capable of operating in the jungle. It could include units stationed in Singapore but not those in Hong Kong. In practical terms this meant that every year two battalions of infantry and about seven smaller units had to visit the Far East for training and we had to make sure that they all had a sufficient number of trained instructors. The Wing Commandant was Colonel Peter Thwaites of the Grenadier Guards, who was also the Defence Advisor to the High Commissioner in Singapore.

On the way home I stopped off in Delhi to give my Northern Ireland talk to members of the High Commission. Stories of India, concerning my grandfather and uncle had been liberally sprinkled in my subconscious mind during my youth so I was interested in seeing the sights. After a couple of days in Delhi I boarded an ancient aircraft, similar to the one in which I had travelled to Kenya twenty years earlier, in order to visit the Indian All Arms Training Centre and School of Infantry at Mhow.

* * *

I arrived back home to find our personal security did not seem to have improved to any extent. On 11 August 1973, the front page of the *Daily Mail* alerted its readers to the fact that a gang of IRA men had been on their way to kidnap me when betrayed by an informer and rounded up by Special Branch. No one told me, but I suppose it was unnecessary to do so once the gang had been arrested. In November of the following year a long article in *The Times* reported an enquiry into the death of a police informer. It transpired that he was the man who had warned the police of the plan to kidnap me.

*   *   *

Up to this time the NCOs Tactics Wing at Brecon had been grafted on to the Parachute Regiment's Training Centre there and had been administered by the Parachute Regiment. It was now felt that the School of Infantry should take over full responsibility for it and a ceremony was arranged to mark the occasion. General Tubby Butler of the Parachute Regiment was given the task of handing it over and after getting him kitted out with various bits of equipment that he had forgotten, we jointly stood on the saluting base as some men marched pass. He then formally handed the establishment over to me. The excellent Jack Thorpe who had been the Parachute Regiment's commanding officer up to that time, now became commandant of the School of Infantry's Tactics Wing and everything continued as before.

A few days later Major General Dunbar who had, as Director of Infantry, been my boss since my arrival at Warminster, departed. The Director of Infantry had his headquarters within the school and Charles Dunbar actually lived in our officers' mess. The arrangement could have been difficult had it not been for the great care he took not to impinge upon my position and in this he could not have been more considerate. Whenever we had a formal guest night, he would arrive as a guest and after dinner take his leave in good time so that other guests junior to himself would not have to wait around for him to go. He then spent a few minutes in his bedroom before reappearing as a member of the mess, after which he could stay drinking at the bar for as long as he liked without anyone else having to worry about him. In every way he had been the soul of kindness and consideration and I was sad to see him go.

His replacement was David House of the KRRC with whom I had worked when I was in the War Office and he was on the staff of the Chief of the Defence Staff. He lived with his wife outside the school but his office was near mine. It so happened that at about this time the Tactics and Doctrine Committee, decided that the army should have a new pamphlet on the subject of counter-insurgency, known then as counter-revolutionary warfare. This committee was chaired by the Vice Chief of the General Staff and consisted of the Director of Combat Development, the arms directors, the commandant of the Staff College and the Chiefs of Staff of UK Land Forces and the British Army of the Rhine. The procedure for producing a new army pamphlet was for the committee to issue terms of reference and select one of its members to lead on the subject. If the matter concerned all arms equally, it would be given to someone known as the Brigadier Author who worked at the Staff College. But if it was a subject that was primarily of concern to one arm, it was given to the director of that arm. In this case it was given to the Director of Infantry. The procedure for producing the pamphlet was ponderous and lengthy, but it should be remembered that the end product would probably represent the army's considered view of the subject for many years to come. In this case it replaced a pamphlet called 'Duties in Aid of the Civil Power' issued in 1935.

Naturally the School of Infantry, which was supposed to be a centre for thought on all infantry matters, was consulted and I was brought in from the start because, having written *Low Intensity Operations*, I was generally considered to have more experience of the business than most. Above all, I was actually present in the building where the work was being carried out and David House who was also well experienced in the matter, enjoyed discussing it with me. I can not remember what the final pamphlet was like, but none of Mr Hattersley's abhorrent bits would have been included.

From the time of my arrival at Warminster, I had been concerned that the school was in no position to carry out its role as a centre of thought for the infantry, because there was no library. At the very least an Arms School should have a library containing all current military publications relating to its arm of service with a security grading below 'confidential'. Ideally it should also include many books of reference together with material designed to help officers working for the Staff College entrance exam or their promotion exam. I wanted a full and useful library and set about agitating for one. Naturally all sorts of problems loomed up when we started looking for a place to put it and when we tried to get money to pay a librarian and buy books. However, in the autumn of 1973 our new library opened.

During November, on my way to visit the Jungle Warfare Wing, I stopped off in Cyprus where Hew Butler, now a major general, was commanding the troops. The purpose of my visit was to give my Northern Ireland talk to his officers. Next day Hew invited to lunch our old friend Petros, who had been commanding the Greek fighters in Nicosia when we had been there ten years earlier. Petros was very interesting about recent events in Cyprus. Amongst other things he said that a delegation from the IRA had visited some former EOKA men to discuss tactics and had also asked whether anyone had information that would help them to get at me. According to Petros the EOKA men told the IRA that it was 'not cricket' to pursue me now that I was no longer involved in their contest.

Soon after my return, the School of Infantry was visited by a team of officers from the Sudanese army who wanted to buy the latest infantry anti-tank weapon that we were trialling at the Support Weapons Wing. I accompanied them when they watched a test firing from an armoured personnel carrier on the range, to see how it worked. Unfortunately the first missile looped the loop and crashed into the ground with a loud bang a short way off. Seeing what was happening, we all ducked. As the smoke and dust drifted away on the wind we straightened up and I sheepishly said that such a thing had never happened before. They agreed to try again but the next missile did the same thing, landing even closer than the first. Luckily most Sudanese have a good sense of humour and all adjourned happily to the mess for lunch. After a few modifications, this weapon, known as Swingfire, became highly successful, but I don't know whether the Sudanese ever bought it.

*   *   *

In April 1974, I heard that I would have to leave Warminster at the end of August and go on leave until the following January when I was to attend the 1975 course at the Royal College of Defence Studies. I did not at all mind going on leave for four months but had no desire to spend a year on a course which by all accounts was a waste of time.

As it turned out the course was not unduly exacting. It meant catching the train at Farnham in time to reach the college in Belgrave Square for the morning lecture which started at 10 o'clock and after a break and discussion period, finished in time for lunch. After lunch one could work on projects with several other students or research and write a paper set by the Directing Staff. Sometimes if no other members were involved one could go home to work. There were about seventy-five students of whom nearly half were from Commonwealth or foreign countries. The UK students were drawn from all three services with representatives from the Diplomatic Service, Home Office and police. An important purpose of the course was to give British officers a chance to meet and become friendly with their contemporaries from overseas and we were naturally encouraged to take them home and let them meet our families.

In addition to the lectures, we went on a number of visits to meet workers in factories, trade-union officials, local government Civil Servants, and various other people who appeared to be more or less irrelevant to our likely future appointments: a further dose of mind-broadening. Obviously senior officers need to realise that all military activity, with particular reference to the procurement of weapons and equipment, is dependent on political, financial and industrial backing, but most officers know that anyway. Personally I did not enjoy these visits, travelling around in a bus with a crowd of smoking and sometimes singing fellow students, as we made our way from one place to the next. On these occasions I usually teamed up with a thin, like-minded diplomat who had been in the Rifle Brigade in his youth and who did not sweat or take up too much room in the next door seat.

The best part of the course was the extended tour that we did in the autumn, when half a dozen different groups went to different parts of the world. I rather fancied the group that was going round Africa, but the very interesting and stimulating commandant of the college, Air Chief Marshal Sir John Barraclough, wanted me to accompany his group, which was touring Europe. By this time I knew that my next posting was to command the 2nd Division in Germany so that it made sense for me to get up to date with 'Cold War' issues. We went to Bonn and Stockholm and then to Yugoslavia and Italy, all of which turned out to be very worthwhile.

The publicity that had been given to *Low Intensity Operations* led me to believe that there was a need to outline those of my personal experiences that led to the conclusions reached in that book. I therefore decided to write another book called *Bunch of Five*, which was started at Warminster and finished in the train between London and Farnham. My initial intention was to cover my time in Kenya, Malaya, Muscat, Cyprus and Northern Ireland; hence the five components of the bunch. But clearly with the insurgency in Northern Ireland still going strong, the Ministry of Defence would not have permitted an account of my doings there. So the book finished up as a 'bunch of four' plus a summary of the lessons learnt. By the end of the course, Faber & Faber were almost ready to publish it.

Chapter 11

2nd Armoured Division and Staff College 1976–1980

In January 1976 my family and I left Horsley House for the last time and moved to the headquarters of the 2nd Division at Lubbecke in Germany. Lubbecke was a small market town between Osnabrück and Minden on the northern slopes of the Weserburger Walde.

The overall situation in the British Army of the Rhine at the start of 1976 was rather different to that existing at the time of my departure in 1953. Then, NATO was vastly superior to the Russians with regard to nuclear weapons, so there was little temptation for them to make use of their undoubted superiority in terms of conventional forces, since to do so would rapidly lead to the total annihilation of their homeland. But by 1965 they had caught up in nuclear terms. Now, it was felt necessary for NATO forces to demonstrate that they could hold a Soviet assault using conventional forces for long enough to enable a settlement to be reached, before being obliged to resort to nuclear weapons, a strategy known as Flexible Response. NATO, greatly reinforced by the reformed West German army, was therefore constantly trying to improve its conventional forces, but as soon as it did so the Russians improved theirs in order to restore a balance more favourable to themselves. But the strain on the economy of the Soviet Union was beginning to tell and NATO was concerned that the Russians might risk attacking the West before being obliged to give up the race for financial reasons.

That was the big picture, but closer to home the United Kingdom's economy after several years of Mr Wilson's stewardship, was causing concern and the government felt obliged to reduce expenditure on defence. This led, as usual, to another re-organisation. There was to be a reduction in the size of each of the three divisions resident in Germany, but an extra division, currently in England, would join BAOR so that we could fulfil our treaty obligations to the alliance. My division was to be reorganised first, which meant that its manpower would be reduced by around 30 per cent, the four armoured regiments reduced to two and the four infantry battalions to three, although each of the regiments or battalions would have four squadrons or companies instead of three. There was also to be an armoured reconnaissance regiment. The new divisions would be known as 'armoured divisions.' When the arrival of a fourth division is taken into account the total reduction in armoured squadrons throughout the corps was only three. This was more than offset by an increase of two armoured reconnaissance squadrons and twenty infantry companies, especially as the infantry companies were being re-equipped with a new and powerful anti-tank missile. This re-organisation would be my principal concern while in Germany. There was to be a major exercise at the end of the year, to discover what adjustments might be needed to make the new arrangements work.

It is perhaps worth mentioning that at the time of my arrival there was a great deal of bad feeling at the way in which the business was being forced through without proper concern for the views of the Commander-in-Chief, Harry Tuzo, and the Corps Commander, Jacky Harman. And of all the people critical of the new arrangements, none had better reason for their misgivings than the officers who had been appointed to command brigades. They were now supposed to regard themselves as garrison commanders in peacetime whose wartime role was to be deputy divisional commanders, ready to act as task force commanders by taking under command a varying number of units to carry out particular tasks. There was a lot of complicated military thinking behind this, but it made little difference in peacetime, because the units that would have been in their brigades were still in their garrisons and they merely had to call themselves task force commanders when on training. Nonetheless I had much sympathy and a bit of reassuring to do. Luckily, so far as my division was concerned, neither Brigadier Desmond Langley, Commander Munster Garrison and Task Force Charlie, nor Brigadier Mike Reynolds, Commander Osnabrück Garrison and Task Force Delta, was going to make themselves unhappy on the strength of a title. They were more interested in getting on with their jobs and enjoying themselves.

Inevitably most of my time in the early days was spent driving around, getting to know people. By great good fortune Colonel Keith Burch, the Divisional Chief of Staff (officially Colonel GS), had a firm grasp of the problems involved in the dreaded re-organisation to say nothing of facing the Russians. In addition he had the knack of preparing for likely future eventualities well ahead, so that we were never reduced to dealing with matters on the spur of the moment, which made life easier for all concerned. There were two other stalwarts in the headquarters, Loyd Body who was the brigadier commanding our three artillery regiments and Tony Baxter who handled the administrative and logistic side of the business. The other two divisional commanders were longstanding friends. David Alexander Sinclair was at Verden to the north and Nigel Bagnall was at Herford, to the south. Not long after my arrival Dick Worsley took over as Corps Commander from Jacky Harman. We had often met socially since we worked together in Malaya, but our relationship there, had not been of the easiest. It would be interesting to see how we would get along in the rarefied atmosphere of I Corps. Soon afterwards Harry Tuzo left to become the Deputy Supreme Allied Commander Europe and the highly intelligent Frank King took over as Commander-in-Chief of the British Army of the Rhine (BAOR).

In this connection it must be said that BAOR was like nowhere else in the army. For years, while nothing had actually happened, people had been keyed up and trained to fight the great battle for the country's survival. Many of the important players had spent their whole careers oscillating between I Corps, the Ministry of Defence and the Staff College. To these people the operations that had taken place in far off corners of the world were side-shows and those involved in them could not be expected to understand proper soldiering. Life in Germany revolved round a regular progression of study days and training exercises, interspersed with social and sporting occasions, all conducted in style and regulated according to long standing custom. One needed to adjust.

*   *   *

During the early summer of 1976 we became friendly with Clemens von Nagel who lived on a sizeable estate near Warendorf which was one of the main centres for equestrian sport in Germany. Clemens was a generous host and in addition lent us an elderly horse called Frankie. One morning, on returning from a family trip to Berlin, my ADC, Robert Martin, met us with the news that my horse Frankie had collapsed in the stables. The local vet declared that he had suffered a heart attack and should be put down. Robert had rung up von Nagel to tell him the sad news, only to discover that he too had had a heart attack that morning and died. Our children declared that God had arranged matters so that Clemens could ride Frankie to heaven. Poor Gabrielle was distraught. We continued to see her often until we left Germany and she remains a great friend and a regular visitor. But much had occurred from a military point of view before these sad events took place.

*   *   *

The business of validating the new organisation started to gain momentum at the end of April 1976 with a visit from General Peter Hunt, Chief of the General Staff. In the course of briefing him I said that the main problem was likely to be the reduction in the number of battlegroup headquarters i.e. armoured regiment and infantry battalion headquarters, from eight to five, rather than in the replacement of brigades by task forces. I also pointed out that although the width of the front would be reduced by the increase in the number of divisions in the corps, the depth of the front would remain a problem. The shortage of battlegroup headquarters would make it difficult for the Divisional Commander to control the defence of the area behind his front, with particular reference to securing bridges and defiles against enemy airborne forces. This would be especially awkward in the period before the arrival of reinforcing battalions from England, should the war start before they were in place. The fact that each battlegroup would have an extra company or armoured squadron, though of vital importance in terms of capability, would not assist in terms of control. Another important question would arise regarding the management of re-supply, as the new organisation had greatly reduced the logistic capacity of the division and was based on the assumption that the logistic units would be controlled by divisional headquarters direct and not by the task forces. There were heaps of more detailed problems to be sorted out, including the changes in tactical procedures that would inevitably follow on from the way in which the new division was put together. A day or two after General Hunt departed, we held a divisional study day to explain and discuss the new arrangements and to tell everyone how we planned to test them out during the coming year. In May the Supreme Allied Commander Europe (SACEUR), General Al Haig of the US Army, held a study day at his headquarters outside Brussels for all his subordinate commanders down to the level of divisional commander.

* * *

Two months later the newly reorganised 2nd Armoured Division went out on a skeleton exercise which meant that the divisional headquarters and the headquarters of the task forces and battlegroups went out, but not the men. Such exercises allowed the staffs at every level to be practised, while the expense of moving tanks and guns and vehicles would be avoided, not to mention the colossal damages that had to be paid out to landowners whenever a sizeable number of troops were operating on the ground. For this exercise we weeded out many of the unnecessary vehicles that the divisional headquarters had accumulated over the years, based on Nigel Bagnall's experiments in 4th Division designed to make the headquarters easier to move and less vulnerable to air attack. Although it meant that I had to exchange my sumptuously appointed caravan for a Land Rover, I was happy to make the changes. Hitherto the movement of even a small headquarters had resembled a circus travelling from one place to the next. At one stage in the exercise when I was tucked away comfortably in a barn, General Al Haig appeared and we had a lengthy talk about the way in which my division would be working when restructured.

After a while he said that he would like to visit a battlegroup headquarters so I took him to the command vehicle of the Irish Guards which was close by.

For the big autumn exercise the other divisions in the corps would have to lend us enough companies, and armoured squadrons to bring our battlegroups up to the new strength. Other units and sub-units such as an armoured reconnaissance regiment, would be provided from corps troops. What was left of Nigel Bagnall's division plus some Dutch and Canadian troops would provide the enemy, while the remains of David Alexander Sinclair's division would provide the umpires and control mechanism for the exercise director who was the corps commander, Dick Worsley.

On one such exercise I remember talking to Desmond Langley and his brigade major, Christopher Wolverson, by the bank of a river which his task force was supposed to cross during the coming night. I wondered vaguely whether it would be a fiasco like the time when 7th Armoured Brigade tried to put a pontoon bridge across the Weser in the large-scale exercises of 1950. I was reassured by the fact that times had changed and that the Langley/Wolverson team was supremely competent. To the left of where we were standing was a steep hill with a castle on top and Desmond said that he had taken the owner up for a ride in a helicopter to see how much damage was being done to his land. Everywhere they looked, the fields were scarred by tank tracks and there were great holes in the hedges. Far from being upset, the owner was rubbing his hands with glee, saying that the compensation he would get, would keep him in funds for years to come. Apart from these flashes of memory, I do not remember much about the exercises.

*   *   *

At the end of 1976 the Royal United Services Institute asked me to write an article on the new armoured division. Having discussed the strengths and weaknesses of the new division, I concluded that providing that it was reinforced as planned from the United Kingdom before the outbreak of war, it should be able to do what was required of it. After discussing the ways in which it could carry out the various tasks that might confront it after reinforcement, I switched to what might happen if the war started before the reinforcements arrived. In this case the division would not only be much smaller, but also of a totally different shape so that it would have to be used in a different way. The Corps Commander and Commander-in-Chief approved the article, but the Ministry of Defence asked that reference to the situation that would exist before the reinforcements arrived should be cut out. Although everyone was well aware of our dependence on reinforcement, the feeling in the Ministry of Defence was that the article went into too much detail as to the form the reinforcement would take and the capabilities that depended on it.

The big exercise was followed by various discussions and conferences designed to digest and disseminate the lessons learnt at such great expense to the taxpayer. It was during this time that I became involved in talking to a number of German officers. Each of our divisions was paired with a German division for the purpose of exchanging views. Some of their officers would attend our study days and vice versa. The 2nd Armoured Division, as we were now called, was paired with the 7th Panzer Grenadier Division, which was fortunate because its commander, Major General Doctor Ferdinand von Senger und Etterlin, known as Deidi, was both knowledgeable and friendly. He also knew far more than we would ever know about the Russians, having invaded their country as a subaltern in July 1941 and having fought them until losing an arm after which he became adjutant (ADC in English terms) to the famous General Guderian. Guderian finished the war as Hitler's Chief of the General Staff after which he and Deidi were in a prisoner of war camp, where he was visited by Liddell Hart. Long discussions ensued. Guderian flattered Liddell Hart by saying that he was one of his disciples, which surprised Deidi as he had never heard Guderian mention the man. When asked, Guderian said that he did not know much about Liddell Hart, but that they needed to 'chat him up' to get extra cigarettes and chocolate. After the war Deidi was one of the first Germans to go to Oxford as a Rhodes Scholar, thereby following in the footsteps of his father, another distinguished general, who had commanded the German Corps at Monte Cassino. Needless to say, Deidi's doctorate was academic, rather than medical.

*   *   *

By 1977 Mr Wilson had handed over the job of Prime Minister to Mr Callaghan and General Hunt had handed over the job of Chief of the General Staff to Roly Gibbs. In April the new Prime Minister accompanied by General Gibbs paid a visit to BAOR, which included a stop off with 2nd Armoured Division. They met us in the field and as he was obviously cold in his London suit, I lent him my combat jacket which was rather small for him, but which protected him from the elements. He was certainly a more impressive man than his predecessor and having been a naval officer in the war, he knew how to talk to the soldiers without 'turning them up' by trying to be matey. It was also good to see Roly Gibbs again. With his vast store of combat experience and common sense, he was eminently suited to calming down the disquiet caused by the recent organisational turmoil.

Later in the year we were visited by the Secretary of State for Defence, Mr Fred Mulley and his wife. They arrived one evening, spent the night with us and next day I took him to see various regiments. Mr Mulley, was pleasant and impressively knowledgeable about defence. He had joined a Territorial Army battalion of the Worcestershire Regiment at a young age just before the war and quickly rose to the rank of sergeant. He was wounded and taken prisoner when his battalion was part of 2nd Division, during the retreat to Dunkirk. He was genuinely interested in the welfare of the soldiers.

The Queen's silver jubilee was in 1977 and it was decided that the army's contribution would be a grand military review to be held in Germany. Because of the time and money that this would cost, there would be no large-scale military exercises during the year, although skeleton exercises and low-level training would take place, which gave me plenty to do. Furthermore in addition to the units in my division, I had been given responsibility for training and administering an infantry brigade, recently renamed a 'Field Force', which would be commanded directly by the Corps Commander in the event of war. In charge of it was my old friend, Bob Pascoe. One of its battalions was 3 Para, whose commanding officer, Peter Morton, I had last met at Ayios Sozomenos in 1964 when he was trotting around with Brigadier Roly Gibbs.

For the Queen's Jubilee I was appointed Army Review Commander, which was not a particularly arduous task. Nigel Bagnall was in charge of the main event, that is to say the parade itself. The first item planned was a display of massed bands comprising over 800 bandsmen, which would give the Germans something to think about. This was to be followed by a march past of hundreds of tanks, armoured personnel carriers, armoured reconnaissance vehicles and artillery pieces with Army Air Corps helicopters dashing hither and thither overhead. Nigel's divisional headquarters staff would work all that out. My headquarters would be responsible for building the stands, organising tents and marquees, arranging for the movement of the participants and guests in and out of the parade area and of course for security. Keith Burch was still fully occupied with the re-organisation and its aftermath, so Tony Baxter took charge of the arrangements for the jubilee celebrations and handled them magnificently. Whatever befell, I would be held responsible, but as ceremonial was definitely not my strong suit, I felt that the best chance of a successful outcome would be for me to keep as far away from the inevitable meetings and planning as possible. Only in the last few days did I put in an appearance at Sennelager where the review was to take place, moving with my caravan to a secluded spot by the side of a lake. Here I was close enough for Tony Baxter to get hold of me should he need me, but well placed to do a bit of fishing when not otherwise engaged.

It pains me to think how little I can remember of the historic events of the next two days. The dress rehearsal was probably the most stressful part, thanks to one of the few decisions that I had made personally, which was to make 3 Para responsible for security. In doing so I had said that literally no one was to be allowed in, who did not have the requisite pass. On the morning of the rehearsal I was in a boat fishing away when a party appeared on the bank waiving their arms frantically. On approaching the shore I discovered that Nigel Bagnall was being held by 3 Para, because he had forgotten his pass: they would not let him go without my personal authorisation. After that I decided to put on my dress uniform and hang around a bit. I remember the conference after the rehearsal because Frank King wanted to make the helicopter display more spectacular by having them dive towards the spectators as the tanks went past. I wondered whether our medical arrangements would cope with a helicopter crashing into the Royal Stand but said nothing. Frank King was, after all, the Commander-in-Chief and the Chief of the General Staff, Roly Gibbs, who was also at the meeting, just laughed as usual.

Despite the problems of reorganising the division, by far the greatest part of my time was spent visiting regiments and battalions on training and in barracks. These visits involved listening to the views of countless numbers of people of all ranks and specialities. This is the standard way in which commanders through the ages, have gathered the information that they needed to handle their day-to-day business.

*   *   *

In September 1977, I heard that my next appointment was to be commandant of the Staff College. I was to take over from John Stanier early in the coming year. My last few months in Germany were spent making sure that everything we had learnt about the restructuring and its affect on the corps were fully recorded.

Although the recent restructuring of the corps had been the main topic of interest during the past year, another major change had been going on for some time, resulting from the alteration of the nuclear balance between NATO and the Soviet Union. When NATO had total nuclear superiority, our tactics had been based on a form of defence that involved battlegroups drawing advancing Russian detachments into small nuclear killing grounds. By 1976 with the improved ability of the Russians to reply in kind to a nuclear attack, it was felt that these tactics might not work because there might be too long a delay before the initial use of tactical nuclear weapons was authorised. The tactics described could only work if there was very little delay between asking for political clearance and getting it: if delayed, the target would have moved before clearance arrived.

NATO's reaction was to replace the old tactics with a policy of holding a main position as firmly as possible as far to the east as possible. The idea was that the time it would take the Russians to build up a concentration of force sufficient to penetrate such a strongly held forward defensive position, would be enough for our commanders to get the authority to use a nuclear weapon. Furthermore a weapon used in this way could possibly be directed against enemy concentrations to the east of the border, thereby saving the West German population from sustaining more harm that necessary. For these reasons the Commander-in-Chief of Allied Forces Central Europe decreed that all plans should be based on this policy of forward positional defence. In this context it has to be remembered that Allied Forces Central Europe consisted of one corps each from Britain, the Netherlands and Belgium, two from America, but three large ones from Germany. In addition there were some German territorial forces, not under NATO's command, but which would play their part in the defence of Germany in the event of war. Although it was the United States that provided and authorised the use of the nuclear weapons, it was Germany that produced the most number of men on the ground and it was over West Germany that the battle would mainly be fought. Their views were thus bound to receive a lot of attention especially as the Commander-in-Chief Allied Forces Central Europe was always a German.

During the summer and autumn of 1977, the staff at corps headquarters carried out an examination of the ways in which the reshaped corps should work. Their immediate problem was to formulate a new concept of operations and accompanying tactical doctrine that would fit the new NATO policy and the shape of its reorganised divisions. All of this gave rise to many papers requiring comment and a number of high-powered meetings were held to consider the implications.

The 2nd Armoured Division's Study Day, held in July designed to keep people abreast of events, was attended by von Senger. Whilst accepting that the old idea of small killing zones was outmoded, he suggested an alternative. His idea was that the British, German, Dutch and Belgian corps might all be used to contain a large number of Russians in one huge killing zone for long enough to get authority for the release of one or more tactical nuclear weapon. Probably no one present, including von Senger, actually thought that it might happen in exactly that way. What he implied was that we needed to stop thinking that major operational decisions would necessarily be made by divisional or even corps commanders. In the event of a Russian invasion the way in which the battle would be fought would probably be determined at a higher level.

In any case within the British Corps there was little scope for deciding where at the start of a war, the main area of defence, consisting of numerous positions and alternative positions many miles deep, should be because this would be laid down from above. But the British still thought that within the main position there was some latitude to decide whether it should be defended by a system of mobile or positional defence. The difference between these two concepts is that for positional defence the main strength is held well forward, designed directly to damage the enemy's attack, with limited reserves held back to plug any holes that the enemy might make. For mobile defence the forward part of the main position is held with fewer troops and is designed to channel the attackers into places where they can be advantageously attacked by strong reserves moving forward. The mobility of mobile defence refers to the move of reserves forward, not the move of the front backwards, which amounts to a withdrawal. Some years earlier, plans for a withdrawal from the border between East and West Germany to an obstacle formed by the River Weser, had sometimes wrongly been described as mobile defence, which caused certain German officers to regard the term with suspicion.

Another matter which we in 2nd Armoured Division studied at this time, was the use that could be made of the large number of small towns and villages that existed throughout much of the area that we would be trying to defend. Broadly speaking a sizeable built up area can only be used in isolation, if it is situated in such a place that the enemy must attack it and if it is big enough to absorb a worthwhile enemy force. But some small built up areas could be exploited by being incorporated into normal defensive layouts and others could be used for harassing, damaging and delaying the enemy even if circumstances did not permit of them being put into a full state of defence. Before reinforcement, the 50,000 men of I Corps had twelve mechanised infantry battalions and the three non-mechanised battalions of 5th Field Force. But when reinforced to its full strength of 120,000 men the number of non-mechanised infantry battalions would rise from three to twenty-two. It seemed to us that more thought needed to be given to using some of them to take advantage of built up areas.

By August 1977 most of these matters had been fully discussed at HQ I Corps and I prepared a paper which I intended to use as a basis for bringing the teaching at the Staff College up to date. My main conclusions were that our most pressing weakness did not stem from shortage of units or equipment once the corps received its reinforcements from England. Nor did it stem from our new organisation or from our operational plans or concept. I reckoned that our weaknesses lay in the time needed for our reinforcements to arrive and also from the fact that there were logistic shortages in terms of transport, ammunition and spares, not to mention insufficient time available for training, the maintenance of equipment, and the erosion of training facilities.

I cleared my paper with Dick Worsley as Corps Commander. The next thing to do was to make sure that it fully represented the views of General King, the Commander-in-Chief. For this purpose I had a very full discussion with his Chief of Staff, Robin Carnegie who took my paper away to think about it and get it examined at his headquarters. After a certain amount correspondence and amendment it was given the go ahead shortly after my move to the Staff College.

*   *   *

In February 1978 we bade farewell to 2nd Armoured division and moved to the Staff College at Camberley. Outwardly the Staff College did not seem to have changed much since my time there in 1956. One thing that had not changed at all, was the commandant's secretary Monica, who had arrived when General Hull was commandant thirty years earlier. She was highly efficient and controlled entry to the commandant's presence with unflagging devotion so that no one should disturb him when he was trying to concentrate on complicated aspects of military thought, so necessary for the preparation of the many speeches that he would have to deliver. In fact there was plenty of time for higher thought, as Brigadier Alastair Dennis, the deputy commandant, ran the place on a day-to-day basis, being the person who prepared the programme and directed the teams responsible for drawing up the various aspects of instruction. From an administrative point of view Colonel Gerry Hulme the Chief of Staff, officially known as the colonel GS, did everything else. Both these men were top class and good company into the bargain.

The student body was divided into three divisions, each commanded by a colonel supported by a number of lieutenant colonels who did the day-to-day teaching. Colonel Peter Inge ran the Junior Division of the Staff College, based at Warminster. From our time together in the Ministry of Defence I knew that I need not concern myself too greatly with this division, but visiting him gave me an opportunity to keep up with many of the friends we had made when we were at the School of Infantry. One advantage of being the commandant was that I was entitled to chose the members of the directing staff and during my time I managed to collect together some first class officers.

Although the way of life had not changed much since 1956, the subject matter had altered to keep up with the times. It was part of my job to see that it continued to do so, which in 1978, mainly meant ensuring that the recent changes in BAOR were understood and incorporated into the syllabus. Many people thought that the main reason for my appointment was to bring the teaching on counter-insurgency up to date, but in fact this had already been done very effectively and was now extremely sophisticated.

A task that went with being commandant of the Staff College was membership of No. 2 Board, which selected officers for promotion to the rank of full colonel and brigadier and allocated them to appointments in these ranks. Another was membership of the Combat Development and Tactical Doctrine Committee, which met under the chairmanship of the Vice Chief of the General Staff. The decisions made by this committee were relevant to the Staff College because once adopted as army policy they had to be incorporated into its teaching.

Quite apart from the speeches that I had to give within the college, I was often asked to speak on topical matters of interest to many and varied military and civilian audiences outside it. One of my earliest invitations was to explain to representatives of the press how recent innovations in BAOR had affected the organisation of 1st British Corps and its method of operating in the event of war. This I did on the basis of the paper I had prepared in conjunction with the Chief of Staff at BAOR Headquarters.

Hans Hinrichs with whom I had been friendly when we were both students at Camberley in 1956, was one of the first people to come to stay with us at Staff College House. He had recently retired as a lieutenant general and was now the director of the German equivalent of our Royal United Service Institute. He was concerned that the middle-piece German officers were not well informed about the way the British Corps was organised, or about its tactical ideas. During his visit he asked me to write an article for his magazine to enlighten them. Accordingly I drafted an article and sent it to the Ministry of Defence to get their approval, which they gave. It then transpired that BAOR Headquarters were not happy with it, because they thought that it might inhibit efforts that they were making to get the commander of Allied Forces Central Europe to accept a degree of mobile defence within the forward position occupied by the British Corps. Later in the year General Franz Josef Schulze the current Commander Allied Forces Central Europe, stayed with us for the night before giving a lecture to the college. My impression of his feelings on this matters was that, as most of the soldiers throughout his command at the beginning of a war would be conscripts or reservists, it was best to keep things as simple as possible. Added to this, he also had the political angle to consider.

Two years after retiring from the army, I published a book called *Warfare as a Whole*, which contains my views on confronting the Russians and can be read by anyone wishing to know more about that. I will desist from writing further on the subject, as the circumstances have long since made it irrelevant. Nonetheless it was the main preoccupation of those involved in the defence of the country during my time at Camberley and consequently provided much of the matters discussed at the Staff College.

The first of these was to keep in touch with the members of the directing staff and students. There were altogether 173 students of whom 45 came from overseas countries. Each of our courses lasted for one year. Of the British students, a few of whom came from the other two services, about half had been educated at state schools and half from public or direct grant schools. And of the ones from public or direct grant schools, not more than twenty-five to thirty came from what might be called the traditional public schools, at that time associated with providing the army with its officers. In short the view normally expounded by the press and television that army officers come from a narrow and privileged background was wide of the mark. Another relevant statistic is that only about one third of the UK officers had attended a university.

A highlight of the of the course was the battlefield tour that took place in August and which I remembered so well from my own days as a student. It was great fun, but some of those who had over the years been describing the battles in which they had taken part, had died and others were getting a bit forgetful. Realising that there was a limit to the time that it could go on, it had been decided in the Ministry of Defence that there should be no more tours after 1979. It was my sad duty to preside over the last two to take place and we made the most of them. Travelling with us were many of the great performers from the war such as General Pip Roberts who commanded 11th Armoured Division during the breakout battles, Robin Hastings who commanded the Green Howards during the days immediately following the landings and Hans von Luck who commanded the Germans opposing 11th Armoured Division's advance. None of them were in the least bit forgetful. As a parting gift to the performers, Elizabeth did a pastel picture of each one as he was delivering his talk.

*   *   *

On one occasion during the running of the course I was visited by John Stanier, now Vice Chief of the General Staff, who said that General Roly Gibbs would like me to look into the way in which our forces within the United Kingdom were commanded. This involved examining how Headquarters UK Land Forces and the headquarters of the various districts and brigades were organised and worked. It was not a subject that had impinged on my consciousness in the past, but I was aware that many people were concerned that it needed bringing up to date. I particularly remember that when Bill Scotter who had recently relieved Frank King as Commander-in-Chief of the British Army of the Rhine, came to stay with us, he was critical of the lack of supervision and training opportunities available to the regiment of which he was colonel. After looking at the problem, my opinion was that there were too many senior officers in the command headquarters and too few below district headquarters looking after the units. I also felt that units of the Territorial Army were not sufficiently integrated into the formations designed to reinforce the British Army of the Rhine in the event of war. To my mind it was necessary to separate all the operational and logistic units, whether regular or territorial, from the training, administrative, and UK base units. They should then be incorporated into a field army or corps, with a proper chain of command running from UK Land Forces through districts to brigades and thence to the units. The arms directors and district commanders could continue to direct and administer the non-operational schools, depots and establishments as at present.

Not long after passing my views to John Stanier, I was told that I was to hand over the Staff College to David Alexander Sinclair in January 1980 and take over as Deputy Commander-in-Chief of UK Land Forces and Director General of the Territorial Army. I was sorry to leave. The Staff College was the very epitome of military excellence. Everyone had to work hard, but because of the traditional efficiency with which it was run, there was none of the friction that arises from people wondering what was going to happen next. The syndicate system of teaching used at the college, was designed to allow students to learn from each other as well as from the directing staff. And because there was such a wide divergence of experience amongst the students, there was much that they could pick up from each other. Many of the foreign students had useful operational knowledge, some having been involved in the Arab/Israeli or the India/Pakistan wars.

Above all the Staff College taught people to think straight and express themselves clearly and concisely. The college crest consisted of an owl perched on crossed swords. Underneath was written '*Tam Marte Quam Minerva*' which, though concise, was incomprehensible. For my closing address I had the crest prominently displayed on a screen but to discourage those who asked silly questions at the end of lectures when everyone else wanted to go to lunch, I had the motto changed to 'Ears Open Mouth Shut'. One year at the Staff College was worth any number of university degrees.

*   *   *

Perhaps its worth mentioning here that in 1975 I had become chairman of the Mounted Infantry Club which had been founded after the Boer War, to perpetuate the comradeship that existed within the Mounted Infantry, then a distinct branch of the service. When the Mounted Infantry was abolished as an arm of the service in 1922, its non-public funds were handed over to the club to use for the purpose of encouraging infantry officers to take part in horse sports such as hunting, chasing and point to points. Whilst at the Staff College I had a perfect opportunity for researching the club's background, as a result of which I produced a short history of the club for the benefit of the members.

Chapter 12

High Command 1980–1985

In the 1980s New Year Honours List I was made a Knight of the Bath, which meant that Elizabeth became a Lady. She deserved it many times over considering what she had put up with since marrying me. In February 1980 we moved to Havelock House, Tidworth and in March I became Deputy Commander-in-Chief in the rank of lieutenant general. Tim Creasey had recently taken over as Commander-in-Chief and Micky Tillotson as Chief of Staff. So far as reforming UKLF was concerned, John Stanier had by now not only prepared the ground, but he had also sown a good handful of seed. It would be up to the three of us to foster the growth.

In the letters that I wrote to John Stanier from the Staff College, I had restricted myself to discussing the problems relating to the command of the formations and units stationed in the UK. It is now worth looking at the overall situation of UK Land Forces, in order to get the job I would be doing into perspective. UK Land Forces had three functions. In the first place it had an operational responsibility, in conjunction with the other two services, for the defence of the United Kingdom and for mounting operations abroad if required. Its second task was to prepare the regular and Territorial Army formations and units stationed within the United Kingdom for their wartime roles, either as reinforcements for overseas commands or for home defence. Its third task was to administer all the troops within the country including the schools and depots of the Individual Training Organisation and the Ministry Defence controlled base installations. All told there were around 88,000 regular soldiers and 74,000 members of the Territorial Army.

During the years when the West had nuclear superiority over the Soviet Union and when any war was expected to last for a very short time, neither home defence nor the business of reinforcing overseas commands was given a high priority. The main role of UK Land Force was seen as being administrative. But with the change in the nuclear balance and the expectation that a war might have to last for weeks as opposed to days, the reinforcement of NATO by troops from Britain, became vitally important. This greatly increased the need for the formations and units concerned, to be carefully prepared and properly equipped for their planned roles. Home Defence also merited a higher priority, because it was assumed that the enemy would try to interfere with the despatch of these reinforcements and with the massive movement of United States troops in and out of the country during the early stages of a war. In short the change in the nuclear balance not only affected the concept of operations in Germany but also the strategic outlook throughout the NATO Alliance.

It is worth noticing that our commitments to NATO were not restricted to the Central Region. We had also agreed to assist in the defence of Northern and southern Europe as well. Of these two, it was the situation in the north that most concerned us. Within Allied Forces Northern Europe there were two separate threats both connected to the movement of American and British troops to Europe and to the defence of the United Kingdom itself. In order to stop the move of Americans across the Atlantic, the Russians needed to deny us the use of the Norwegian Sea and its outlets into the Atlantic. But their airfields in the Kola Peninsula were too far away for their aircraft to cover such operations. It was therefore considered likely that Russia would try to occupy the northern coast of Norway in order to operate from airfields there, which would also bring them within reach of the United Kingdom itself. The other threat was of an attack on the Baltic Approaches, that is to say the Jutland Peninsula, Zealand and that part of Germany lying north of the Elbe. This area was not only the homeland of Denmark, a member of NATO, but it also contained airfields the possession of which by the Russians would greatly increase the air threat to the United Kingdom and therefore the movement of reinforcements to the continent. Furthermore enemy possession of this area would pose a serious threat to the left flank of the Central Region.

Tim Creasey gave me the task of preparing those troops within UK Land Forces involved in carrying out all these various roles. The idea was for me to create and command a new formation called the UK Field Army, which would combine all operational units whether regular or Territorial Army, within an effective chain of command. There were a total of 159 major units (lieutenant colonels' commands) and 271 independent minor units that would be included in the new Field Army, 106,000 strong. Of the major units, 58 were from the regular army and 101 from the TA.

For some years lip service had been paid to the so-called 'one army' concept, meaning that units of the regular and Territorial Army were part of one united whole. As virtually all of the Territorial Army would be in the new UK Field Army its formation would add strength to this concept. The Deputy Commander-in-Chief had for some time held the parallel appointment of Inspector General of the Territorial Army but hitherto his role had been mainly to represent the interests of the Territorial Army in a general sense and to give encouragement to its officers and men. Under the new arrangements the TA would be fully under my command which would enable me to adjust its organisation to suit the interests of the army as a whole. A major general in London was responsible for the link between the Ministry of Defence, the TA Council and the Regional Associations (TAVRAs), which had the statutory duty for recruiting, also for handling the financial affairs and administering Territorial Army units and their drill halls. Each of these Associations covered a group of counties, the chairman being the Lord Lieutenant of one of the counties, with the Lord Lieutenants of the other counties being deputy chairmen. The chairman of the TA Council was always a very distinguished retired officer so that all in all, the Territorial Army had considerable influence in Parliament and in the country as a whole.

My first task was to get all the units of the combat and supporting arms into brigades of one sort or another, so that they could be properly trained for whatever task they were earmarked to carry out in war. Under current arrangements only eighteen out of sixty-eight of the combat arms units (armoured corps and infantry) were looked after in this way, as opposed to thirty-one out of thirty-seven of the supporting arms units (gunners, sappers and signals). There were at the time four operational brigade headquarters and a number of group headquarters commanding units of the supporting arms. The needs of the many units not under any of these headquarters were looked after in an ad hoc way by the districts within which they were stationed. Within a few weeks we worked out that we needed an extra nine brigade headquarters, although those not required to take the field in war would only need a small number of staff officers. The Ministry of Defence made it clear that all the officers and men to staff these headquarters would have to come from our own resources, including the brigadiers themselves, but there were fifteen brigadiers in the headquarters of UK Land Forces which was far more than we needed. Just to make things easy for us we were also told that in order to save money we would be expected to give up 115 staff officer posts from within the command, which would have to be accomplished in addition to the re-organisation that we had in mind. Thanks to Micky Tillotson's negotiating powers and super-efficient staff work we made the savings and got nearly all that we needed for the UK Field Army within a couple of years.

The next problem was how to get the brigadiers under the command of major generals, qualified to support and supervise their efforts. It was these major generals who would have to work out what was needed in the way of training, equipment and logistic support for each of our reinforcing formation, including those that might find themselves involved in home defence or as part of a national force sent overseas. Fortunately there was a perfectly good set of generals with their own headquarters already in existence in the form of the district commanders, installed originally by Oliver Cromwell who used them to collect taxes and suppress unrest during his dictatorship. The slight complication was that they were also the people responsible for the administration of all troops within their districts and would remain directly responsible to the Commander-in-Chief for those establishments not in the Field Army. It might take time for them to regard themselves as being primarily the two star commanders of the UK Field Army under the Deputy Commander-in-Chief.

* * *

A particularly important part of my job would be to visit the various NATO commanders to discover precisely what they wanted from us. There would not be difficult with regard to those troops earmarked for the reinforcement of the British Army of the Rhine. But we were also responsible for providing a formation known as the UK Mobile Force, consisting of a brigade group with its full logistic backing which, when fully made up with TA and individual reservists, would amount to almost 15,000 men. The UK Mobile Force had to be prepared to operate either in Italy, or in the central region of NATO or under command of Allied Forces Northern Europe. But the only way that a force of this size could reach its destination in time, would be for some of its heavy equipment to be stockpiled before the outbreak of war. This meant that a decision as to its destination, needed to be made in advance. Also a major general with some staff officers would have to go to the NATO headquarters under which this force would be operating, to look after its interests and control its lines of communication with the United Kingdom, thus allowing the brigade commander to get on with fighting the battle. On a smaller scale we were also responsible for contributing to the ACE Mobile Force, a brigade sized formation that could be sent to reinforce any NATO country threatened by the Soviet Union to underline the fact that an attack on it, was an attack all the countries of NATO.

As soon as I started visiting the district commanders and units in different parts of the country I came face to face with the problem of distance, a matter that I had overlooked hitherto. To give some idea of the way it would affect my life it is only necessary to point out that the distance from our northernmost brigade headquarters in Perth to our headquarters at Wilton near Salisbury is roughly the same as the distance between Hamburg and Florence. Another interesting statistic is that the whole area covered by the British Army of the Rhine would fit comfortably into South West District. It would have taken me many years to get round the UK Field Army by car, but luckily I had a call on the helicopters of the Army Air Corps. The Royal Air Force was also very helpful in providing a twin engine, six-seater aircraft called a Dove which had been built for £840 soon after the end of the Second World War.

In the first two months I got round all eight of our district headquarters, visiting a number of smaller headquarters and units at the same time. Tony Farrar-Hockley was now Commander-in-Chief Allied Forces Northern Europe and my next port of call was to his headquarters in Oslo. There was a dinner party at his house where I spent the night and afterwards we sat on the patio outside his dining room where at 11.30 pm, two weeks before midsummer's day, the sun was still bright and hot enough to be noticeable. From there I was off to Denmark to be briefed by the Commander Baltic Approaches and the Commander of Land Forces Jutland. During our discussions the importance of the timely arrival of the UK Mobile Force was stressed many times over.

My next visit was to Allied Forces Central Europe now commanded by Deidi Senger. Elizabeth came with me and we spent the night with him and Ebba at their house, before our discussions next day at his headquarters. As most of the Field Army would be deployed to the Central Region in the event of war, I suggested that next year he might come and stay for a few days with us and visit some of the Territorial Army that would be fighting under his command.

When still at the Staff College I had chosen an officer of the Royal Irish Rangers called Willie Burke to be my Military Assistant. He was an excellent choice. Not only was he very thin and therefore comfortable to sit next to in a car or aircraft, but he was also a former special forces man with a flair for knowing what was going on in our headquarters at Wilton and in the Ministry of Defence. My ADC from the Royal Green Jackets, was Alexander Nall, also reasonably thin, a cousin of Elizabeth's and a pleasant and quiet companion. One or other of these officers came with me on my travels, often accompanied by Lieutenant Colonel H. Jones of the ASD branch when we were dealing with organisational matters.

* * *

During the summer of 1980, Dwin Bramall told me that the he might have to find someone to take charge of the armed forces of the newly independent Zimbabwe. The job would be to make one army out of the two rival terrorist organisations plus the old South Rhodesian Army. It would have been a bit like trying to combine two wings of the Mau Mau murderously hostile to each other, with the Kenya Regiment! He said that it was possible that I would have to do it. Later, in a letter, he said that the Secretary of State for Defence (Francis Pym) and the Foreign Secretary (Lord Carrington) both agreed with him that I was best suited to the post, although all three of them seemed to think it would be very unlikely to work. He went on to say that the Prime Minister had ruled me out as being too high profile for the job, but that she might change her mind. Eventually Mugabe settled for the commander of the old Rhodesian Army, until an African general was ready to take office.

The majority of my work was not the contacts with the overseas commands, but with the endless visits to our regular units, to Territorial Army drill halls, or to meetings of the local TA Association. On one occasion having spent the night with the Commander of North West District at Preston I had a full day in and around Manchester. That morning, to save, time I set off in a helicopter despite heavy mist. Just outside Manchester we realised that the fog was so dense that we could go no further, so the pilot put me down on a traffic roundabout, which was a good place for thumbing a lift. Strangely enough the first person to stop was an air traffic controller from Manchester Airport, returning home after the night shift. He kindly and quickly delivered me to my destination which was the drill hall of the Duke of Lancaster's Own Yeomanry. The helicopter joined me when the fog dispersed. Often I would visit three or even four units in a day, which could be a bit wearing, especially as they were all most hospitable.

In my travels the thing that struck me most forcibly was the immense enthusiasm of the Territorial Army. Not only did the men happily give up many of their weekends, but the key players put in an immense amount of time to keep the show on the road. Nowhere was the enthusiasm more pronounced that in the north-west of the country where the TA Association chaired by the Earl of Derby seemed to have the whole community behind it. And the community was most important. Amongst many who supported the Territorial Army in one way or another, none were more significant than the employers who had to put up with the absence of their men when they were training. Once when visiting a TA company in the hills above Preston I found a sergeant wearing First World War medals, instructing some recruits. In conversation he said that he had taken part in the famous landing of the Lancashire Fusiliers at Gallipoli in April 1915. Clearly he must have been well over 80 years old and on mentioning this to his company commander, I was told that although he may have passed his prime with regard to fighting the Russians, he was invaluable in terms of raising the men's morale.

In September there was a big exercise the first part of which was to practice the reinforcement of BAOR. This would be followed by a full-scale exercise in Germany in which the reinforcements would take part. I decided to go with the reinforcements, travelling initially with a battalion based in Leicester and moving all the way to its destination at Sennelager. This took five days after which I returned to see how the collection and despatch of other elements of the force was working. A few days later I returned to Germany to watch some of our non-mechanised forces taking part in to the corps battle.

After another three days I was off to Turkey to see how the ACE Mobile Force might be used there, should the Soviet Union threaten NATO's eastern flank. There had recently been a change of government in Turkey and a general was the new President. At a reception I was approached by our Ambassador and told that I was to be presented to the new President and that I was to offer him the congratulations of the British Army, which I duly did.

*   *   *

And so life went; on endlessly moving round the country, sometimes accompanied by Elizabeth who took the chance to discuss with the wives of the District Commanders the problems confronting service families and where possible meeting and talking to members of the various wives clubs in the area. My travels were interspersed by periods at our headquarters in Wilton. These were partly taken up with negotiations regarding the forming of the Field Army but not exclusively so, as there was the normal turn round of our units in Great Britain with those in Northern Ireland, Germany, Cyprus and other overseas places, such as Belize, to be catered for. All these moves involved some re-training of the units concerned, for which I was responsible. Indeed one of my tasks as Deputy Commander-in-Chief was to act as the superior commander, in terms of reporting and discipline, for small detachments throughout the world.

By the end of 1980 we were all clear that certain things needed to happen in addition to the provision of the extra brigade headquarters. First, that it should be the General Officer Commanding South West District who would become the commander of the UK Mobile Force in war and go with part of his headquarters to wherever it was sent, leaving his deputy to handle Home Defence within his district. Second, that the General Officer Commanding South East District should be prepared to take part of his headquarters and command any overseas operation that might happen in peacetime, leaving his deputy to look after his district while he was away.

The Chief of the General Staff's conference in January gave me a chance to explain to the army as a whole what the setting up of the UK Field Army involved and how it was progressing. Although it was now accepted as being necessary, it was not exactly welcomed in some quarters because in order to find the resources we needed in one area, we had to cut back in others. In particular we greatly reduced the number of arms and service advisors in headquarters UK Land Forces, which was unpopular with the arms and services directors in the Ministry of Defence. As someone once said, 'you can't make an omelette without breaking eggs' and when trying to make an omelette it's only too easy to finish up with scrambled eggs anyway.

One of the small overseas detachments for which I was responsible was the staff of the Kenya training areas where each year a number of battalions went to train. In February 1981, with a sigh of relief, I flew out there with Elizabeth and visited all the training areas, and also detachments of the Scots Guards and 34th Field Squadron, Royal Engineers. In addition there were meetings with the British High Commissioner and the Kenya Department of Defence in Nairobi. Neither of us had been in Kenya since our honeymoon and it seemed a good idea to take some leave there after my work was done. We had a wonderful time meeting many old friends.

Soon afterwards I paid a quick visit to BAOR and then returned to say farewell to Tim Creasey who was supposedly retiring from the army. It fell to me to make the speech at his farewell dinner and I foolishly repeated what he had been saying for ages, which was that nothing would induce him to stay in the army any longer. 'Hear hear', he said in a loud voice. A day or two later when packing up, he was contacted by the Prime Minister who begged him to respond to a request made by the Sultan of Oman that he should take on as his Minister of Defence. Tim had commanded the Oman army some years earlier in which capacity he had finally defeated a very persistent and savage insurgency. Like the great soldier he was, he reluctantly agreed, so that his desire to retire had to be postponed. The sad thing was that soon after he left Oman some years later, he died before being able to enjoy the many things he wanted to do.

*   *   *

John Stanier was the new Commander-in-Chief of UK Land Forces which was very pleasant from my point of view. We had known each other since we were both in 7th Armoured Division in the late 1940s. As the Director of Public Relations when in the aftermath of Ireland I was being harassed by ridiculous stories in some of the weirder newspapers and badgered to give talks ands interviews, he could not have been more helpful. Of more immediate importance was the fact that he had been in on the Field Army idea from the start and, having just come from being Vice Chief of the General Staff, he was well placed to get what we wanted from the Ministry of Defence. For a week or two after he arrived I did not travel far afield, apart from six days in Scotland getting round the various units and headquarters there, but then I was off again, this time to America.

Every year in memory of an American officer called Kermit Roosevelt, the United States Army arranges for one of its generals to speak to a number of military audiences in the United Kingdom and for a United Kingdom general to do the same thing in the United States. In May 1981 it was my turn to visit the six selected destinations in America. Elizabeth came with me and we had an interesting and enjoyable fortnight. But all too soon it was back to visiting units and headquarters throughout the United Kingdom.

There were now two additional problems regarding the Territorial Army that needed sorting out. The first related to its peacetime deployment. As a result of many years of cuts and amalgamations, some battalions had their headquarters in one place and their companies spread over a vast area. For example one had a battalion headquarters in Shrewsbury and companies as far apart as Yorkshire and Cornwall. This was madness run amok. The second related to the way in which Territorial Army regiments were supported by regular regiments, which needed adjustment. Needless to say making the required changes aroused fierce opposition from the TA regiments themselves, or from the associations supporting them. In the end, we managed to make some alterations where they were essential for operational purposes, but for the rest we let sleeping dogs lie on the grounds that another re-organisation was bound to take place within a few years. It always does.

A major problem was getting enough money to pay members of the TA for the days that they spent training. The system was that every member of the Territorial Army was paid for a maximum of thirty-eight days per year but some key people needed to put in more days if the unit was to function properly, while most did less. What we wanted was authority to transfer one man's unused days to someone who needed to do more than the permitted thirty-eight. Obviously this would cost more and over a few months I tried to persuade the Parliamentary Undersecretary of State, the Minister of State and eventually the Secretary of State of the need to get the extra money out of the Treasury. Eventually approval was given, but then the Ministry of Defence tried to purloin some of it for a different purpose altogether and one unconnected with the Territorial Army. The TA Council and TAVR Associations were naturally furious. Not long afterwards the government tried to get a bill unconnected with defence, through Parliament where it got stuck. In some inscrutable way it got unstuck as soon as the Territorial Army got all the money originally allotted to it. It was a fine example of democracy at work and of the influence wielded by the Territorial Army's supporters in Parliament.

*　*　*

While all this was going on I continued in my attempt to visit as many of the major and minor units of the Field Army as I could. By now I had a new ADC in the form of Jamie Gordon, slightly thinner than his predecessor and a good deal more interested in the military profession. In August we set off together for one of my visits to Nigel Bagnall who was now commanding I Corps in Germany. After our business was done, I spent a day or two with 2nd Royal Green Jackets at Minden. Two years earlier I had taken over as the colonel commandant of this battalion from Roly Gibbs and I visited them on a number of occasions.

Whereas most regiments had a senior or retired officer as colonel of the regiment, each battalion of a rifle regiment had a colonel commandant, an arrangement that dated from the Cardwell Reforms of the mid-nineteenth century. When I became colonel commandant, the Royal Green Jackets had three battalions. Each colonel commandant looked after the interests of his own battalion and in addition one of them, at this time Dwin Bramall, was the representative colonel commandant who dealt with the Colonel-in-Chief and the outside world. One of the other two, at this time me, was responsible for officer recruiting for the regiment as a whole. Finding the right officers was an interesting task and one that involved interviewing a number of young men who hoped to join the regiment: there were always many more wanting to join than we could accommodate. In 1982 we all changed round. Roly Guy selected the officers, I became the representative colonel commandant and Dwin Bramall who was fully occupied as Chief of the Defence Staff, gave us advice when we needed it.

For the first few months of 1982 my travels continued as before. The troops in Northern Ireland, including the Ulster Defence Regiment, still came directly under the Ministry of Defence rather than UK Land Forces, but as Inspector General I was responsible for the Territorial Army units in the Province. In February 1982 I set off there on a tour of inspection. Ever since the start of The Troubles, the Territorial Army had been kept well away from the security forces. Their job was to be ready to repel the Russians and neither the IRA nor the Protestant extremists wanted the Russians in Ireland. Probably as a result of this, neither side interfered with the Territorial Army. This was brought home to me when I found myself handing out a British Empire Medal to an individual from that IRA stronghold, Ballymurphy. The ceremony took place in the drill hall at Girdwood Park, where the detainees had been taken on the day of internment ten years earlier. After the presentation he and some of his family together with other members of his unit joined me for a drink and a friendly chat.

By now Headquarters UK Land Forces had been reduced and reorganised: most of our brigadiers had gone. Some of the new brigade headquarters were up and running, while others were still being established. In February and early March I was busy with our NATO contacts visiting various headquarters in

Belgium and Germany and the German Ministry of Defence. Later in March I visited Cyprus.

Since taking over as Deputy C-in-C two years earlier I had twice visited the headquarters of the General Officer Commanding Commando Forces at Plymouth and also the headquarters of the Commando Brigade. Although the Royal Marines belonged to the Royal Navy, the commando brigade included an artillery regiment, a field squadron of the Royal Engineers and a logistic support regiment which was manned mainly by the army. Furthermore, when not embarked, Royal Marine Commandos were usually acting as soldiers, as in Ireland for example, and there were many matters where close liaison between the army and the Royal Marines was required. For these reasons I had arranged a further visit to Major General Jeremy Moore in his headquarters at Plymouth for 2 April 1982.

That morning the news came through that Argentina had invaded the Falkland Islands and that a naval task force was being prepared to deal with the situation. Clearly the Royal Marines would be busy so my visit was cancelled: we would soon be fully occupied as well. When an operation of this sort is foreseen, a contingency plan to deal with it, is drafted by the Commanders-in-Chief Committee, sent to the joint planning staff in London, agreed by the Chiefs of Staff Committee and filed. As a result of a political decision, this had not been done in the case of an Argentinian attack on the Falklands, but clearly plenty of people had thought about the possibility over the years because decisions were quickly made. On the very day it happened the Ministry of Defence announced that the Commander-in-Chief Fleet, Admiral Fieldhouse, would command the operation, that Air Marshal Curtis would be his air force commander and that Jeremy Moore would be his land force deputy. The Commando Brigade, commanded by Brigadier Julian Thompson, was nominated as the landing force and next day UKLF was told to reinforce it with 3 Para, two troops of the Blues and Royals and a battery of 12th Light Air Defence Regiment. Shortly afterwards 2 Para and 29th Field Battery were also added to the brigade.

Thereafter things moved at breakneck speed. The immediate task facing UK Land Forces was to get vast quantities of combat supplies from the depots around the country to the ships assembling at Portsmouth, Southampton and Devonport. Regular soldiers, members of the Territorial Army and the civilian workforce in the dockyards laboured to get the job done. Merchant ships were commandeered following an order in council. Arguments about civilian working conditions and man-days for the TA were put aside as everyone pulled together to get the fleet to sea. Some ships even sailed with dockyard men still aboard, adapting them to their wartime role. These men were returned to the shore in small boats as the ship passed Land's End.

Our newly slimmed down headquarters worked well thanks to the excellent work done by Micky Tillotson's staff and in particular by his right hand man, Brigadier Christopher Airey. There were occasional protests from the Ministry of Defence when generals there who had previously only spoken with our brigadiers, had to deal direct with more junior officers. But the very fact that we had reduced the number of levels between the people who did the work and those who took the decisions, speeded up the whole process. On 6 April, I visited some of our men as they embarked in the liner Canberra and watched as she put to sea on the first stage of her long voyage to the South Atlantic. Soon afterwards I looked in on H. Jones, now commanding 2 Para, as his battalion was leaving its barracks in Aldershot. I watched the men march off to war as the band played 'Don't Cry for Me Argentina'.

*   *   *

A slightly unreal feeling set in after the fleet sailed. There was a lot of diplomatic activity designed to get Argentina to withdraw and many people, supposing that some compensatory deal would be stitched up, felt that there would be no fighting. Others felt that we could not possibly accept the sort of concessions that would lead to an Argentine withdrawal. As the intelligence picture built up, it became plain that 3 Commando Brigade, even though it had been enhanced by our extra units, would be too small to take and hold the Falklands. It was therefore decided that we should get another brigade ready to assist in this task.

The 5th Brigade was the formation earmarked for overseas operations, but as two out of three of its infantry battalions had already gone to the Commando Brigade, we would have to replace them. At this time virtually all the infantry battalions in the United Kingdom had either just returned from a tour in Ireland or were preparing to go there, or they were involved in imminent changeovers with battalions overseas. Although battalions on public duty in London are not normally considered to be in peak condition for operational tasks without a period of retraining, 2nd Scots Guards had recently returned from training in Kenya and 1st Welsh Guards were the Spearhead battalion, that is to say on stand-by for a move at short notice, so these two battalions joined 7th Gurkha Rifles in 5th Brigade.

It was also clear that when a second brigade was deployed extra artillery, engineers and signals support would be needed for the force. It was easy enough to work out what the scale of this support should be under normal circumstances, but there was one overriding factor to consider, which was that the task of freeing the Falklands had to be completed before the worst of the South Atlantic winter weather made operations impossible. If we were to wait until a full sized force could be assembled and enough shipping provided, it would be too late. It was therefore necessary to cut out every single inessential man or piece of equipment, which often meant sending small detachments with a particular capability, rather than a whole squadron or regiment. Who went and who stayed was worked out between Admiral Fieldhouse's headquarters, the Ministry of Defence and Headquarters UK Land Forces. Resulting decisions arrived at after much careful consideration, led to disappointment amongst those left behind and some criticism regarding the risks being taken.

An important aspect of preparing to send a second brigade was that, if deployed, it would be necessary for Jeremy Moore to take command on the ground in the Falklands. To do so he would need a headquarters large enough for him to conduct a two-brigade operation and look after the base area behind them. Although headquarters South East District had been constructed in such a way as to enable it to hive off an operational headquarters to go with the commander, should he be chosen to lead such an expedition, Jeremy Moore's peacetime headquarters in Plymouth was not. I therefore asked him to visit me at Wilton and over lunch in my office we worked out what he would need and I agreed to provide it. Another aspect of Jeremy Moore's projected move was that John Fieldhouse would have no land force deputy with him in his headquarters. It was therefore decided that when Jeremy Moore left, he would be replaced there by the general officer commanding South East District, who was Lieutenant General Dick Trant.

Meanwhile it was very necessary to get the newly re-constituted 5th Brigade, commanded by Brigadier Wilson, a chance to shake down and train together before it set sail. We therefore moved it to the Sennybridge Training Area in Wales for two weeks and Dick Trant put them through their paces. This gave time for them to absorb some extra equipment and it gave me the opportunity to meet their commanding officers and some of the other officers and men. By 1 May it was clear that efforts to negotiate the Argentinians out of the Falklands were not going to work. On that day the Royal Air Force based on Ascension Island bombed the runway at Port Stanley and the war can be said to have begun in earnest. Next day a Royal Navy submarine sank the *Belgrano*. 5th Brigade would be on their way within a matter of days.

At this point John Stanier departed for the United States to carry out the Kermit Roosevelt lecture tour, as I had done the previous year. He would be away for the next three weeks during which time I would be the acting Commander-in-Chief. My first act was to visit John Fieldhouse in his bunker at Northwood from where the war was being directed, to discover whether there was anything he wanted me to do. In the course of our talks I expressed the view that although Jeremy Moore would take his own Chief of Staff to help him fight the battle, he needed a senior officer who thoroughly understood how to manage the large base that would build up behind the front. Such a person could also act as his link to Northwood when Jeremy was away from the force headquarters. He could also keep in touch with Rear Admiral Woodward who commanded the naval task force and Commodore Clapp who commanded the amphibious warfare ships. Fieldhouse and Moore agreed that this was a good idea and I undertook to find a suitable officer. It seemed to me that what was wanted was someone who had been Chief of Staff of a division in BAOR and I thought that I knew exactly the right person. The officer concerned was Brigadier John Waters who had been Chief of Staff of 1st Armoured Division at the end of my time in Germany and who subsequently commanded a brigade. He was now a student at the Royal College of Defence Studies. The problem would be to get hold of him as although he would be doing nothing of importance, the college hung on to its pupils with great tenacity. He was flown out to Ascension Island where he joined the force as deputy commander to Jeremy Moore.

When 5th Brigade sailed from Southampton on the *Queen Elizabeth 2*, I was there to see them off. Walking up the gangplank I noticed a familiar figure ahead of me in the form of my cousin Linda Kitson. She said that she had been appointed the official war artists and she had a number of pencils hung round her neck. She was wearing a thin pair of cotton trousers and a blouse and was carrying a small case of some sort. When I asked whether she had warm clothes and strong shoes she said that she thought it was very warm where she was going, but she knew little about it. She had no idea how long she would be away but had parked her small yellow car under a crane on the dockside to get her home when the ship returned. I had lunch on board during which I commended her to the care of the brigadier, expressing the hope that she might be adequately kitted out before landing.

*   *   *

With the departure of 5th Brigade the day-to-day pressure of events dropped back a bit, but we continued to take a great interest in the daily briefings we received from the intelligence department. These had kept us informed of the threats posed to the fleet, first from enemy submarines, then from their surface ships and after the sinking of the *Belgrano*, from their land based aircraft. From the beginning of May when HMS *Sheffield* was sunk, the Royal Navy had been sustaining casualties and we had been preparing our processes for supporting those of our families who might be confronted with the death or injury of their husbands or sons. The first serious loss happened on 19 May when a helicopter crashed whilst moving some men from one ship to another. Eighteen soldiers and three Royal Marines were killed. Three days later 3 Commando Brigade made their successful landing at St Carlos and although the landing itself was carried out without casualties, the fighting that ensued thereafter caused them to mount up.

On 22 May John Stanier returned. It had for some time been decided that he would take over as Chief of the General Staff from Dwin Bramall and that I would take over from him as Commander-in-Chief. Ted Burgess who had been commanding an artillery regiment in Belfast during my time there, would take over from me with the title of Commander of the UK Field Army. Although that is what I had been in practice, ministers in London had apparently thought it better that I should not have that title in case elements in the press started saying that I would be sure to reconstitute the B Specials and spread them throughout England! Apparently my reputation had not fully recovered from the shock of *Low Intensity Operations*. But what might I not do as Commander-in-Chief? At the end of May I was sent on leave before taking over from John.

It can hardly be said that my time as Deputy Commander-in-Chief and Inspector General of the Territorial Army represented the highlight of my career, but it was at least educational. For the first time I had become immersed in the ways of the Territorial Army and was hugely impressed by their enthusiasm and effectiveness as soldiers. Another aspect of my job had been getting to know a bit more about the problems faced by NATO commanders outside the central front. It was all too easy for those of us who had been mainly concerned with the problems of the British Army of the Rhine, to think that only the central front really mattered. Over the past two years it had been my good fortune to see and talk to many of the NATO commanders from Norway to Turkey and gain some slight understanding of their problems. It forcibly brought home the extent to which failure in one area could adversely affect the alliance as a whole.

Clearly my main task had been to set up the UK Field Army and get its purpose understood. The travel involved had been tiring in the extreme but I felt that the idea was now widely accepted. Our efforts had certainly enabled many units to focus on and prepare for the sort of operations that might come their way should the Russians decide to chance their arm by attacking the West. The Falklands campaign had been a timely reminder that our many overseas commitments should not be ignored and that preparing for them was still as important as ever.

At the end of June I became Commander-in-Chief and at this point I would like to discuss a matter that became crucial during my time as Deputy Commander-in-Chief and remained highly relevant for the rest of my time in the army. I refer to the vitally important business of maintaining the support of army families not only when their husbands are away on active service but also when they are at home. In peaceful times it is necessary in order to ensure that men do not leave the service prematurely because their families can not stomach the conditions under which they are obliged to live. In wartime failure to look after the families properly not only undermines the morale of the men themselves but can also lead to a lack of support for the war on the part of the population as a whole. Events in the Falkland Islands focused our attention on this issue.

By 14 June, when the campaign came to an end, the army had lost 167 men. More would have died had it not been for the magnificent work of the medical officers and nurses manning the makeshift hospital at Ajax Bay in the St Carlos Settlement area and the Hospital Ship SS *Uganda*. Equally valuable was the skill of the helicopter pilots who evacuated the casualties from the forward area. Of the 1,000 wounded that got back to the hospital at Ajax Bay, only three died.

The problems of looking after those whose husbands were killed or wounded, was the job of the families officers, helped by the wives clubs of the units concerned. Luckily, whilst touring the United States for the Kermit Roosevelt lecture the previous year, Elizabeth had talked to many of our hosts wives, to discuss how they handled general problems relating to the families. As a result she had conceived the idea of setting up a federation of the many unit wives clubs that existed in the United Kingdom, by getting representatives of each one to a meeting at which she could get an idea of the sort of problems that most bothered them. The first meeting was held at Bagshot Park in the autumn of 1981, then the headquarters of the Royal Army Chaplains Corps. As a result, a small committee selected by these representatives was set up with Elizabeth as chairman. The Federation of Army Wives Clubs as it was then called, was to blossom over the years. At the time of the Falklands War it was in its infancy but it did at least exist and it provided a communication link which enabled Elizabeth to bring matters that were worrying the wives, to the notice of the authorities. One of her main concerns was to reduce the apprehension felt by the wives in the early stages of the conflict when the BBC cut in on their programmes to announce the fact that a ship had been sunk or a battalion engaged in heavy fighting. The uncertainty caused by the irregularity of these announcements was causing wives to sit glued to the television all day and Elizabeth was vigorous in trying to ensure that announcements were only made at specified times in conjunction with the regular news broadcasts. She also knew the wives of some of the commanding officers in the Falklands well and understood from her own past experience what they must be going through. During the war and in its aftermath, Elizabeth worked hard to alleviate problems and sorrows thrown up by the conflict.

It came as no surprise to find that there were odd pockets of resistance. Despite the obvious advantages that it brought to the army and the families, some resented the influence that such a powerful organisation would wield when it came to allocating the army's scant financial resources. Others, such as some staff officers in district headquarters, could see that dealing with it might well increase their workload, while others thought that, as we had always got along all right without it in the past, there was no sense in setting it up now. Over the next two years I made it very plain that, unlike King John at Runnymede, I had not signed the charter under duress and that I was fully behind it.

As the years went by this great organisation became accepted as its value became clear for all to see and the Federation's AGM was usually attended by a minister and often by the Chief of the General Staff and the Adjutant General. It now calls itself the Army Families' Federation and remains a magnificent tribute to Elizabeth's vision, energy and determination to overcome all obstacles in establishing something that she could see was urgently needed. Both the Royal Navy and the Royal Air Force now have Families Associations and other countries such as Italy have taken an interest in it. At a party given in 2007 to celebrate the twenty-fifth anniversary of its founding, in the presence of its Royal Patron, the Minister and the Chief of the General Staff, the President started her speech by saying that they had come together to celebrate 'firstly the courage, vision, and tenacity of one phenomenally special person, Lady Kitson – Elizabeth – who twenty-five years ago not only recognised a need, but acted upon that need, and the Federation was born.'

During its infancy, its progress was seldom far from my thoughts.

*   *   *

I must now return to the time when I took over as Commander-in-Chief and explain what the occupier of that office was supposed to do. His most important function was to prepare for such operations as would be required in the event of war with the Soviet Union and, separately, to prepare to deal with such troubles as might arise in other parts of the world. In both cases C-in-C UK Land Forces worked in conjunction with the Commanders-in-Chief of the other two services based in England.

In order to handle these eventualities there were two separate Commanders-in-Chief Committees. The first known as the Home Committee, dealt with matters concerning a Russian attack on NATO, including home defence, the move of reinforcements to the ports, and the reception and onward delivery of US forces passing through to the continent. The second, known as the Overseas Committee, planned for operations outside the NATO area. Some overseas operations might be on a similar scale to the Falklands War, whereas others would be on a smaller scale such as evacuating British and friendly nationals from trouble spots throughout the world. A tri-service staff headed by a Royal Navy Commodore was stationed at Wilton to do the planning for both of these committees. Plans, once agreed by the Commanders-in-Chief, were presented to the Chiefs of Staff's Committee in London.

In addition to these two primary functions the Commander-in-Chief was of course responsible for the activities of the Field Army Commander and, through the District Commanders, for assistance to the civil authorities and looking after all the base logistic and administrative units that were directed by the Ministry of Defence.

None of this posed any particular problem, but there was confusion regarding the command of the Individual Training Establishments and Depots throughout the country. For some unaccountable reason the Adjutant General was in charge of places like Sandhurst and the Staff College while Arms Directors and District Commanders shared command of the Arms Schools and Regimental Depots. Having myself commanded both the School of Infantry and the Staff College, I realised that it worked well enough after a fashion, but was a mess. Over the past year Dwin Bramall as Chief of the General Staff and John Stanier as Commander-in-Chief had been trying to sort it out by producing another lieutenant general's post in the Ministry of Defence known as Director General of Military Training. I pointed out that it would all work more smoothly if he became the Commander of the Individual Training Organisation, within Headquarters UK Land Forces. In that way the C-in-C, the Army Commander and the Training Commander, all using the same staff, and with the District Commanders and the Arms Directors subordinate to them, could deal with any problems efficiently and economically. This was eventually agreed and to my great satisfaction another of my Belfast associates, Charles Huxtable, was given the job, arriving at Wilton shortly after I took over as Commander-in-Chief.

Naturally the Commander-in-Chief UK Land Forces had a number of lesser functions to perform. In the first place he was, together with the Commander-in-Chief of the British Army of the Rhine and the Adjutant General, required to meet with the Chief of the General Staff to discuss overall army policy before meetings of the Army Board. Second, he was a member of No. 1 Selection Board whose job it was to select brigadiers for promotion to major generals and appointments in that rank. The system was exactly the same as that followed by No. 2 Board when selecting men for promotion to the rank of brigadier. There were various representative tasks to perform within the army, and in relation to the army's links with the civil community. The Commander-in-Chief was also called upon to host senior military visitors from overseas from time to time.

In 1983 I became the representative colonel commandant of the Royal Green Jackets which involved an expansion of my duties with regard to the regiment and additional travelling. At the same time I became Honorary Colonel of the Oxford University Officers' Training Corps, a unit of the Territorial Army. Also in 1983, I became aide-de-camp general to the Queen. This was basically a great honour rather than a job, but it involved me in a few pleasurable ceremonial functions, such as walking behind the Queen at the opening of Parliament.

There was therefore plenty to do, but providing the Russians did not attack the West, there would be time enough time to prepare for further adventures such as the recent Falklands campaign. Indeed sorting out the legacy of that excursion would be my most pressing task during the first few months of my time as Commander-in-Chief.

*   *   *

It is now time to look at the extent to which lessons from the Falklands War affected the way in which future overseas operations would be commanded and controlled. In the year preceding the campaign, a significant change took place in the status of the Chief of the Defence Staff. Hitherto he had acted as the spokesman for the Chiefs of Staff Committee, co-ordinating their views and representing them to the Secretary of State and Prime Minister. Under the new arrangements, he became responsible for formulating an opinion on matters of defence after consulting with the service chiefs and then for presenting it to the politicians as the view of the armed forces. Each of the service chiefs retained their constitutional right of direct access to the Prime Minister, which they had always possessed. The change may seem like splitting hairs, but in fact it ushered in a new way of exerting control of operations.

When the Falklands campaign got going, The Prime Minister set up a sub-committee of the Overseas Defence and Policy Committee of the Cabinet to handle the war, consisting of herself, the Secretary of State for Defence, the Foreign Secretary and one or two other senior politicians. It was officially known as the Overseas Defence Committee (South Atlantic), but was usually referred to as the War Cabinet. Technically decisions taken by the War Cabinet should have been passed by the Secretary of State for Defence to the Chief of the Defence Staff, thence via the respective service Chiefs of Staff to the commanders in the field. What happened was that the Chief of the Defence Staff, Admiral Lewin, was actually made a member of the War Cabinet and he sent its decisions direct to the Commander-in-Chief of the Task Force, Admiral Fieldhouse, who passed them to his relevant subordinate commanders. The requirements of the forces taking part, together with accounts of what was happening, passed back up the same chain of command. Naturally Admiral Lewin kept the other service chiefs informed so that their staffs were ready to provide Admiral Fieldhouse with what he needed. It was a brilliantly effective system, but by side-stepping some of the usual filters, it involved taking more risks than usual. The Falklands War was of brief duration, but for this system to work in a more prolonged conflict, it would be necessary to increase the Central Staff i.e. the staff, which looked after the Chief of the Defence Staff. This was still small compared to the staffs of the existing Service Chiefs.

During the second half of 1982 when I was the chairman of the UK Commanders-in-Chief Overseas Committee, we made recommendations to the Chief of the Defence Staff for putting the system that had worked so well in the Falklands War on a regular basis. Under these arrangement the Chief of the Defence Staff would nominate one of the Commanders-in-Chief as the designated commander. Certain officers from all three services would be earmarked in advance to move from their normal appointments to form a joint force headquarters for the designated commander, while others would form a joint force headquarters for whoever was appointed to command the force sent overseas. In other words the process which occurred in an ad hoc way during the early stages of the Falklands War would be pre-planned.

All of this clearly indicated a further increase in the power of the Chief of the Defence Staff at the expense of the Service Chiefs. Although the Chief of the General Staff, as head of the army, would retain responsibility for the army's performance, his power would increasingly pass to the central staffs. John Stanier, now Chief of the General Staff, had no illusions as to the way in which the wind was blowing. With his rare ability for encapsulating a situation in a memorable phrase, he pointed out that the position of the Service Chiefs would soon be the exact opposite to that of the 'mistress' who traditionally exercised power without responsibility: they would find themselves with responsibility but no power. Over the years his prediction has largely come about. During the 1990s even the Commanders-in-Chief were excluded from the operational chain of command and relegated to the position of 'providers,' their tri-service staffs forming the nucleus of a permanent Joint Force Headquarters set up on the outskirts of London through which the Chief of the Defence Staff can directly control operations.

But although the Falklands War had been successful, once it was over people spent much effort deploring the things that went wrong. Listening to the allegations of incompetence and mismanagement that were bandied about, anyone would think that we had lost. I spent much time during the latter part of 1982 listening to this sort of talk. My constant refrain was that all operations seem at the time to be a shambles, but what matters is the outcome. Our forces had pulled off a remarkable victory in the face of all sorts of difficulties and we should be thankful indeed. Some set-backs may have been the result of miscalculation, but others could well have been the unavoidable precursor of success. Conflict is like that. This time even the politicians had got it right.

*   *   *

At this time our home, Bulford Manor, was a lovely old house beside the River Avon just outside Bulford Garrison on the road to Larkhill, home of the Royal Artillery School. Security for us remained a problem. There was a full military guard on the house together with a complicated alarm system, which sometimes went off at the wrong moment.

Soon after taking over as Commander-in-Chief I was asked whether I would like to become NATO's Deputy Supreme Allied Commander, Europe. If I agreed, I would have to give up my present job after about eighteen months. I was reluctant to do this because I felt that UK Land Forces needed some continuity. Both Tim Creasey and John Stanier had only held the post for one year, which was far too short a time to get to know what needed doing in such a vast and complicated command. Another point was that my father-in-law had recently given us his house in Devon and wanted us to take over so that he could move to the farm in the not too distant future. He was fully prepared for me to finish my three years at Bulford, but if I wanted to go on much longer than that, we would have to get someone else to look after the house until we arrived. I explained all this to John Stanier and hoped that he might be able to find someone else to fill the appointment. I also said that if he really needed me to fill that, or any other post, after my time at Bulford I would do so, but that I would prefer to retire at that point.

*   *   *

At the end of March I went with my new Military Assistant, Myles Frisby, short, thin and highly organised, to Belize where we kept a small garrison commanded by a brigadier. There was always a possibility that Guatemala might invade the country and it was necessary to keep enough troops there to act as a deterrent and to hold the fort until reinforcements could arrive. We naturally wanted to keep as few troops there as possible, but with the example of the Falkland Islands very much in people's minds we had to be sure that we had enough. An incidental advantage of having troops there was that they could be given some jungle training. I spent the inside of a week visiting our men and discussing the problem with the commander and our civil representatives in the country. My visits to overseas detachments such as Belize were relevant to the work being carried out by the Commanders-in-Chief's Overseas Committee.

Much of our work on the Overseas Committee related to the running of joint exercises, some of which were elaborate and extensive. Usually one or more of the Commanders-in-Chief visited them: sometimes all three together. One case springs to my mind when the three of us went by jet to Lossiemouth where we transferred to a helicopter for onward transmission to an amphibious task force at sea off Cape Wrath. By this time John Fieldhouse had been replaced as C-in-C Fleet by an athletic man called William Staveley. On arrival the weather was too rough for us to land on the flagship so the helicopter hovered overhead while Staveley invited us all to climb down a rope onto the deck. As I saw David Craig, the Air Chief Marshal, disappear down the rope, I was tempted to say that I would be happy to watch the exercise out of the window. But lunch was at the other end of the rope so, reluctantly, I grasped it and descended the 20 or 30 feet to the deck which was heaving around to such an extent that I wondered whether I would even want any lunch. Anyhow the rest of the day went well and by the evening I was safely back at Bulford Manor. The next time I went to sea the weather was favourable and we landed successfully on the deck of an aircraft carrier in the Channel.

The spring of 1983 saw two events of considerable importance to me. First David Tobey replaced Jamie Gordon as my ADC and then a few weeks later Bob Pascoe replaced Micky Tillotson as Chief of Staff. Jamie had been an excellent companion to me on my travels and I greatly enjoyed the interest that he took in his profession. Micky's departure was even more painful as he was the true architect of the many changes that had taken place within UK Land Forces over the past three years. He knew so much and had so many contacts that I feared his departure would leave us exposed to assault from those who did not fully appreciate the value of our recent reforms. Luckily the senior members of Micky's staff were competent and well trained and Bob Pascoe, in his calm and quiet way soon proved himself more than capable of handling the job. So much was this the case that two years later he was promoted to lieutenant general and sent to command in Northern Ireland.

As a result of yet another re-organisation in Germany, the 2nd Armoured Division commanded by Peter Inge, had recently been moved to England, where it had merged with North East District. The Queen decided to visit it in its headquarters at York in May and in accordance with the normal procedure I met her on her arrival and presented the Divisional Commander. After that my duties were complete and I could sit back and enjoy the party. After lunch we moved to the nearby barracks where selected units of the division were to march past the Queen. This was Fulford Barracks where I had arrived as a raw recruit in January 1945. I watched as the troops marched past the Queen who was taking the salute from where Dick Poole had been standing when we passed out at the end of our training. My thoughts went back to Sergeant Capper and Acting Corporal Hole telling us that we were the biggest shower they had ever had the misfortune to train.

*   *   *

Although I have said a good lot about the Falklands War and the reforms, which had been put in place regarding the way in which future overseas adventures might be handled, the Cold War remained top priority in terms of defence. Indeed the Cold War was thought to be in a particularly critical condition at this time as both sides were struggling to keep ahead of the game, with more and more expensive technology being introduced to overcome Russia's nuclear advances. No one could foresee that the bubble would burst by the end of the decade when the Soviet Union realised that its economy would no longer allow it to keep up with the West. On the contrary, in 1983, 1984 and 1985, during which the three Russian leaders, Brezhnev, Andropov and Chernenko died one after the other, NATO felt that an insecure Soviet leadership might well take advantage of their superior conventional strength combined with their nuclear parity, to launch a pre-emptive attack.

All this meant that the business of reinforcing NATO both from the UK and from America became increasingly important, so that it was the affairs of our Home Committee that most frequently occupied our minds. And although steps had been taken to enable BAOR to fight in accordance with the concept of flexible response, and although the UK Field Army now existed to prepare reinforcements for their task, little had been done to ensure that they could get to their destinations in time. This was one of the most important aspects of home defence but when it came to spending money, it had a lower priority than financing our forces in Germany. The fact that 62 per cent of the army destined to fight on the continent in the event of war was in the UK and would never get to where it was wanted if our home defence arrangements failed to work, was usually overlooked. (NB: the 62 per cent included Reservists as well as regulars and members of the Territorial Army.)

Should war appear imminent, UK Land Forces would have to call out the Territorial Army and the 70,000 individual reservists. It would also have to receive back into the UK, army families and dependants evacuated from Germany and elsewhere abroad. It would have to move those brigades and units earmarked as reinforcements for NATO, to the ports and despatch them to their destinations: roughly 60,000 to BAOR, and 16,000 to Denmark and Norway. It would also have to deploy the formations and units earmarked for home defence tasks, amounting to a further 35,000 men supplemented by a number of independent companies formed from the Individual Training Organisation. Finally it would have to out-load some 40,000 tons of stores and move it to the ports or to destinations within the UK.

When the war started, the immediate threat would be from air attack and raids by Soviet special forces, designed to hamper the move of UK and US reinforcements to NATO, followed by further air attacks designed to damage the country's ability to wage war. Our job included protecting installations such as airfields, communication centres, dockyards and ports and a large number of other key points related to the well being of the country as a whole. We had to ensure freedom of movement, route maintenance and traffic control, including control of the movement of civilians trying to escape from urban areas which were being attacked from the air.

In 1983 there were 27,000 US servicemen in the UK, a number that would increase to 120,000 in the event of war not counting a further 50,000–60,000 that were expected to pass through the country en route to the continent. The USA had 250,000 tons of stores in the UK in peacetime, which would have to be out-loaded and a vast quantity of extra stores would be passing through the country thereafter. We needed effective links with US forces in order to co-ordinate our activities with them in three main areas. First, to co-ordinate the defence of the American Key Points in the UK with our own. Second, to tie in US movements within the UK with our own movement plans. Third, to ensure that US divisions and brigades in transit through the UK could be made available to help in home defence tasks while they were in this country.

Hitherto our point of contact with US forces was with the headquarters of the 3rd US Air Force, which looked after the American servicemen in the UK in peacetime, but it would be fully occupied in fighting the air battle in the event of war. What we needed was direct contact with the headquarters of US Forces in Europe stationed in Stuttgart and it was agreed that we should deal direct with General Smith who was in charge there. Our first meeting was in January 1983 and thereafter we met him every six months, alternately in England and Stuttgart. In the intervals our planning staff worked with his, to produce practicable plans for our joint approval.

Another essential aspect of home defence concerned the links that we had with the civilian authorities which were totally inadequate and took little account of the effects that conventional bombing was likely to have on the population. Over recent years a certain amount had been done to improve matters, but much remained to do. It would be tedious now that the whole idea of an attack on the West by Russia has long since disappeared, to go in detail into the way that we and the civil authorities and the Americans set about rectifying the situation. Suffice it to say that it involved a great deal of planning by the staff of the Commanders-in-Chief's Committee and our subordinate headquarters, who also had to conduct meetings with the civil authorities at regional and county levels. Every six months our committee met in full session to iron out difficulties after which, accompanied by as many of the Commanders-in-Chief as wished to do so, I reported to the Chiefs of Staff Committee in Whitehall. Undoubtedly it was the interest and strong line taken by the Chief of the Defence Staff, Dwin Bramall, that resulted in progress being made, particularly in the political field. Our planning was supplemented by a series of exercises that took place over the next two years.

*   *   *

During the summer of 1983, I was kept busy moving around the country in addition to which there were visits to the British Army of the Rhine and to General Smith in Stuttgart. By October things had eased off a bit and we both enjoyed a visit to Desmond Cassidi who was the Commander-in-Chief Naval Home Command at Portsmouth during which we attended a Trafalgar Day dinner on board HMS *Victory*: a great occasion. Of all the Commanders-in-Chief with whom I had dealings whilst at Bulford, he was the one who was most congenial to me personally and who I most enjoyed meeting. He had a splendid wife who was a doctor in Londonderry. Somehow she always managed to be present when duty called in Portsmouth and then, by travelling at night, she was back in her surgery next morning in time to see her patients.

A few days later I got a message to contact the Chief of the General Staff urgently. On doing so John Stanier told me that a large number of US and French soldiers belonging to the Multinational Force in the Lebanon had been killed by two separate explosions in the Beirut area. I was to go at once to Cyprus, spend the night there, going on to Beirut next morning in a helicopter. My task was to visit our contingent and assess the risk of leaving it there. I was also to recommend ways in which it could be made safer. Before returning I was to visit the French and US contingents to offer the condolences of HMG on their losses. Within a couple of hours I was airborne. Desmond Langley who was now the Commander British Forces in Cyprus, met me at the Akrotiri airfield and took me to his house for the night.

Next morning I flew by helicopter to the Beirut airfield where I was met by the commander of the British contingent in his Land Rover and we set off through the streets of Beirut to his headquarters. From him I learnt that two bombs had gone off almost simultaneously the previous day. The US contingent, consisting of a battalion of US Marines was in a large building alongside the airfield. Such was the force of the explosion that the whole building collapsed killing about 250 men and injuring a lot more. The French contingent consisting of a company of parachutists located several miles away in west Beirut, lost nearly sixty men. President Mitterand was even now visiting the survivors and the US Vice President was due to arrive next day, all of which according to my informant, was making the authorities a bit jumpy. I told him that he was lucky that he only had me to worry about and not Mrs Thatcher.

On arrival at his base he gave me an excellent rundown on the way in which the multinational force worked. Apparently the Lebanese government was opposed by a considerable number of terrorist groups all of which could and did resort to violence from time to time. He also pointed out that although calling themselves peacekeepers, the multinational force did not meet the criteria for a peacekeeping force, which required it to have been invited by all parties to the dispute in order to assist them to find a way through their differences. In this case they were in fact working on behalf of the Lebanese government to help it out of its difficulties. He also pointed out that each of the contingents had their own ways of doing business; the larger the contingent, the more likely it was to resort to direct action. The British contingent, which only consisted of an armoured reconnaissance squadron was the least likely to throw its weight around. He also said that he had good relations with all the opposing parties and that he was in frequent contact with them, because he was responsible for protecting the peace talks that were supposed to be going on. He considered that there was very little risk of his men being attacked. Although agreeing with his analysis, I felt that he might have overlooked the fact that many of the groups were sponsored and supported by outside countries such as Iran. Should one of these countries want to get at Britain for any reason, possibly totally unrelated to the affairs of Lebanon, it could do so by getting its client group in Lebanon to blow up our contingent there. Naturally I did not cheer him up by mentioning this: he had probably worked it out for himself anyway.

We then walked round his position looking for improvements that could be made to increase security and talking to the men, many of whom had been involved in helping to rescue US servicemen from the ruins. As was to be expected they were in great form. In the course of our discussions he said that he could get air support from Cyprus within four hours and gunfire support from the heavy guns of US ships at great speed. After a quiet lunch I stood with him on the balcony looking out over the rooftops of Beirut. As we did so, we heard a single rifle shot fired a long way off. It was the last shot that I heard during my military career and I have no desire to hear any more.

On the way back to the helicopter I visited the embassy which Britain shared with the US. I then went on to see the colonel commanding the US contingent.

The devastation was indescribable. The commander of the French contingent was unable to see me owing to other commitments. After that I returned to Cyprus to visit the RAF hospital where many of the wounded US troops had been taken. During the night I flew back to England, writing my report for the government on the way. This was a lengthy document as in addition to making an appreciation and recommendation as to whether we should withdraw our contingent or not, I had to answer a number of specific and detailed questions. My conclusion was that provided we carried out certain improvement to the security of the base, the risk of leaving our people there was acceptable. Next day I went to London and reported my findings to Dwin Bramall and John Stanier after which I did the same for the Secretary of State in the House of Commons. During their visits to Beirut, both President Mitterand and Vice President George H.W. Bush publicly announced that there would be no withdrawal. By May 1984 the whole of the multinational force had been removed.

*   *   *

By the end of 1983, the large scale restructuring of UK Land Forces was largely complete. In the Field Army the new brigades were in place. The Individual Training Organisation was up and running within UK Land Forces. Headquarters UK Land Forces, having been reduced in size by 35 per cent and completely restructured under one Chief of Staff, was now capable of serving the Commander-in-Chief, the Field Army commander and the Training Commander. This was hugely economic as well as being efficient. It was particularly helpful to staff officers at district headquarters who did not need to worry whether something they were dealing with concerned the Army Commander or the Commander-in-Chief, because the same staff looked after both of them. The concept of one staff looking after several commanders at different levels was not new, because in the overseas 'unified commands' of the 1950s and 1960s, a combined staff looked after the Commander-in-Chief and his subordinate army, navy and air force commanders. It had not previously happened within the army because commanders at different levels were seldom co-located.

After this welter of change it was now important to provide a period of calm during which people could go about their business without worrying whether their job would still be there when they came down to breakfast next morning. This I was able to provide within UK Land Forces, but within the Ministry of Defence confusion reigned supreme.

The trouble arose because, as the Chief of the General Staff set off a study designed to restructure the army's chain of command, the Secretary of State launched a separate study designed to strengthen the central staff in the Ministry of Defence at the expense of the single service staffs. Michael Heseltine was now Secretary of State and his study was necessary to enable the changes made by his predecessor, John Nott, to work. But it went further than was needed for that purpose. Both the Chief of the Defence Staff and the three service chiefs felt that the reduction in the single service staffs suggested by the Secretary of State, would prevent them from carrying out their remaining functions in a crisis. At the same time John Stanier felt that he would be unable to carry out the reductions he wanted to make in the army's chain of command outside the Ministry of Defence. This was because his own staff in the army department would be too greatly reduced to take on the work previously carried out by the people that he wanted to remove outside it.

As one of the principal advisers to the Chief of the General Staff, I was sometimes involved in discussing how to resolve these problems. Clearly neither the re-organisation of the Ministry of Defence nor details of how the army's chain of command worked in the 1980s, would be of much interest now were it not for the fact that the discussions going on in 1984, led directly to the way things work today. For this reason it is worth having a brief look at what was happening at the time.

The problem was that if the central staff was to be increased and the single service staffs decreased to the extent that the Secretary of State envisaged, the allocation of resources as well as operational matters would have to be taken away from the individual services and handled by the central staff. My personal opinion was that in the long term this would probably be advantageous, but I made it plain that it should be done gradually over a period of years. The single service staffs could only be run down when the central staff had built up enough expertise to deal confidently with the three Service Chiefs of Staff and the various Commanders-in-Chief. Even then, although the long-term aim of the Secretary of State's proposals was sensible, they would needed adjustment to make them safe. The Commanders-in-Chief's Committee had recently discussed the matter at the request of Commander-in-Chief Fleet. He felt that the Secretary of State's proposals were a step in the right direction that would be painful for three years, after which they would leave us in a stronger position. Commander-in-Chief Strike (RAF) felt that they would lead to chaos for three years, followed by something worse than we now had.

During the last few months of 1984 Secretary of State Michael Heseltine interviewed individual Commanders-in-Chief and other senior officers regarding the way in which their various areas of responsibility were being handled with particular reference to their cost effectiveness. It is interesting to see how, over the years, many of his ideas have been adopted. Now the central staff handles vastly more than it did in 1984. How well it works is another matter.

During 1984 and the early months of 1985 the discussions that we had with John Stanier took up a lot of time but were basically frustrating because what he would have liked to see happen was so constantly being sacrificed to fit the Secretary of State's plans. By contrast, the day-to-day business of the Commanders-in-Chief working to the Chief of the Defence Staff for operational matters, was anything but frustrating and forged ahead to good purpose. Great strides were made in terms of home defence, and preparation for future overseas operations and a number of tri-service exercises, some on a massive scale took place. Our contacts with the Americans also bore fruit as our planning and meetings developed.

One hugely important matter continued to be debated throughout my time with UK Land Forces. This was the question of whether the United Kingdom should continue to have an independent nuclear deterrent when the time came to replace Polaris missiles. On several occasions Dwin Bramall discussed this matter with me privately as for example when we were sitting in the back of a vehicle moving from one peg to the next on the Tidworth shoot. As usual he liked discovering what other people thought, although he was pretty reticent when it came to letting them know what he thought. In the case of the nuclear deterrent there were in fact two major issues. The first was whether we needed one at all and the second one was what form it should take. Although I had no informed opinion as to its exact form, my view was that it was essential to keep a national nuclear deterrent, despite the fact that it was expensive.

The opposite view was that our deterrent was so small compared to that of the United States that we could safely leave that part of the business of confronting the Soviet Union to the Americans. We could then use the money saved to buy more tanks and guns, although if past experience was anything to go by, the treasury would have swallowed it up rather than allow it to be used to buy extra weapons. My feeling was that, although abandoning a national deterrent may have been a tenable view in the 1970s, the position was now different because various other countries such as China, Israel, South Africa, India and probably one or two others, were assumed to be getting nuclear weapons. How, for example, would we have been placed had Argentina had just one primitive weapon when she invaded the Falklands, if we had none? We could not then have been sure that the United States would protect us if the rulers of Argentina had said that they would use their bomb against us in self-defence, should we attack them. In retrospect we now know that the Thatcher government was determined to keep a national deterrent and that the argument really centred on the precise type of weapon to be selected. Nonetheless there were some important advocates for abandoning it, including some of my associates and I took every opportunity to plug the need for the United Kingdom to retain it.

Another matter of almost equal importance to my mind was the fact that ever since the end of the Second World War nuclear weapons had, so far, been influential in preventing a major war breaking out between Russia and the West. At the same time they had not stopped smaller wars such as the Arab/Israeli conflicts, nor had they prevented numerous outbreaks of insurgency around the world many of which had been instigated by outside powers trying to damage their competitors without actually going to war with them. We had endlessly become involved when the insurgencies had been directed at us or at countries whose interests we needed to protect and there seemed no reason to suppose that this situation would not continue indefinitely. But ever since the 1960s when the British government ordered the withdrawal of our forces from east of Suez, they had laid down that our forces should almost entirely be organised, trained and equipped to carry out their NATO obligations or the defence of the homeland. For this reason we had been obliged to deal with every other commitment on an ad hoc basis borrowing troops from our NATO forces when necessary. Thus in the early stages of the Northern Ireland troubles armoured and artillery regiments from Germany had to be used as infantry as indeed they had been used in Cyprus as peacekeepers when the Greeks attacked the Turks in early 1963. For practical reasons I had always felt that these limitations made it important that our NATO contribution should as far as possible be arranged in such a way as to make it compatible with the needs of the sort of situations that might blow up elsewhere.

With this in mind I took a particular interest, in the question of the research and development costs of new weapons and equipment with particular reference to the research and development costs of a new battle tank. It was not that I thought that tanks were obsolete or becoming less important because of the anti-tank potential of helicopters and the new range of infantry anti-tank weapons. But we needed so few tanks compared with the numbers being produced by Germany or America that I felt we should buy from one of those sources rather than pay the vast cost of researching and developing a further generation of tanks for ourselves. It seemed to me that we could make better use of this money by increasing the capability of the UK Mobile Force. This would not only help to defend Denmark and therefore ourselves in the event of a major war, but increased assets, particularly in terms of artillery, engineers, signals and logistic resources, would improve the army's ability to take part in operations outside the NATO area if required.

*   *   *

During 1984 there were two major exercises. In April there was a Home Defence exercise attended throughout by the Minister of State at the Home Office. Then in the summer there was a massive reinforcement of NATO exercise that lasted for a whole month in September and early October. It involved regulars, Territorial Army and even the call out of reservists together with the requisition of shipping, the despatch of large numbers to the continent and the practising of troops on home defence tasks around the country.

In May of 1984 the Queen as our Colonel-in-Chief visited the Royal Green Jackets. As two of the battalions were in Germany, we decided that the visit should take place at Celle, which was where the 3rd Battalion was stationed. Because it was a regimental visit rather than a visit to that battalion, the other two battalions and the Territorial Army battalion all sent strong contingents. As representative colonel commandant I was the host in one sense, but the three of us took it in turns to look after the Colonel-in-Chief. The whole visit went off well and was much enjoyed by us all. No one who has had official dealings with our present sovereign can have failed to appreciate her complete mastery of the job and the humanity of her approach to people of all sorts. For many reasons I have always been a strong supporter of the monarchy, not least because the very existence of a sovereign puts the pretensions of other exalted people, particularly politicians, into a proper perspective.

*   *   *

In the 1985 New Year Honours List I was made a Knight Grand Cross of the Order of the British Empire and soon afterwards attended my last investiture. My children who were never over-impressed by awards of this sort, summed up my achievements as 'Seven times round the track (meaning the investitures): four BEs, two MCs and a Bath'.

By the beginning of 1985 I started to work out how best to prepare for handing over on 1 June when I was due to retire. To my great satisfaction my successor would be Jimmy Glover, another former Rifle Brigade officer who was serving as Vice Chief of the General Staff. In order to allow Jimmy's Chief of Staff to get well worked in before Jimmy arrived, Bob Pascoe handed over to him in March. I was sad to see Bob go. It is always pleasant when your right hand man is also a friend and our association went back to the fireworks at Kophinou in 1967. Being the Chief of Staff of UK Land Forces was a particularly difficult job, as it involved looking after the Army Commander and the Training Commander as well as the Commander-in-Chief. Furthermore his task was not confined to running the headquarters, as he was often busy contacting the staff of the naval and air force Commanders-in-Chief in order to iron out as many differences as possible before the Commanders-in-Chief met in committee. At these meetings which were held in front of many officers and Civil Servants representing a wide circle of interested parties, it was important to keep disagreement and discussion to a minimum if only to get through the agenda in time for lunch. Anything that could not be resolved in advance, would usually have to be recorded and passed on to the Chiefs-of-Staffs Committee in London for a decision. It is also of interest that an insoluble disagreement in London, was sometimes passed down to us to see whether we could recommend a course of action that they could accept. Bob Pascoe was a wonderful 'behind the scenes' fixer, as indeed had been Micky Tillotson.

Before leaving I naturally had to visit many people within and outside the UK. My final overseas trip was to Denmark where I was profusely thanked for my efforts to improve our ability to come to their assistance in the event of war.

During the run up to my departure I naturally found myself obliged to give an even greater number of talks than usual. Throughout my army career I had used formal speeches to a great extent to put over my views, always writing my own and often going through several drafts before being satisfied. Although some of my speeches lasted no more than a few minutes, as when introducing a subject or entertaining the assembled company at the end of a meal, many lasted for half to three quarters of an hour. Having kept a copy of most of them I am able to get an idea of the extent to which preparing speeches had increasingly impinged on my existence. For example during my time in the Ministry of Defence in the mid-1960s I only gave five talks. During my command of 1st Royal Green Jackets, ten. While commanding 39th Brigade in Belfast the number rose to twenty-six. After that it was thirty-seven at the School of Infantry, eleven in Germany, thirty-four at the Staff College, thirty-one as Army Commander and eighty-five as Commander-in-Chief. Many of these talks were given at schools or universities or to societies expressing an interest in various aspects of service life and an appreciable number were given to service audiences abroad. Despite the labour involved, I did receive one major advantage from it. The very business of preparing the speeches meant that I had to collect information on the subject matter and arrange it in a clear and logical manner. This greatly helped when subsequently faced with the need to think about or discuss the subject concerned. All the same the thought of not having to make many speeches when retired, was one of the most attractive aspects of leaving the army.

*   *   *

As the time approached for our departure, Elizabeth worried that I would find it difficult to adjust to civilian life after a little over forty years in the army especially as I had been preparing myself for a service career ever since I was a child at Portsmouth. My view was almost the exact opposite. I felt that I had already spent too large a proportion of the only life I was ever likely to have in this world, in the services. I was very keen to try something else, especially to have something quite different to think about. But I realised that Elizabeth had thrown herself so completely into working for the army and supporting me, that she might miss it more than I would. On the other hand if we were going to fit into Devon after so long away, the sooner we started the better.

Our last day was spent saying goodbye to the many people who had looked after us so well over the last three years. We were due to leave Bulford Manor first thing in the morning of 1 June, but as we had everything packed and ready, we left after supper the night before. It was still light as we drove across Salisbury Plain and through the countryside south of Warminster where we had enjoyed such good hunting in the past. Soon it got dark; and that was that.

Epilogue

All through my military career I looked forward to returning to Devon and since doing so have never wanted to be anywhere else. We sometimes go away for a week or two but I always heave a sigh of relief on re-entering the county, especially when reaching the top of Haldon Hill from where one can see the outline of Dartmoor rising up in the distance.

For some time we were fully occupied in getting the house arranged to suit our needs. After a few years we gave up the horses and thereafter became immersed in the sort of activities that confront those who are thought to have plenty of time to spare. In addition to maintaining contacts with my former regiments I became the President of the Mounted Infantry Club and County President of the Royal British Legion. In a civilian capacity I became a deputy lieutenant of the county, a governor of Stowe School and the chairman of a small limited company concerned with running a fishery.

Elizabeth rapidly became immersed in the affairs of the county to a far greater extent. In addition to becoming a deputy lieutenant she has served on numerous committees and for the last twenty years, has run a short course to enable those who specialise in painting horses to be able to do so while looking at the real thing rather than at photographs. She has also continued to paint horses, landscapes and people and has become a wonderful sculptor of animals, birds, fish and the occasional human. Her energy is breathtaking.

Our children went out to work and in due course married. They remain in close and loving touch and constitute our greatest source of interest and satisfaction. We are lucky to have three friendly and sensible sons-in-law and a number of grandchildren. Nearly all the people who played such an important part in my early days in the army have now passed away and the same can be said of the senior officers for whom I worked and who tolerated my eccentricities during my military career. I remain grateful for what they did for me with particular reference to Mike Carver, John Mogg, Roly Gibbs and Dwin Bramall.

Shortly after retiring I wrote two short books to expound my views on how the army should be organised and run to fulfil its functions in the modern world. I envisaged them as being companion pieces to *Low Intensity Operations*, which was still selling well at the time. The first, called *Warfare as a Whole*, was designed to show that the various categories of war stretching from one in which all weapons might be used, right down to counter-insurgency, were part and parcel of the same business. It explained why the army must understand how to conduct all these activities and how it should be organised, trained and equipped to do so. It emphasised the vital importance of retaining our own nuclear weapons. Based on my experience in my last two appointments and conscious of the necessity of being able to switch forces stationed in one area to operate elsewhere, I recommended some fairly drastic re-deployments. My idea was to thin out in the central region of NATO and fulfil our NATO commitment in an area where the type of units needed would, in addition to carrying out their NATO function, be available for use in other parts of the world should the need arise. Had my readers foreseen the collapse of the Soviet Union, which was still three or four years away, my ideas might have been more sympathetically received, especially as the rest of the book was generally acceptable, except to those who wanted to scrap our nuclear weapons.

The purpose of the second book called *Directing Operations*, was to examine the way in which operations should be directed in the modern world. The business of directing operations involves working out how to apply resources within a given set of circumstances for the purpose of achieving a specific aim and then seeing that the arrangements decided on, are put into effect. I set about doing this by looking at the qualities that commanders need in relation to what they have to do and then identifying what is required to prepare them for their task in terms of structuring their careers and giving them the required experience and training. Amongst other things, this involves organising the army in such a way as to balance the need for producing the best commanders against other requirements such as the provision of staff officers and people to run training and administrative units. Any student of English military history can hardly fail to notice what little regard has been paid to this vitally important matter in the past. All too often totally useless people have been given senior command appointments, either to give them the experience they might need to fill staff jobs in London, or just because they are good company. All too often the results have been disastrous. There were few objections to this book and some of its recommendations have been adopted, although not necessarily because I wrote about them.

Not wishing to pontificate on military problems once divorced from an up to date knowledge of what was going on, I then turned to military history. My first attempt was to produce an account of Prince Rupert's doings as a leader of the King's forces in the Civil War 1642 to 1646. This seemed to go quite well so I wrote a follow up volume outlining his subsequent career as an Admiral and member of the government of Charles II. My next effort was to write the story of Oliver Cromwell as a soldier, ending before he installed himself as England's military dictator. All of these three books reflected the conclusions that I had reached when writing *Directing Operations*. Subsequently I put together a short biography of my father together with a collection of his paintings under the title of *When Britannia Ruled the Waves*. In addition to these books, I have contributed to various other publications. Furthermore a number of academics and writers from various parts of the world have visited me to discuss the military operations in which I had taken part and my books on the subject. I have even, on occasions, accepted invitations to speak on these matters, but am now too out of date to be of much use.

In conclusion I would like to underline the fact that the best thing I ever did, was to persuade Elizabeth to become my wife. It may be that in some quarters I am regarded as having moved the army forward in the field of low intensity warfare, but I believe that Elizabeth's work for the families and dependants will be remembered long after my innovations have been forgotten.

Index

Dear Reader,

We hope you have enjoyed this book, but why not share your views on social media? You can also follow our pages to see more about our other products: facebook.com/penandswordbooks or follow us on X @penswordbooks

You can also view our products at www.pen-and-sword.co.uk (UK and ROW) or www.penandswordbooks.com (North America).

To keep up to date with our latest releases and online catalogues, please sign up to our newsletter at: www.pen-and-sword.co.uk/newsletter

If you would like a printed catalogue with our latest books, then please email: enquiries@pen-and-sword.co.uk or telephone: 01226 734555 (UK and ROW) or email: uspen-and-sword@casematepublishers.com or telephone: (610) 853-9131 (North America).

We respect your privacy and we will only use personal information to send you information about our products.

Thank you!